Limerick County Library

30012 00458041

D1631553

n Chortac

WITHDRAWN FROM STOCK

The Magic Spring

The Magic Spring

My Year Learning to Be English

Richard Lewis

LIMERICK
COUNTY LIBRARY
00458047

Atlantic Books
London

First published in Great Britain in 2005 by Atlantic Books,
an imprint of Grove Atlantic Ltd

Copyright © Richard Lewis 2005

The moral right of Richard Lewis to be identified as the author of
this work has been asserted in accordance with the Copyright, Designs
and Patents Act of 1988.

All rights reserved. No part of this publication may be reproduced,
stored in a retrieval system, or transmitted in any form or by any
means, electronic, mechanical, photocopying, recording, or otherwise,
without the prior permission of both the copyright owner and
the above publisher of this book.

The author and publisher wish to thank the following for permission to
quote from copyrighted material:

'Living Doll' words and music by Lionel Bart, copyright © 1959, reproduced
by permission of Peter Maurice Music Co. Limited, London WC2H 0QY.

'The Moving On Song' by Ewan MacColl. Copyright © 1968 Stormking
Music Inc. Administered by Harmony Music Limited. Reproduced by
permission of Ewan MacColl Limited.

Every effort has been made to trace or contact all copyright-holders.
The publishers will be pleased to make good any omissions or rectify
any mistakes brought to their attention at the earliest opportunity.

9 8 7 6 5 4 3 2 1

A CIP catalogue record for this book is available from the British Library.

ISBN 1 84354 307 9

Designed by Richard Marston
Printed in Great Britain by Creative Print & Design, Ebbw Vale, Wales

Atlantic Books
An imprint of Grove Atlantic Ltd
Ormond House
26–27 Boswell Street
London WC1N 3JZ

For Rosa

Contents

Author's Note

The Magic Spring took more than three years to research. However, events have been condensed to reflect a single calendar year. As a result, one or two meetings have changed time, location or both for the sake of continuity. In some cases the reportage reflects not one instance of an event but several. In addition, a few names have been changed in the interests of privacy or discretion. Aside from this minor cosmetic surgery, the events retold are true. A selection of further reading is included as an appendix. However, the work of one writer proved particularly valuable in appraising the sum of historical information available to non-historians such as me. I am greatly indebted to the authoritative writing of Professor Ronald Hutton, in particular his history of the British ritual year, *Stations of the Sun* (Oxford, 1996) and his history of modern pagan witchcraft, *Triumph of the Moon* (Oxford, 1999). Hutton can be taken as the primary historical source for British folklore in *The Magic Spring*, although any errors are of course my own.

Richard Lewis, London 2004

The Magic Spring

Giant

A gust takes me. I slide down the wet grass and chalky slurry until I come to a halt in a heap, halfway down the slope. I try to stand up but my foot slides away. Again I fall face-forward onto the mud. What now? Against all popular advice, I look down.

One hundred and twenty feet below, in the black beyond, lie clumps of hedgerow, hawthorn and the Cerne river. Above me are gorse patches and howling wind. Beyond the valley the downs rise up darkly into the early morning sky as the village sleeps, unaware of my torn tendon. My cheap shoes are soaked through. I am trivial among the elements: a tiny part of something massive and unknowable with the power to shake trees, make rain, give life. I lie for half a minute, perhaps more, to regain my breath, my heart pounding against the clay. I should never have attempted this climb with an injury. But I have to go on. I ask Hele for strength – why not, as long as he's here? – and drag myself slowly up the hill. Eventually I reach a neat strip of white chalk and gravel, one of the Giant's ribs, I think. It is difficult to make it out in this light. Then another. Yes, I am on Hele himself. The sun is rising over his hill, casting an eerie blue light onto the grass. Then I see it.

First: a pair of horns, rising over the horizon, out of the grass, into the liquid blue light. The horns are followed by a pair of eyes, monstrous and huge, set into a giant head of grinning teeth and animal hair. I blink and see six pairs of hands reaching up to the creature, which bobs and dances in the dawn. I drag myself closer. The wind is blowing a gale, flattening the gorse against the down.

At the very top of the hill, in the ancient site, the giant masked man sways in a sackcloth, his carved wooden mouth set in a grotesque smile, his horns black against the dawn sky. He seems to look directly at me. He seems to leer. Around him, in a ring, dances a group of men in black and white, dwarfed by his size, long sticks in their hands. They raise their sticks up to the horned giant in an act, it seems, of demonic deference.

It's sunrise on the first of May. And here before me, at a sacred place high on a hill, is a group of costumed characters performing an ancient rite. I turn up my collar, brace myself against the wind and limp towards them.

What on earth am I doing here? I ask myself. Looking back, it all started with a casual visit.

1 | DJs, Pies

The road bridge was up at England's most easterly point, so I stopped and watched a trawler put out from Oulton Broad. When it had inched into the North Sea, and the road had fallen once more into place, the electric gate twitched into life and let us past – the pair of young women with prams, hair pulled back in taut ponytails, the dog-walker with pink dreadlocks and sandy boots, flushed from the beach, and the white-haired man in a quilted anorak from Chadds who had suddenly leaned towards his friend and said, 'Sod 'em. I'll just become a magician.'

Lowestoft is a working port, far removed from the gentrified postcard cottages of Southwold, a few miles south down the Suffolk coast, or the seedy kiss-me-quicks of Great Yarmouth to the north. It's a town of narrow, terraced houses, large industrial cranes and fish-finger factories. But I ignored the scale-covered gate offering me 'Real Bloaters' and the pub with boarded windows boasting 'DJs, Pies'. I shunned the Sea Breeze Social Club, the South Pier that offered 'Family Entertainment and Fried Food'. Instead, I knocked on the door of an unassuming house next to a dark, abandoned gas appliances shop and waited for a reply.

I was here to visit a friend. A friend who had recently moved to Suffolk and had, in a moment of characteristic largesse, promised me an entertaining evening at the local folk club. I wondered if this could possibly be a promise too far, but the invitation had awoken in me a question I'd been mulling over for some time.

I'd been having a problem with roots.

Mine, I mean. Frankly, I wasn't sure I had any. And I'd racked my brain, searched back in time. But the more I thought about it the more difficult it was to pin down. And for some reason I'd been thinking about it a lot.

In my earliest memory I was an outsider. My family had moved away from south London to the West Country and, as they tried to plant the new garden, stow boxes and redecorate, I knew we didn't really belong. It wasn't just the accent that I would never learn to pronounce, or the street names I would always forget. It wasn't just the legacy of local history I could never assimilate – miners, Methodists, people who said 'gert' and wore daps. Along with our tea-chests and family photographs, we had carried with us an indelible sense of otherness. I absorbed the anxieties of my parents as they grappled with unfamiliar surroundings, and made rootlessness my starting point.

I did try saying 'gert'. I tried saying 'tomottoes' and 'suck-'ee' as well, but I failed to pull it off. I was self-conscious. It wouldn't stick. When I was old enough to explore on my own I felt like smoke between the paving stones. From the cast of a face or the code in a gesture to the way a person walks, the new town was a loyalty card I would never fully redeem.

I kept having a go at it, though. My adolescence was a string of naive bids for identity and I hung around in strange and diverse groups, hoping osmosis would cause a defining cultural kernel to grow deep within me. I wore a leather jacket but was too cerebral to develop the punk spirit. I grew my hair long but was too uptight to be a hippy, too underendowed in the moped department to be a biker. I bought an onion but it failed to make me French.

One day I heard an Irish jig played on a solitary fiddle and the lonely, soulful sound captivated me. Like one or two English before me, I resolved to become Irish. The history, the poetry, the mythology, the politics, religion and famine – they could all wait. I was going to get on the fast track by learning the diddly songs. I bought record after record, distilling my taste to a cherry stone of perfection that existed in three or four treasured vinyl discs. I learned to play guitar.

But it soon became clear that I was on a hiding to nothing. Apart from the fact that it was another accent I couldn't do, the songs spoke of a history, of political and economic struggles, that didn't belong to me. Though they spoke to me, I couldn't pass on their message. What did I know about fleeing my home for a better life and ending up in America? It wasn't part of the collective memory where I grew up. No, these songs were meant for others. But surely there had to be some English songs I could relate to. Surely it was my duty to be at least sincere.

But I had no idea where to begin. We – I mean the English – had done a good job of burying our fundamental ways under a veneer of sherry and industry. We'd hidden ourselves behind war, empire and a flawed notion of cultural superiority. The embrace of progress meant we had stifled our folk traditions. We had brushed our ethnic foibles under the colonial rug with the rest of the savages. We could go to the Last Night of the Proms all we liked, but there must have been something organic once. Something that had grown out of the land, had been communicated among people, among themselves, at work, in the inns and fields? Surely England had its own folklore.

By 'folk', I meant the music and customs we had always had, since the dawn of time, the songs, dances and plays performed by ordinary people, rather than professionals. The songs that fathers passed down to their sons in the cornfield, the lullabies that mothers sang to infants in the crib. The bawdy tales of derring-do swapped in alehouses or the gritty sea songs telling of brutal press-gangs and the cruel life on board a man-of-war. The songs that tell us about ourselves and our history, passed on from one generation to another, their authors lost in the mists of time. Ritual songs. Magic songs. Songs about the land.

Frankly, I was jealous. Every other place seemed to have its own folklore. In Mongolia it is customary to drink fermented mare's milk, make a low feral growl in the back of your throat and whistle at the same time, while beating four on a yak-skin tambourine. Aboriginal Australians prefer to do their growling down a long pipe while banging two bits of wood together. It's not much but it is wholly their own and I wanted a shot at it.

Clearly, not every Irishman was a fan of the Dubliners, nor

could every Swiss turn his hand to a quick yodel before setting off for the bank. But when the chips were down this sense of tradition was something ancient, permanent and binding that belonged to them and helped them belong. When they were away it reminded them of home. When they were home it reinforced their identity and helped forge communities. When they were oppressed it only added to their strength. The French had the accordion, the Greeks had the bouzouki. And the English?

I marched my adolescent self into George's Bookshop and requested *The Penguin Book of English Folk Songs*. I'd read about it on the sleeve of a record from the sixties. They didn't have it. It was out of print. That was the end. I found other clothes to wear and filed the question of roots away at the back of my mind. Evidently it had fermented.

A dog barked and the door opened.

Louis was eating dried hops out of a plastic bag.

'The hop,' Louis said, offering me a bite. 'Nature's finest bittering agent.'

'Yes.'

'And what do we call English beer?'

'Bitter,' I said, accidentally stepping into a shallow bucket of filth-coloured water on the kitchen floor. The dog, which had been drinking out of it, gave me a look and waited for me to take my shoe out of its evening toddy.

'Don't worry,' said Louis. 'That's only sedimentary waste. The real stuff is in the bathroom.' He proudly showed me a large keg full of a black sludge called 'mild', conveniently positioned next to the lavatory.

'We'll decant that and take it with us to the sing-a-round,' he said.

Sing-a-round? Home-brewed ale and a folk club. My heart was sinking.

I knew why. A decade before, I had been living in a small, rural town in the Midlands, unemployed and stony broke. At length I had found a job at a car-seat factory where I sat for a year putting one bit of metal into another for eight hours a day and developing an interesting dermatitis. I saved enough money to move to London to look for work as a writer, and eventually I found it. I was an economic migrant, but I was also a cultural migrant.

In London you could visit galleries and operas, see plays and musicals; you could listen to something called the LPO at some place called the RFH or watch an evening of stand-up comedy. And the next day you could slate them all for a newspaper and take home a cheque for your efforts. For London was England's centre for art and media, for poetry and punditry. It was also the UK's most cosmopolitan city. You could buy Moroccan sausages from a French deli and sit drinking Turkish coffee at an Italian pavement café while speaking Portuguese to a Brazilian. Felafels, plantains, guavas and yams, they were all waiting for your patronage, and you could get your pastrami on rye bread, ciabatta, pumpernickel or pitta.

People in London were always busy, working on 'projects' or rushing from business lunch to crowded bar. Everyone was calling up everyone else on mobile phones and they were all promising to get back to one another just as soon as they got finished with their projects. Permanently braying, London-dwellers said things like: 'That skirt is *so* post-Kylie' and 'I hope your juicer's insured'. It was the most pretentious, self-regarding city on earth and I was proud to call it home. After all, simply being there meant I'd made it, didn't it? And wasn't that what it was all about? That feeling of superiority? Surely I hadn't bust my chops at the car-seat factory just to drink beer the dog had licked and sing about sailors? Well, it was too late now, we were going. And that itchy question was tickling at me again.

Waveney Folk Club was just that. A club. Like a bridge club or cross-stitch club, it was a place for like-minded individuals to gather, safely removed from those who wouldn't understand, and take part in their chosen hobby. At Waveney the hobby was singing folk songs. When they weren't singing folk songs, the members were silent. There was a bar, but no licence. There was no smoking either. You could make yourself tea, quietly, if you wanted, but I noticed at least one Thermos flask. People here brought their own.

'Why do you think I decanted the mild?' Louis winked, pouring me a glass. I drank it. 'Mild' was a misnomer. Still, it went down all right if you didn't think about the dog lick.

The good folk of Lowestoft had arranged themselves in a loose circle and sat silently waiting for Graham, the leader, to get things started. Graham was a retired man in a sailor's cap with a large leather fob on his belt. He was wearing a knitted sweater, with a picture of a concertina and the words 'Waveney Folk Club' emblazoned across top and bottom, and drinking from a pewter tankard. Waveney is a river. Graham was an amiable man who took charge with good humour and solicited performances from around the circle. Everyone did a turn.

As the folk conch made its way from one person to another I came to a frightening realization. They were good. These were all polished performers, accomplished enough to be on stage. In fact, many had the air of seasoned pros. A couple on piano and concertina sang a lilting waltz, two guitarists mesmerized the room, squeezeboxes polkaed and jigged. No one played wrong notes. I was trying to make myself invisible behind a chair when suddenly, as I knew he must, Graham pointed at me.

'I've forgotten your name, Paul,' he said.

'Richard,' I mumbled.

'All right, John, sing us a song.'

The request aroused in me a curious feeling of dread. I hadn't played the guitar for an age. I had rather hoped just to drink the 'mild' and observe quietly from the back, but now I had the conch. I was in the ring. This was the way it was going to be.

I searched through the dusty vaults of my memory. Something English, something old. Why hadn't I been taught things? There must be something. Well, there was the theme from *Captain Pugwash* – but I couldn't just hum 'Diddly dee, de-diddly dee – ' Surely I could do better. 'Four and Twenty Virgins'? Er, no. 'Heave-ho, blow the man down?' That's the only bit I know. 'What Shall We Do With the Drunken Sailor?' What indeed? Something old, something English. I needed help, but who would save me? I heard someone clear his throat impatiently in the silence and, hoping against hope that sheer momentum would bring forth a song, I closed my eyes, opened my mouth, and this came out:

> I got myself a crying, talking
> Sleeping, walking
> Living doll . . .

Something old, something English – in my darkest hour, Cliff had rescued me from the wilderness. I had been chosen. Through me, the voice of Cliff had spoken, but would it let me off the hook

with the higher powers? I had heard about folk clubs. I had heard
of people getting barred for singing songs in a non-traditional
way, ostracized and ceremonially drummed out (on the spoons)
for rendering a 'too-rye-ay' as a 'wack-fol-me-daddio'. I imagined
Graham gently leading me to the door and saying: 'I think we both
know this is for the best, Nigel.'

But Waveney wasn't like that and I wanted to keep an open
mind. There *were* beards, yes, and Graham *was* wearing a sailor's cap.
But wasn't Lowestoft a seafaring town after all? Facial hair is not a
crime, except in a few states in America, and surely an honest man
is entitled to choose his own headgear? The club members afforded
me the same courteous applause they gave to all the others, and the
conch moved on. Louis gave an informative song about the origins
of the phonograph, which I suspect he had composed himself.
A group of women with squeezeboxes played jaunty tunes. A man
with a beard sang a song called 'Brimbledon Fair' and another man
with another beard sang a song called 'Dorothy Drew'.

This last one struck a chord. It was set in Manchester and
involved the sudden elopement of the eponymous Dorothy with
an unnamed calico printer's clerk. My forebears had been calico
printers in Manchester. I glowed with sudden pride at the idea that
it could be genetically my fault that this song even existed. It may
have been the effect of the 'mild', but for the first time it seemed I
had heard a traditional song from England that I felt could actually
belong to me. It was a good song and at no point did the singer
place his finger directly into his ear.

The next morning I discovered that Louis's dog, aroused by the reek of beer, had eaten my footwear during the night, which left me in a predicament with regard to the four-hour train and Tube journey that lay ahead of me. I tiptoed barefoot into town and discovered to my glee that Foot-Rite were having a sale on flimsy deck shoes – the sort that, were it the height of summer, might be just right for the beach. But it was far from the height of summer. New Year, in fact. I purchased a pair for £5.99, reduced from £10.99, sang a triumphal bar of 'Auld Lang Syne' and made a resolution to return to Lowestoft for future shoe bargains.

I had enjoyed myself, but on the way home I couldn't help mulling over the whole idea of the folk 'club'. If this music belonged to us all, why did it need its own club? Why was it a *hobby* to sing folk songs? Why weren't we all just doing it all the time? How had this part of England's heritage come to be hidden in a darkened room full of Thermos flasks and crisps?

The story begins with an Edwardian composer called Cecil Sharp. Sharp was born in south London and had a Cambridge education but only modest means. A teacher of music and composer in the classical vein, he had experienced a personal revelation as the nineteenth century had drawn to a close.

And what a century it had been. In the space of a hundred years, England had reinvented itself entirely. Machines such as the spinning jenny and the shearing frame had transformed the woollen and cotton trades from modest cottage industries to giants of commercial manufacturing. As wealthy capitalists built factory upon factory, the arrival of steam power and the railways enabled ordinary people to travel up and down the country as never before. Industry moved away from the countryside and centred in new, purpose-built towns like Leeds and Huddersfield which sprawled over the land, darkening the skies. Ordinary country people, stricken with poverty, found themselves moving to the large towns in search of work – a migration that changed the shape of rural life for good. It was a century of innovation, of industrial and political advances that put England and the United Kingdom streets ahead of other nations. It was a time of rabid patriotism, of militaristic bravado, when Britannia claimed to rule the waves, 'the dread and envy of them all'. And it was at this moment that Cecil Sharp became disillusioned with classical music.

He was tired of the way the scene was dominated by German composers. He was adept at mimicking the likes of Schumann, whom he admired, but had achieved little success with such compositions. He had come to feel instead that English music should have an identity of its own. In Hungary, Bartók was reclaiming classical music for his own country by searching within its indigenous musical traditions. In Czechoslovakia, Dvořák had been inspired by folk dances to create new sounds for the classical orchestra. Sharp felt a corresponding need to perform the same task for English music. But where to look? What was English?

It was time to get out of the city, time to dig in the country soil and unearth England's true cultural heritage. Carrying only a notebook and a giant portable phonograph, Cecil Sharp got on his bike. He would eschew the highbrow pretensions of the capital and make it his business to discover the proper England of proper English folk. Country folk in rural hideaways where primitive customs surely remained unchanged since time immemorial. That was his holy grail, his romantic quest. He would deliver unto England its roots and its heritage.

And me?

Although I had moved back to London, the truth was that the vague, anchorless feeling had only intensified. That is to say, I'd brought it with me. Something had to be done. My curious, Cliff-centric evening at the Waveney Folk Club sing-a-round had rekindled in me a hundred questions about my roots that transcended my ill-informed prejudices. I had to face up to my ancestry. It would have been so much more romantic to have really – originally -- been Irish or French or Greek. But what if one is simply English? What hope for romance then?

I was galvanized into action. Out there, beyond the muggy heat, the filth, the social climbing and financial tyranny of the city, I felt certain there was an ancient heart. There were surely age-old places, rites and rhythms that beat to a different pulse. There had to be lessons from the land, devised before the dawn of Christianity. We might have buried it all deep in a mire of lager, Blockbuster Videos and themed pubs, but there was an English folklore as vibrant and colourful as those of Ireland, Scotland and Wales, I was convinced. It was only a question of squelching through the landfill, among the used KFC wet-wipes, and grasping hold. This, then, would be my grail quest. There are so many places such a journey can take you. Would I spend all my life standing on the platform without ever jumping on the train?

2 | Bear Necessities

The man at the travel desk was apologetic. This came as no real surprise. Letting the customer down with a wan smile is a skill taught on the first day of railway school. 'Yes, I know Whittlesey *does* have a station,' he said. 'But I can't sell you a ticket to it.' Of course not, where would be the fun in that? 'I can do you one as far as Peterborough.' After that I'd be on my own, it seemed, lost in the fens, at the mercy of local transport, the malicious whim of ticket collectors with inscrutable faces and secret timetables designed to give you an aneurism, then keep you trapped in a town with only a witch doctor and a well.

The man studied me. Eventually he said, 'Whittlesey, eh? You off to the Straw Bear, then?' I answered yes, although I didn't know what it was yet. I just knew I was going. The man gave a nod of recognition, a faint smile with a hint of complicity, as though I had just joined the Masons by mistake. I didn't know what to say in return, so I simply smiled back.

My presence here was entirely due to a chance sighting a few months before. I had been in Oxford on business – in other words I had raced through the meeting and passed the afternoon strolling along the canal – and happened to glimpse a curious man out of the corner of one eye. He had a long straggly beard and a hat bedecked with flowers. He was wearing a T-shirt that bore the slogan 'I Follow the Straw Bear'. The image had caught my imagination. Was there a parallel community where foliate hats were commonplace? And could this community somehow belong to me? Gradually it had become clear that I, too, needed to follow the Straw Bear.

And so the tiny, two-carriage train pulled out of Peterborough. This is where it would begin, my quest, in this bleak spot in the reedy flatlands of the east, early in January with rain in the air. The train carried an odd-looking cargo. It was filled with seat after seat of identical people. Bearded, balding men of fifty-something years. In sensible coats. They chatted among themselves and I heard phrases like 'Ah! Fetch out your *billets*, John. Here advanceth the stout guardian of the hole-punch!'

The ticket inspector arrived.

'What's this, then? Works outing?' he asked one man.

'No indeed,' came the jovial reply. 'We're going to the Straw Bear!'

'Oh, right.' A pause. 'What's that then?'

What indeed? The man in front of me was no help although he tried amiably, his owlish eyebrows dancing. His name was Keith.

'We're here for the borders mostly,' he confided in me as though I spoke the same language. 'Borders all over town, really. Plus the molly, of course. As for the Bear itself, well!' The Bear clearly needed no further explanation. Keith was from the Greensleeves morris in London. Morris dancers – I did know they existed. As a child I had seen them occasionally at events in town, large, lumbering men with their white hankies aloft, their leg-bells jingling and their incongruous, light-footed music. Although the spectacle had left a lasting impression I, like many English, had ultimately looked the other way. But could there be a connection between this odd early sighting and my own fascination with an unanswered question?

'Before you disappear,' Keith said outside on the platform, handing me his card, 'I'd have a swift peruse of the old *menu de trains*, if you know what I mean. Trains out of here are a bit like French steaks – on the rare side.' I thanked him and studied the timetable. Yes. Best not miss the last one. It's unforgiving here in January. The old brick buildings and white façades looked stark and joyless in this light.

I left the gravel and dead scrub of the station approach and joined a loose band of people, all walking purposefully towards town past rows of little houses. The windows were black, the gardens dead and bare. People rubbed their hands as their breath condensed in front of them. The gloom worked its way into me. The sunshine seemed far away and I had no idea where I was. I wondered for a moment if I hadn't made a mistake. Perhaps I shouldn't have come.

Then, as I reached a car park, I felt a low booming – rhythmic, like a heartbeat. Soon I heard it. It became louder, the unmistakable sound of a bass drum, and then, suddenly, from around the side of a brick toilet came the straw man, capering and tottering, sur-

rounded by his leaping entourage of children dressed in coloured jackets made of rags.

A man dressed as a haystack. No face, no fingers. Just long swathes of yellow straw tied together to look like a human. But he moved, he danced, he rocked from side to side. Clearly there was someone in there, gasping for air. They called him the Straw Bear. Led by a string, he headed a long procession of strange, otherworldly people. Men in farmers' hats, their faces blackened. Solemn, strange figures playing accordions. Dark women dressed in black and wrapped in foliage. A giant hen. Group after group of wild-hued musicians playing sweet, rhythmic music on old instruments, lighting up the dark day. The dancers kept on coming, row upon row, the joy of the music belying the solemnity of the grim faces.

I stood there in the car park, for a while, dazzled and excited. Apparently, this was my culture. So where had it been hiding? Here in the fens? Or did this happen everywhere? I looked again at the ghastly man-woman with sooty face, beard and dress, at the man dressed as a horse, at the groups of dancers with bushes on their hats. After a while I walked into the market square, where the Straw Bear was just returning. I'd forgotten to feel gloomy and I didn't feel so cold. Crowds were thronging and the musicians and dancers had split up into groups to perform. They played small, wooden button accordions. They called them melodeons. They played concertinas, fiddles and drums; brass and banjos. A wood clarinet. A saxophone. A piercing pipe and drum. I found myself outside a pub and I slipped in. They were serving a specially brewed beer called Straw Bear Ale. It was dark and malty. I didn't normally drink this sort of thing. I took my pint outside to watch the dancers.

There were women with steel swords. They each held an end, describing an intricate lattice as they wove in and out. Suddenly the swords fused together in a six-pointed star, which one of the women held aloft while the crowds cheered. I was stunned. I remembered having the same feeling the first time I watched a bullfight. The artistry in the dance of the toreros was a strange and foreign code. The whoops and sighs of the audience showed appreciation for secret things I didn't understand. The difference then was that I had travelled to another country.

The women left and another band of people arrived to take their place before me. With black faces, this group of dancers performed inside a circle of men in country tweeds and waistcoats. These stern-faced gentlemen slowly stalked the perimeter of the arena until they came to a stop at a random point, facing the onlookers – and stared. I counted six men on staring duty alone. More ominous still were their musicians, an all-woman band of black-clad figures, their heads bound around with flowing evergreen foliage. They played the same jolly, bouncy music, their faces immobile. There was, it should be said, something terrifying about them.

Around the edges, men and women laughed and smiled. I watched a young mother grinning and pointing. At her feet three children looked on, transfixed in horror as monsters in feathers and flowers grimaced at them and leaped about, shrieking and banging sticks. In another group of dancers, one of the men appeared to be disgraced former Tory politician Neil Hamilton, in clogs. A small boy turned away in disgust.

More and more came. The ghoulish, primal-looking Witchmen, in dark glasses and feathers. The Red Leicester morris, the red from their faces staining the cheeks of ladies as they stole kisses. The Pig Dyke Molly, in black and white. Longsword dancers and horses. It was a jumble of colour, of sound and motion, drums and whirring rattles. The black faces and costumes seemed to come directly out of the landscape, born out of the severity of January, bringing

LIMERICK
00438047
COUNTY LIBRARY

primal energy to the winter. They seemed to have slipped through the reed beds and out of another time and place altogether, some place bordering on the superstitious. I felt stirred up by the show and my stomach began to rumble.

Whittlesey, I soon discovered, was not overburdened with places to eat. I hunkered down in a Chinese chip shop and ate sausages out of the paper wrapping, my coat wrapped tightly around me as the wind howled through the open door. It wasn't what I'd had in mind, but the curry sauce warmed me and I began chatting to a couple at the next table. They performed with an Appalachian dance team, English people dancing moves created in America by British and Irish immigrants. They told me how the festival brought together enthusiasts from all over the country, enabling them to meet. Enthusiasts?

'English folk music and dance could be happening next door to you,' said George, who played guitar. 'And you wouldn't necessarily know.' She made it sound like a furtive, secret society. Perhaps that's what it was. She invited me to the Bricklayers Arms later, to see them dance.

As I walked through town I saw women with red stains on their faces. The Red Leicester morris called it 'spreading the red'. A lady adjusted her attire in a shop window. 'I can't decide if I look traditional,' she fidgeted, 'or just silly.' Another woman in a cloth cap banged a frame drum, a fag hanging from her mouth. Four boys looked on, shouting 'Go for it'. They were all wearing tweed hats and carrying pewter tankards. A trio of banjo players slipped in and out of some pillars, and a miniature Straw Bear scurried over the cobbles. A man in rags was buying a furry snake from a street vendor. Men in bowler hats strolled along the road. A massive crowd was assembling outside the Bricklayers Arms, watching the dancers on the green.

Inside the pub it was warm and busy. On the wall, next to a straw tableau, a notice advised that 'bad language' would not be tolerated. It was hard to imagine this convivial crowd causing any grief. George's Appalachian group were already performing in the bar. A series of lone step-dancers capered and clicked on a portable wooden platform that captured the sound of their shoes, while the musicians played boisterous, rhythmic music on the melodeon and banjo.

It was English music, apparently. One of the team, Adrian, told me this 'old-time' music had gone to America with the early settlers and developed there. Folklorists collected the tunes from the Appalachian Mountains in the early part of the last century. But I had never seen it played.

'You haven't been to the right places,' Adrian said. 'It's everywhere.'

We had a couple of drinks. Adrian was telling me about the correct price to pay for concertina repairs when I spotted a trio of smiling people with interesting hair. I joined them. One man was wearing a T-shirt that said 'I Follow the Straw Bear'. He had a long, tangled grey beard and a hat bedecked with flowers. I recognized him immediately. His name was Dick Brooker and he made the festival his holiday every year. It's a nice time of year to get away to the freezing east of England.

'I do painting and decorating work mainly,' Dick said suddenly. Quite a bit of his work had found its way onto his shirt. His friend was playing a melodeon in the corner – bouncy shanty tunes. He owned an instrument shop in Oxford. Another arrived, a session began and we sat tapping our feet and chatting.

'What do you think of the show so far?' Dick asked me.

'It's good,' I said.

'No it's not, it's rubbish,' Dick shouted, drunk and happy. 'But it's *English* rubbish!'

It didn't seem like rubbish. But how would I have known? I was still a bit dazed but the beer was tranquillizing me into a state of warm contentment. Apparently the dancers in the rag jackets with sticks were borders morris. That's what Keith had meant on the train. The dances come from the border between Wales and England. They are more energetic and aggressive than the type with ribbons and little hankies. Those come from the Cotswolds. The black-faced other worlders, they were molly dancers, from here – from the fenlands. The molly tradition is characterized by its soot-black faces and hobnailed boots. I picked up a programme from one of the tables. It said they traditionally only appeared in the depths of winter. Mollies would accompany ploughboys on Plough Monday, begging pennies. It's gruff, aggressive dancing, as bleak as the January fens.

I was intrigued by the use of words like 'traditionally', 'was' and 'would' in the programme. It was the language of museums. The tone implied that we were seeing something divorced from its original setting. Some kind of re-creation or revival. I wondered if it was. When *was* 'traditionally', exactly? Where did it go? Has it been gone long? Is it coming back? Why did we do these things once and then stop, and then start again?

The sword dances come from Yorkshire. Some say the Vikings brought them. There is something about them, a kind of art form, like a human haiku. As if to illustrate the point, a group of rapper dancers – with bendy metal swords – came in and performed a dance to a fiddle. One by one they locked swords and suddenly the star was aloft. This time I applauded.

I couldn't believe I had struck so lucky on my first outing. And I couldn't believe this community. This good old country pub filled to the beams with animation and ancient tradition. Up at the bar, I caught a glimpse through the window of the lounge. I hadn't noticed this other room before. It was full of unsmiling people, talking in muted tones among themselves. Keeping separate. There was no colour in there, no music or dancing.

And then, suddenly it dawned on me.

Them's the locals. I looked from one bar to the other. That's right. And we were the weirdos, come from London, Manchester, Newcastle, with our tie-dyed bags and earrings. We'd come from all over. One group of sword dancers had come from Boston. Boston, Massachusetts. We didn't really belong here. We were enthusiasts. Hobbyists. I was at a convention. Even the Straw Bear himself poked his head in, took one look at us and left. I didn't quite understand. I looked around at the motley collection of beards, tankards and hippy hair. Where was this music, this dance,

this tradition – where was it really from? If the locals themselves wanted to keep apart, was it really local? Was it really tradition? Who was really doing it and why? What did it mean?

I had too many questions and none of what I saw was making any sense. I thought about asking Dick and Adrian and the others. Sadly, I was drunk, so I listened to the shanties coming from the squeezebox in the corner and let it all wash over me. There was too much here to take in. I heard someone at the bar saying, 'Of course, all of this used to be a pagan ritual, like most of these customs   '

Really? Animal masks, feathered hats and black faces. A man covered in straw. Could it really be true that here in this tiny fenland market town I was seeing a tradition that stretched back across the ages, to a time when people worshipped corn, the sun, the trees?

The festival programme wasn't much help. The event I had witnessed was only twenty-five years old. Although twenty-five years was a long time – a lifetime's devotion to a hobby, you might say – it was hardly ancient. But the Straw Bear's roots were older. 'A long time ago it was the custom on the Tuesday following Plough Monday to dress a Plough Boy in straw and parade him through the streets,' the programme claimed. There was a reference to it in a newspaper from the home stretch of the Victorian era. Hardly ancient. Could it go back further?

We can't know. There are records of plough customs and superstitions from the medieval period onwards, but not before. In medieval times the ploughing season began here after Christmas. It was about turning over the wet soil, dragging heavy ploughs with oxen, making it good for planting. There were numerous superstitions attached to the process. People sometimes dragged ploughs around a fire for luck. In Tudor East Anglia, churches burned plough lights.

Records, history. The difficulty with records is, you never know if they mark the beginning of something or whether they are merely noting down for posterity what went previously unrecorded.

It wasn't until the eighteenth and nineteenth centuries that so-called Plough Boys began to wear fancy dress in order to make more of the occasion. Here came the blackened faces and farm animal disguises. Not too pagan, really. And yet they did communicate something primal, perhaps something that had always existed here, in one form or another. It was that that I wanted to investigate.

The dance teams were called 'sides', as though they were competitors in a contest to see who could wear the most amusing hat. They had all been created recently, some as recently as the nineties. And yet what they were doing, the way they dressed, the movements they made and the music they played – these all spoke of ancient things. And I wanted to find out more. The Straw Bear alone was not going to answer my questions: a more detailed search was called for. A systematic approach. The music cranked up a notch and I felt at ease here, among the whooping, high spirits and good humour. And so, systematically, I bought pints of dark Black Dog beer and drank them.

•

On the train out of town I sat down at a table opposite a young woman with a two-year-old boy. He was staring out of the window as the rain made mirrors of the buildings. His mother asked me how long the train would take to get to Peterborough. I remembered the outward journey was very short.

'About five, ten minutes,' I said.

I glanced over my shoulder. The carriage was full of the same people from this morning. Returning to their real towns. Day trippers. The woman opposite wanted to know why everyone had been in Whittlesey for the day, what the great interest was, all of a sudden, in her home-town. They told her it was Straw Bear Day.

'Oh yeah . . . Yeah.' A pause. 'What's *that* all about then?'

'Country dancing mainly,' they said. 'Morris men and that, a big bale of straw that walks about the town.'

'Pub sessions,' someone else said. 'Traditional music.'

'Oh . . .' she said. You could see the thought glide through her and escape, like a final demand or a parking fine. 'It's funny,' she said. 'I've lived in Whittlesey all my life and I've never been to see it once.' She laughed at this. But it wasn't so crazy.

We don't live in agricultural communities any more. Ploughing is hardly central to our way of life. We buy our food from Tesco and Asda. It comes from New Zealand, South America, from whoever can deliver it cheaply and consistently shaped. Whoever can supply it with the right kind of wrapper. Churning up the soil – what significance could it possibly have for us now?

We passed a batch of squat, ugly buildings and I watched the signs drift by. Courts. Currys. Carpetright. When we got to

Peterborough the woman stayed seated as the train prepared to go back to Whittlesey. 'Oh, I'm not getting off *here*,' she explained to the ticket collector. 'I live in Whittlesey, I'm only on here because he wanted a train journey,' and the boy ate his doughnut and stared out of the window.

'Look,' said his mother, pointing at a JCB, mashing up the soil outside the retail park. 'There's a dig-dig.'

Today had served to kindle something and I wanted to follow my curiosity. I needed to find out more about this music, see where it led me. But first I needed to get the right kit.

3 | Nasal Problems

Dripping with rain, I slipped into a London shop. The shop sold folk instruments from around the world. They had everything from an autoharp to a zither and I was sure I would find something here. But what? I was fiddling with a tiny drum when the assistant swooped upon me.

'Ha, ha, sir. Now we don't play the *tambourim* with a finger, do we? You'll need a *tambourim* beater, but we are sold out I'm afraid.' I put the drum down. Two steps into the shop and I had already broken a folk rule.

'What can we do for you?' The man asked. The morsel of Chocolate Hobnob sticking to his lip bobbed up and down with the words. I wasn't sure. I had a guitar already but I wanted something more – traditional. Once again I reached into my murky past and this time fetched out an image from childhood: a picture of the toy toad in *Bagpuss*, who had regaled his fellow shipmates with songs of a folksy bent. What did he play? What was it?

'I want a banjo,' I said.

'We have banjos, sir. What sort did you want?'

Sort? What, was this a test? 'The cheap sort,' I said. 'What would you recommend?' The assistant gave the sort of chuckle I had previously only heard from my accountant.

'Ha ha. Well now. That would depend on the sort of music you want to play on it. Bluegrass, Irish or jazz?'

'English,' I said.

'Oh no, sir. If it's English music you want, you'd be better off with a melodeon. We have those too.' He motioned to a rack of the small button squeezeboxes I had seen at Waveney and Whittlesey. They looked complicated and expensive. 'Or a concertina.'

At this point the other assistant looked up from the counter and chipped in.

'Ah, well, careful. You see, the concertina was never *actually* a folk instrument. It was never supposed to be used for *folk* tunes: that's just an invention of *revivalists*.'

He seemed angry at this. I wasn't sure where his argument was going.

'You know, I'm kind of fixed on the idea of a banjo. I'll take the one with the fewest strings.'

The first assistant raised his eyebrows. 'That would be the tenor, sir. Ostensibly a jazz instrument, I think you'll find, although it is possible, with lighter strings, to tune it up and use it as an Irish instrument.'

What on earth did he mean? There seemed to be so many rules and regulations. Surely as long as you've got all the notes you can play whatever you like. If I don't get on too well with English folk I might have a crack at 'The Birdie Song'. But the assistants were only trying to help. I bought a melodeon too, just to confuse them, and took my haul away, wondering whether Cecil Sharp would have approved of my choice.

Actually, I think he would have. Sharp is often remembered as a good-natured if emotionally explosive sort of person, with a genuine love of music, although he did have a hatred of 'noise'. As a child he once cried at the sound of a brass band.

At college he had excelled on the ocarina and jam-jars as well as the piano. While recovering from a bout of typhoid he had constructed a xylophone from his parents' trees and had taught himself the banjo while shaking off some other disease. He was also a freethinker, a political radical, a great storyteller and writer of limericks. In short, although he was clearly not of robust physical health, Sharp was exactly the sort of renaissance man to help rid the nation of its fin-de-siècle soul-searching.

The great industrial leaps made in England during the nineteenth century had given various men of letters pause for sentimental thought. The new cities were fearful, violent and unsanitary places. The factories abused their workers, who lived in miserable poverty and ill health. The writers, artists and thinkers of the day became troubled by an elegiac sense of lost community. Whatever had happened to merry old England, they asked themselves? Where had all the flowers gone? Eyes hazy with romance, their spirits bolstered by economic privilege, these pioneers embarked on the search, notebooks in hand. Their grail was the rural idyll and anything that pertained to the timeless simplicity of peasant life. Maypoles, dances, pipes and drums. They let it infuse their work, and in turn their work influenced wider thought.

It was in this climate that Sharp, in 1899, had his own musical revelation, while convalescing from a unique combination of asthma, pneumonia and gout of the eyes in the village of Headington Quarry near Oxford. It was Boxing Day and the local morris dancers were out. As the men jingled into view, their musician, a young mustachioed fellow called William Kimber, was playing a concertina. The tune he was squeezing out intoxicated Sharp. The delirious musician leaped from his chair, gave half a crown to the morris and had Kimber play the tune again while he noted it down furiously. It was 'Laudnum Bunches', a spry jig with an exciting ascending base line, which Kimber followed with 'Rigs o' Marlow'.

The experience energized Sharp beyond even his own ambition. He found in folk music not simply something quaint that served his purposes; rather, he was galvanized by the ancient spirit of the music. Something that had persisted through time, that was compelling, basic and primal. But he was horrified to think that the ordinary people of England, that is to say urban lettered men such as himself, knew nothing of this wonderful music. It was in danger of dying out and ought really to be saved. His suite of morris dance tunes, scored for strings, bassoon and horn was performed by the Hampstead Conservatoire orchestra, but Sharp subsequently abandoned all plans of composing classical music in an English style. The thing to do would be to conserve folk music, revive it and teach it to children in schools so that they might

benefit anew from their heritage. He decided to publish his own collections of folk songs and so he cycled through the countryside, looking for the songs that had been 'handed down among our peasantry from generation to generation and are still to be heard in country places'.

His rustic informants might have been suspicious at first, but Sharp tended to win them over with his wit. He made friends and kept in touch, exchanging letters over many years. Sharp was patient too. He was happy to sit for hours in some peaty midden, quietly smoking his pipe, waiting for an old woman's memory to come back. And when she finally sang, Sharp would be genuinely overwhelmed. He paid the singers, or would exchange a book of songs, a concertina or some tobacco. It wasn't always easy to coax the singing. These were not performers, they sang for themselves. For many the songs were part of their work. One woman could only sing while ironing. If she sat still, her memory went blank. One man could only sing while scaring crows with a metal tray. Sharp travelled everywhere on his bicycle. He enjoyed the liberation of cycling, which kept him close to the land and enabled him to stop and chat to farmers and gypsies, perhaps collecting a song as he did so.

Sharp was by no means the first person to note down rural folk songs – others had been interested for some time, working in their local areas – but he was certainly the first to imbue the music with universal cultural significance, embarking on a series of lectures and performances that, in truth, never really ended until he breathed his last. So what happened next is a measure of Sharp's contagious enthusiasm.

The country went folk song crazy. Aided by influential allies such as the composer Ralph Vaughan Williams and others in politics and the media, Sharp succeeded in pushing the business of folk song high up the public agenda, kick-starting a concerted revival. Newspapers such as the London *Morning Post* ran articles about the urgency of collecting folk music. It was a call to action, but who would pick up the baton? The musical establishment decided that professors of music should take charge. Sharp's derision was absolute and he countered that academia had shown little interest or aptitude. The media fuss had the effect of resurrecting the Folk-Song Society, a small-scale club which, after having not met for two years, was shamed into publishing new collections. The revival had begun.

And so had mine. Choosing my next venue was easy. I had decided to look in at Cecil Sharp House in London. The building, a charmless brick carbuncle, is nonetheless home to the English Folk Dance and Song Society. It hosts concerts, courses and dance classes, screens films and houses the Vaughan Williams Memorial Library. It also has a small bar, stocked with a disappointing selection of drinks, in which meets, every Tuesday, the fabled Sharp's Folk Club.

I went downstairs to the basement. An invitation to join the Ukulele Orchestra of Great Britain flapped listlessly in the breeze from an open window as I ground to a halt at the closed door.

'Do not open the door while people are singing,' warned an unmissable notice. 'Wait until you hear the applause.' A man was singing and playing a concertina. I could be waiting a while.

I waited. And waited. The singer had embarked on a ballad of epic proportions. At this stage the lovelorn gal had only just made up her mind to follow her press-ganged beloved out to sea. She hadn't yet got round to dressing as a sea boy and – whoops – finding herself in battle on board a man-of-war. From there it could go in one of two directions. The unmasking was almost a certainty. I was hoping the captain would take kindly to her, tell her young William's ship was lost and put her gently ashore. But there are other fates for a girl lost aboard a boat full of scurvy sea dogs. And none of them are pretty.

In the event I got distracted by a flyer advertising something called 'Friday Feet' so I missed the ending. But the applause woke me and I slipped through the door, straight into another era.

In the early fifties a Salford playwright and agit-prop socialist called Ewan MacColl tried to move British music away from the influence of the guitar-based 'skiffle' songs of the American poor. Cowboy songs, railroad songs, songs from the Great Depression. This music had been popularized in America by the likes of Woody Guthrie and Pete Seeger and was seeping into the British consciousness with the help of Lonnie Donegan and others. At the same time the BBC had begun a folk song collecting scheme, and in radio programmes such as *Country Magazine* and *As I Roved Out* had begun to offer British folk song to a wider public. One person who tuned in regularly was the slight, mustachioed man with sandy grey hair who I got talking to at the bar.

'The radio was telling you these songs were recorded in 1952, that they were the last *ever* and no more existed,' said the man, whose name was Doc. 'And yet I was going out onto Dartmoor and hearing them in the pub.' It became clear to him that the thing to do was to collect. So he bought a tape recorder – a grey and purple creation – for £1 17s 6d. It turned out to be the first of many. In fact, Doc Rowe has been collecting and documenting British folk customs, rituals and events ever since.

In 1958, partly in answer to skiffle mania and partly in the spirit of the revival of interest in folk song, MacColl, along with radio producer Charles Parker and musician Peggy Seeger, began to broadcast a highly influential series of what they termed 'Radio Ballads'. Originally envisioning a musical drama with actors, MacColl had interviewed British workers, collecting stories about local working-class heroes. The plan was to work the material into a script and fuse it together with original music written along traditional lines. But it soon became clear to MacColl and Parker that the vernacular recordings were much more vital and human than anything they could achieve with actors. They dispensed with the plummy caption voices and narration of BBC radio, allowing the local people to speak for themselves. Snatches of spoken word were interspersed by Parker with music from MacColl and Seeger, creating a compelling immediacy hitherto unheard. Working people telling their own stories in their own accents.

Later, in the early sixties, MacColl opened a venue for British folk song, the Ballads and Blues Club, in London. But the skiffle influence was still heavy. Doc told me that MacColl was tired of people coming into his club from Peckham and singing 'Get Along Little Doggies'. Anyone who wanted a spot at MacColl's club had to sing a song from their own area. Which meant they had to find them. People from the north-east had been happy singing 'Long Gone Lost John' and were peeved to have to learn 'Keep Ya Feet Still Geordie Hinny' and 'Cushy Butterfield' just to please Ewan. But something caught them and they did it anyway. MacColl had tapped into something that had already been stirring.

In 1959 the singer Bert Lloyd published the seminal *Penguin*

Book of English Folk Songs, which he co-edited with Ralph Vaughan Williams, opening up a repertoire for budding folk singers and helping pave the way for the folk song 'movement' which would shape the popular music of the sixties and seventies – from Pentangle, Steeleye Span, Fairport Convention and the Albion Band to transatlantic intruders Simon and Garfunkel and Bob Dylan.

I looked around the room. It was small and rows of rude, uncomfortable chairs faced the front. A few people sat at wooden tables, nursing tankards. There were one or two young people, but most of the denizens of Sharp's Folk Club had clearly been here since MacColl's time. They still wore the workers' caps and the rustic beards, the sixties' neckerchiefs and ponytails.

Doc told me about another singer who had helped stimulate the budding revival. Martin Carthy was a Hatfield lad who had started out singing skiffle and was first noticed when he filled in for Lonnie Donegan. But under the influence of MacColl, Lloyd and the others, Carthy was drawn into English folk and simply transferred his skills. The unconditionals of the revival scene were still bent on singing traditional songs a cappella, an occasional finger in the ear, the way MacColl did it, to help find the note, wherever it was hiding. This was serious, political business and musical considerations were often cast to the wind. But Carthy was 'like a breath of fresh air', Doc said. A virtuoso guitarist, arranging traditional songs in a creative, forward-looking way. 'And his voice was clear,' Doc said. 'Nasal, yes. It was always nasal, but clear and in tune, which hadn't always been the case before.' Carthy also had a far-reaching influence. Dylan borrowed his 'Lord Franklin' directly from Carthy, and Paul Simon famously copyrighted Carthy's arrangement of 'Scarborough Fair'. Listening to tonight's act, that influence was still being brought to bear.

The guest singer was singing songs he'd found in the *Penguin Book of English Folk Songs*. He sang exactly like Martin Carthy. It was almost a caricature. Nasal and flat, yet clear and melodically uncompromising, a slight problem around the letter 'r' — it's the voice that has come to epitomize English folk music. An untraceable 'rural' accent. 'People either liked it or they didn't,' Doc said. 'And mostly back then they didn't.' But somehow the imitation Carthy voice caught on. It has since come to be considered the 'traditional' way to sing English songs, something that may have done much to keep listeners at arm's length. Even Carthy outgrew it and matured.

I got another drink in and mulled it all over while listening. The songs were old, that was for sure, and beautiful in their own right, but had they been dug up out of the soil? The roots of this particular singing tradition were in the early sixties, not before. I wanted to go deeper. These were working men's songs, helped back to life by a radical socialist with a political agenda. But where were the working men? Why weren't they singing them? The last time I was in a factory I had never heard anyone sing 'Oi'll duwink the bawwel dwy' in a piercing monotone.

Doc told me about a time down in Padstow, in Cornwall, at their May Day celebration, when the cream of the early sixties' folk scene descended on a pub to sing a few songs of the west. 'This was Cyril Tawney, Louis Killen, Anne Briggs and the Watersons, there in the pub, singing.' Surely the locals would have been thrilled to have such eminent figures rendering unto them what was theirs. Doc had overheard one old man who said: 'It were all right until all they hippies come down.'

I liked the music, but Sharp's Folk Club was oppressive. I needed some air. Since no one was allowed to talk, the two old men who had now boxed me into a corner were quietly breaking wind between themselves, as a form of non-verbal communication, it seemed. There was no smoking either. I came to feel as though I was in a museum. The singer struck up a fearsome jig on his melodeon. He was brilliant. We should have been dancing, letting go and whooping, but the drinkers at the folk club put down their tankards of ale, stroked their beards appraisingly and said, 'Nice.'

Nice as it was, this wasn't the folk music I had set out to find. I had never lived in the sixties. These weren't my roots. I was going to have to go further afield to find them. I'd have to get on my bike.

But first I was going to have to make my peace with the tankards and the ales.

4 | The Long Bitter End

It was cold and the wind crept behind my scarf, making me feel transparent. My breath condensed in angry little gusts as the queue inched forward. I was waiting in line outside Stratford Town Hall in east London, stamping my foot against the flagstones, folding my arms against my chest. Stratford is a dour part of London and I was dying to move in out of the cold and get a beer. There were cosy-looking pubs within walking distance, their windows broadcasting the rosy glow of easy companionship. All I had to do was to walk in and shake the winter from my clothes. But here I was, freezing in a queue of sensibly dressed men in spectacles, because I had been told on the best authority that the beer in such pubs wasn't real.

I was disturbed by the concept of 'real ale'. I think what did it was the implication that all my previous choices had been flawed and that I was by extension a charlatan, a fraud, a flimsy half-man. It's a kind of goad and, once the challenge has been levelled, there is no escape. 'Can *you* tell your light from your pale? What *is* the difference between a stout and a porter?' There was an added accusation in there and I didn't like it. In the previous year alone, 437 independently owned British breweries had been to work with the malt and the hops. As a result of their discerning toil, a total of 712 traditional bitters, milds, stouts, porters, ciders and perries had been produced and served, warm and pithy, to . . . who? I hadn't seen one of them, let alone tasted one.

But what really hurt was the term 'traditional'. Pubs that sold beers from independent breweries always boasted that they offered 'traditional ales'. Whose tradition? I had grown up drinking any old rubbish. Double Diamond, Harp, John Smith's. All this was wrong, apparently. Or fake. At the very least I was turning my back on my roots. My real ones, obviously, not the ones I grew up with. What had I been doing all these years? And what had I missed?

My first experiment with alcohol – an unpretentious Sainsbury's red with a robust dizziness on the nose and hint of regret in the aftertaste – had abruptly finished a family Christmas dinner when I was eleven. I had followed up the experience at the age of fourteen when, on a school visit to France, a classmate and I had discovered that French supermarkets would sell wine to children at a cost of 40p a bottle.

So it was, then, that in a back alley, conveniently close to the village urinoir and with twenty minutes before we were due to rejoin the coach bound for England, my compatriot and I got outside of two bottles of 12 per cent proof red and white vinegar with a sense of urgency and anarchic abandon seldom seen in that quarter of the world. Such an entertaining spectacle was this, in fact, that a group of local boys gathered on bicycles and mopeds to watch us and offer us tentative cigarettes. When we could stomach no more, we ran in faulty, giggling circles back to our coach to develop full bladders and maudlin. It was a rite of passage and we resolved to become hardened drinkers.

And life certainly presented opportunities. In my teens I took to busking in the city centre with my guitar. I suppose I could have got a Saturday job, but practising music somehow beat saying 'Cheeseburger *meal?*' three thousand times a day. There was an established community of musicians who worked the streets and the better subways. Competition for pitches was sportsmanlike and a gentleman's agreement was soon reached about the orderly rotation of good and bad spots. We generally deferred to an avuncular figure called Paul who played gentle folk songs in the Bob Dylan vein. He mediated in any disputes and dispensed a range of advice from dealing diplomatically with the law to selecting the right sort of plectrum. It was a peaceable, self-regulating micro-community. We never solicited money, that was the first rule. Buskers were musicians. If people placed a value on what we were offering, they were welcome to make a small donation. My favourite pitch was close to the bus station and I enjoyed spending a day there, working on my playing and watching the shoppers and travellers go by. The 'work' brought me in contact with many different types of people, some of whom were generous and friendly. None more so than Detox Dave.

Dave was a wino. You wouldn't have thought it at first, not to look at him. For a start he was young, in his late teens like me. He was mostly shaven, mostly smart. Not for Dave the time-ravaged face, the homeless tan, the matted beard and plastic bag full of string. Not for him the pin striped jacket and vest, the unlaced black boots and incoherent ravings. No arguing at shapes in the Devon Savouries window for Dave. No, he was just starting out. Though his eyes darted, he had so much to learn.

But the wino community worked the other way round from that of the buskers. The older homeless men were generally too far gone to give advice and often too busy talking to themselves to mediate any dispute. There were no disputes anyway. Just a group of people in the same boat, keeping each other company and trying to stay alive. There was Jock, who had been 'just tryin' tae get back tae Glasgow' since 1979. There was Boardwalk, who always sang 'Under the Boardwalk' in a subdued growl. There were two men dressed in threadbare suits and ties who always played chess and maintained a dignified silence. Then there was Old Smiler, who earned his name the easy way.

In this context it's easy to see why Dave enjoyed my company. He was always ready with a grin and a hello each time he saw me. He loved to hear my songs and sometimes helped me with the structure. 'Put another chorus in,' or, 'Not sure about the middle eight, Rich. Feels a bit random.' And, of course, he always had a plentiful supply of very strong cider. 'Tuck in,' he would say. 'Tuck in!' It became a catchphrase. And so gradually I fell in with Dave and the homeless men, who whiled away the countless hours in drink. When I was playing on the street I always found it interesting to watch the reactions of the passers-by. Many assumed I was on my uppers. For some, the assumption gave them a feeling of uneasy superiority and they jingled their change. Some were openly contemptuous, spitting sometimes or jeering. Others simply drew their children closer to them, as if the music were somehow catching. The wandering ancients with pipe and tabor, or 'whittle and dub', were equally undesirable. The bagpipe players more so, for obvious reasons. But buskers have always been with us. In 1891, the *Strand* magazine had obviously seen enough: 'There are two kinds of street musician: those which can be tolerated and those which simply cannot.' It's an interesting piece of journalism, as it captures not only the spirit of street life but society's judgements too.

But the winos never judged. I felt accepted and oddly at home among this shifting band of forgotten stories. As long as my parents were blissfully unaware of the people I was mixing with, I never really felt the need to question this association and, most surprising of all to me now, I never asked how a boy of nineteen like Dave came to be drinking himself to death down the subway.

But Dave had, evidently. One day he said, 'You won't see me next week.'

I said, 'Why's that?'

'Going down the detox, in't I?' Dave replied. 'Might be in for a while.'

He was. In the next few months I drifted away from playing in the street. The subways had changed. A new type of beggar had appeared. Aggressive, dreadlocked and armed with anarchist slogans, the rebellious, middle-class kids descended in groups, bullying the buskers away. 'Fuck you,' they said. 'We're on the streets. We're travellers.' It was a lifestyle choice. The quiet, dignified homeless disappeared through the cracks in the concrete. The musicians stopped coming. No one wanted a fight.

One night I got a call.

'Rich! Remember me?'

'Who's that?' A short silence. Then that upbeat voice again.

'It's old Detox Dave. Fancy meeting up?'

I was busy. He never called again.

Whatever the reason, hardened drinker I was not. I took a long look at my drinking habits. I hadn't been near a British ale since I was seventeen, when I had been traumatized by the fabled 'bad pint'. More recently I had been ashamed to admit to a market researcher that my favourite drink was absinthe. It was no way for an Englishman to carry on. Something had to be done.

I decided to carry out an immediate audit of my drinks cabinet. It was the only way to assess the damage. Continuing the aniseed theme, the cabinet contained three bottles of imported Turkish state raki plus a bottle of French pastis, all for immediate use. Behind them lay a dusty bottle of Jameson Irish whiskey. A sorry state. How could this have happened? If I was to find my English roots I had better get onto the native brews.

But where to start? That figure again: 712. I was playing catch-up and I knew it. But if the number was daunting, the names were something else. Mildew, Teflon, Agent Orange. It was as though the brewers – grimly resigned to the fact that no one would ever stock the fruit of their labours – felt that they could hardly harm sales by naming the beer after a well-known poison.

49   The Long Bitter End

Back in the Stratford queue, bearded men from the Campaign for Real Ale, CAMRA to its friends, walked up and down the line in pink fleece jackets offering out-of-date copies of the *Good Beer Guide* to keep our spirits up. I took one. The book is a cornucopia of exotic-sounding alcohol, liberally sprinkled with esoteric descriptions, such as 'long bitter end', 'residual roastiness' and 'fruit on the nose'.

Wetting one's whistle becomes a logistical challenge in itself when faced with, say, the 'long-lasting dry aftertaste' of Beartown's Wheat Beer. Perhaps I would be better off with a pint of Durham White Gold, 'thirst-quenching with citrus aromas'. Some promise erotic adventure, but be warned: Daleside's Old Legover, the guide reveals, leaves revellers with a 'bitter aftertaste'. Such an experience can be harrowing. If so, what better way to drown your sorrows than in the company of Bateman's Salem Porter, which offers an appealing if apocalyptic 'mellowing of all the elements in the finish'?

A large crowd seemed to be leaving the building, which meant we would be let in. On second glance, it turned out to be not a large crowd at all but two men to whom a lifetime's devotion to beer had clearly given form and substance. The Victorian building, with its period wallpaper and restored chandeliers, seemed a sad anachronism in this dismal part of the capital. Opposite the Town Hall squatted the shopping precinct, its brick-box buildings harbouring KFCs and Pizza Huts.

I was asked to pay £2 for nothing, plus another £2 to borrow a glass and £5 for a sheet of beer tokens. I pushed up the carpeted stairway and across the balcony, flanked by men with their coats on.

Yes. What first struck me was the complete absence of women. The only reason I had ever gone into pubs in the first place was to try to meet women and I didn't really notice what the beer was called. But looking around the main hall at the range of dark check shirts, steel-rimmed glasses and facial hair, I realized that while, perhaps, a few of these men had become connoisseurs as a way of consoling themselves, more potent was the fact that this was the ultimate masculine escape from domestic bliss: 'We drink the beer and then we discuss it. You're welcome to come, dear . . .'

All along one wall the barrels loomed large. Their contents were dispensed by good-natured men from CAMRA. Although the crowd along the makeshift bar was a few deep, there was no pushing or shoving. No bar-side face-offs. As I took delivery of a delicious 'mild' brewed with honey, I heard two men behind me discussing the best scale of Ordnance Survey map.

The men stood around drinking halves out of pint glasses – so as to have room for as many beers as possible – and talking quietly. Anthropologically speaking, we fell into two broad categories: those with amusing beer-related slogans on their T-shirts and those in sports casuals. On the other side of the room there were some such T-shirts for sale. I heard two men debating the merits of the one with 'I Ate All the Pies' emblazoned across the front.

'This is a good one, Derek,' said one.

'Yes,' said the other, 'but I do feel you would need quite a large belly to carry it off.'

If T-shirts are not your thing there are plenty of other opportunities to kit yourself out with manly accessories. There were a number of belt salesmen in situ, offering a range of large, heavy buckles, designed to represent either different types of dragon or the logos of various other beer festivals. There was a range of pewter tankards, lighters, hip flasks and other essentials such as character figurines from fantasy films and books. There was no music in the hall, no band or jukebox. Just men and beer.

I began to feel hemmed in. To ease this, I went for another drink. Of course, had I been really hard-core I would have drunk mead. Mead is the oldest alcoholic drink still to be brewed here, although not much of it is brewed, on account of it being singular in taste. Interestingly, the old Nordic word for the honey-based drink we now call mead was *øl*, pronounced *ale*. As honey became more expensive, the ale was watered down to make a much weaker brew. Finally, the honey was replaced with the cheaper malt, and bitter hops were added to give us the ale we drink now. To begin with, the brewers left the hops floating on the top and drinkers sucked their nectar up through a reed straw, no doubt pleasantly amplifying its effects.

My next choice was an ale called Old Tosser. It was a bad choice. At 5 per cent alcohol it was not remotely refreshing and it tasted too much like my dad's pipe to be any fun. I dispatched it swiftly and swayed towards the cider stand with a view to cleansing my palate. But apples could wait, it was perry I was after. At its worst, perry is Babycham. At its finest it's pear scrumpy. I got some in.

It was served to me by a hobbit, working alongside Merlin, complete with long, flowing locks and beard.

'Where would I have to go to find this in a pub?' I asked the hobbit.

'Well – you know the Wenlock Arms?'

I didn't. His face fell and he gave me a disapproving look. I knew I had broken the first rule of the beer-drinking hobby.

'So you *don't* know the Wenlock Arms?' He was just making sure.

I still didn't.

'Well. I dunno. Brentford's your best bet then.'

Brentford? No good things happen there. I couldn't imagine going to a grim part of town, where I knew no one, just to get a better class of drink. The beers on offer tonight were exceptional and I was glad they existed. But beer drinking, even cider drinking, was a social thing for me: an accessory to a night out. It could never become a hobby in itself, as it had for these men.

Or could it? The perry was good and rather stronger than I had anticipated when I swallowed it. The room began to revolve and I caught tiny, jumbled glimpses of the labels on the barrels. My mind was swamped with beer names, their brewers and their relative strengths in a gumbo of unwanted trivia. Monkey Magic 3.4, Muttley's Revenge 4.8.

Someone suggested I 'neutralize' the perry with a porter. This sounded like abject folly but I was game and, as the dark, rosy liquid went down I did indeed reach a kind of euphoric lucidity.

'Tell me,' I asked a passing drinker. 'Does it bother you about the lack of women here?'

'Gosh,' he replied, looking around as if for the first time. 'It does seem to be rather a male-dominated arena, doesn't it.' His friend wanted to expand.

'You see, the more anoraky CAMRA gets, the more it's going to appeal to blokes, but there's no reason why women should feel excluded. It's not remotely threatening. There's no hassle here, no fight at the end of the night.' This was true, but I wondered if he'd missed the point. The atmosphere was not helped by the cavernous, echoing hall but, certainly, as long as it was filled with good-natured, discerning beer fetishists nothing was going to kick off . . .

Then I bumped into Tia, the only woman I had seen so far. She was young and blonde and happy. I asked her the same question. 'Not at all,' she replied, with a wink. 'I don't mind the company of blokes.' And that was that. The gender issue was entirely my problem. Everyone else was perfectly happy. And none was happier than the elderly CAMRA activist who rested his head on my shoulder as I sat.

'We don't see many of the young getting involved,' he sighed. 'Are you . . ?'

'Young? Yes I am,' I replied. 'Relatively.'

'No. Are you involved?' He clutched my arm.

'Oh. Well no – ' I hesitated. 'To be honest I'm not really sure what CAMRA does.'

'I've been active for five years,' he said, unleashing a faint smell of cooking. 'It's a traditional thing. It's part of our culture we're trying to keep alive. Succeeding.' CAMRA was not a hobby club for beer nerds, he said. It was a serious and weighty campaigning force that had single-handedly 'saved' real ale. By 'real ale' he meant beer that was not mass-produced using cheap, tasteless ingredients by large brewers in search of ever more profit. He meant beer that was brewed lovingly by craftsmen, where quality was not reduced to boost margins. CAMRA, he claimed, had saved a lot of breweries too. Before the group was set up, no new brewery had been founded for fifty years. Since then, more than three hundred independent brewers had felt sufficiently valued to risk a venture into the business. An ancient craft and custom was being revived.

CAMRA had forced brewers to declare the strengths of their beers, had succeeded in achieving more liberal licensing laws and, a real breakthrough, had obliged brewery pubs to stock a 'guest' ale. It was all about greater consumer choice and the well-being of a traditional craft. Rather than buy in mass-produced branded beer from abroad, CAMRA wants to see pubs stocking well-fashioned beverages from their local areas, supporting local suppliers and local people.

'There has been a massive revival of interest in proper ales,' the man whispered into my ear. 'But we don't see so many young, no.'

'Why do you think that is?' I whispered back.

The man from CAMRA leaned forward conspiratorially, as though he were about to impart the world's biggest secret.

'They just want to drink piss,' he breathed. That smell of cooking again. We looked at each other and started to laugh. In Germany beer festivals often end in a fevered mêlée of half-naked women and polka music. In parts of France drinking festivals can last all week and often cause policemen to jump in the river. But if it's English roots you're after, then look no further than this charmless municipal building, full of affable men being polite to each other.

'Of course,' the man said, 'we owe a lot to the morris.'

The morris?

'Oh yes. You wouldn't ever catch a morris man drinking piss.'

I looked at him without speaking. This, evidently, had to be verified.

5 | The Blue-Eyed Stranger

Once, at a primary school disco, I won a prize for doing a chicken dance of my own devising to the Specials' ska-tinged Coventry lament 'Ghost Town'. The prize was having my name read out by DJ Colin, who, I suspect, was not a full-time entertainer. I was proud of my achievement and felt sure all the prettiest girls had made a mental note of exactly who had won the chicken dance prize. They were probably shy of approaching me straight away, but I imagined in the weeks that followed that lemonade-soaked summer evening that the girls would soon begin to form an orderly queue. They would probably want to know my opinion on the issues of the day, perhaps invite me to tea.

A year later, on holiday, I found myself in the hotel bar. My parents had left me to my own devices for the evening and, on hearing the house DJ begin to spin 'Ghost Town', I launched into the chicken dance once more, hoping for a similar accolade. It's true that the girls had not exactly beaten down my door since my previous moment of triumph, but who could resist a twice winner? I put my chin on my chest and got down to it. About midway through the song, I looked up from my blue funk to see that the other revellers had left the dance floor and were standing at the margins, arms folded, watching me with their eyes slightly widened as I convulsed in time to the infectious ska beat. How swiftly was the adrenal rush of chicken dancing followed by the deep welt of humiliation.

This is roughly how I feel about dancing. As a direct consequence of this formative episode, whenever in adult life I am coaxed, tricked or bamboozled onto the dance floor, I go all wooden and adopt what I imagine to be a suitably masculine stance. That is to say, I dance without actually moving, perhaps nodding in a perfunctory way towards the beat, as though acknowledging a good snooker shot. It is important to maintain this attitude while dancing and not to drink too much. For too much alcohol will allow the beast within to come out unchecked, viz: the chicken dance.

How strange, then, that I should find myself ringing up a man who was known to coach young chaps in the ways of the morris. What could I have been thinking? I clearly remember the first time I saw the spectacle of English traditional dance. It was in the city centre and I was a small child. Several very large men dressed in bells and baldrics had assembled and were shaking handkerchiefs at each other, skipping and leaping in a way I had until then imagined to be chiefly the domain of newborn fawns. They terrified me. They clearly also threatened the crowd, a large portion of which was pointing and laughing in deep embarrassment.

There is a reason for this. As I have outlined above, the correct way for a gentleman to dance does not involve the ornamental use of a hanky, so the morris had transgressed from the outset. Add in the leg-bells, the man with a bladder on a stick and the squeezebox, and you've got a very dangerous brew. One that challenges the very foundations of English masculinity. Especially when – look furtively from left to right – we find ourselves liking it.

So it was with some trepidation that I dialled the number for 'Cotswold morris classes (beginners)'. For all my journalistic curiosity, I might as well have sneaked into a phone box and dialled up 'Brazilian she-male – all services'. The feeling of dirty, forbidden love was just the same. How would I explain to my wife that she had married a latent morris dancer. Should I just come out with it? 'Darling, there's something you should know. I am not *as* other men.' Would she understand and wash my hankies? Iron them on a Sunday? I felt the chagrin seep into my skin and wither my muscles. The man on the other end was delighted by my overtures.

'You'd be very welcome,' he said. 'It's mainly ladies at the moment, I'm afraid, so we certainly need more men.'

How had I reached this point?

Well, the comment from the man at the beer festival had aroused my curiosity. So I had tried to contact my local morris side for information. When you live in London, the word 'local' takes on a figurative quality. My area did have a side, I found out, but I asked around and no one had ever seen them. All I got were bemused smiles and raised eyebrows, as though I had asked if, by chance, anyone knew where I could be whipped locally. So I took out the card Keith Duke had given me on the train to Whittlesey and dialled the number for the Greensleeves Morris in Wimbledon.

I told him about my search for English folk roots and my interest in understanding the morris. I told him I had a melodeon and wasn't afraid to use it. I told him I was keen to accompany a dance side.

'I want to see if it can be learned,' I said.

'Of course it can,' he replied. 'Just give it twenty years or so.'

I had arranged to meet up with the men in a pub called the Sultan, but my train had been delayed so I made straight for the church hall. I pushed open the swing door and was met by the sight of about fourteen stout, middle-aged men, all in shorts and T-shirts. All except Keith, who was dancing in a striped business shirt and braces.

'Ah, here's our man,' he announced, and came to shake my hand. He introduced me to Tim, the 'squire' and Gerald, the 'bagman'. The squire is the boss. The bagman assumes a secretarial role. Bert, one of the musicians, had fallen backwards into a chair with his pipe and tabor drum and appeared to be asleep, although, curiously, he was also playing a jig.

The men were pleased I had come and, seeing their open, friendly welcome, I was pleased to be there. I felt a little self-conscious at first. I felt out of place. Apart from Lev, who was nine and fixed me with a grin, there were few men under forty-five in the room, and most were rather older. Although I had char-acteristically forgotten to shave, I lacked the more assertive style of facial hair ornamentation, which, in this company, struck me as noticeable and perhaps not quite the done thing. And I do like to fit in. It's true that, since the Stratford festival, I had been working hard on my beer belly. But I had a long way to go before I could match the sterling efforts of some in this group. They had clearly searched the land for fine English ales. And fine English ales had clearly found them. They wanted me to dance. Just like that. Straight away. Terror struck. It wasn't going to happen.

I dislike sitting on the sidelines. The thing to have done would have been to throw myself into the dancing and enjoy it for what it was, but something deep-seated held me back. Chicken dance wounds might heal, but the scars still linger.

'I'll only slow you down,' I protested.

'This lot couldn't get any slower,' came the response. 'Come on, have a go.'

'Ah . . . well . . . I'm not really ready . . . To be honest it's mainly the music I'm keen on.'

It had been the same for Cecil Sharp in the beginning. When he collected tunes from William Kimber of Headington Quarry Morris that Boxing Day in 1899, Sharp had little interest in the dances. He was a musician and, although he appears to have cut something of a dashing figure on the waltz scene – when his legs weren't paralysed with typhoid – he considered the morris dance itself beyond his remit.

In 1905, a few years after his conversion to folk music, Sharp was asked by a woman called Mary Neal to teach some songs to the Esperance Club for working girls, a social group mainly for seamstresses in St Pancras. Neal was somewhat beguiled by Sharp and his songs, and such was the enthusiasm among her young sewing girls for this new folk song fad that she asked him if he might not also have a few dances to teach them. He hadn't, but he knew a man who had.

Neal paid for William Kimber to come down from Headington to teach morris dances to the Esperance girls, who had a fine time with them, leaping and lolloping with bells and hankies. They enjoyed them so much that they began to teach the dances to others. Mary Neal was so delighted at the outcome that she suggested a society be formed for the propagation of folk music. Sharp was defensive and decreed that the society should not collect folk songs. That, he said, should be left to 'experts'. In the event, so demanding and finicky was Mr Sharp that a society was indeed formed, in 1907, but without him.

Could there have been a connection between this slight and what happened next? Sharp began to disparage what he considered the sloppiness of the Esperance girls' dancing. Neal, to her lasting credit, gave Sharp as good as she got. She wanted her girls to enjoy themselves and thought the dances should be easy and fun. Sharp expected excellence and accuracy. They had to be done just so – in other words, the way he said. The man who had once claimed to dislike the 'mental loudness' of the girls at Girton College now became irritated with what he saw as Neal's lack of 'artistic discipline'. In turn, Neal came to regard Sharp as a pedantic naysayer: the dead hand of scholarly folklore stifling her organically expanding new morris. It was a battle of two strong wills. The scramble for the morris had begun – and Sharp, who had originally only seen a use for the music, now became glued to the dance as well. As any morris dancer will tell you, you can't really separate the two.

'Best way to get the music right is to dance,' came a voice. Others agreed. There seemed no way round it, but still I remained cemented to my seat. The men weren't standing for me not joining in somehow, so I was told to take out my melodeon and try playing along. This I did and the dancing began.

It was a curious sight. There were no bells and no bladders. There wasn't a floral hat in sight. This was morris hard-core and with the shorts and bulging T-shirts the whole scene resembled nothing so much as an oversized PE class, in which I was without doubt the snivelling oik who had forgotten his kit. Alan, the 'foreman', was leading the practice, as the most experienced dancer. He spoke in a loud, clear voice and managed the fine juggling act of keeping an authoritative tone without antagonizing the men. He needed to be firm, though, as many of the men were giggling among themselves, Bert was drinking steadily and some at the back were not working as hard as the others.

'You know you should be dancing a double caper there,' he accused the idlers. 'Instead of a single caper.'

'There's always one,' someone chided.

'You're the worst offender,' Alan rounded on him. The man giggled.

Then there was trouble with the hankies. Too many of the men were lifting their whole arms to get the necessary whipping sound, but 'that is not what I'm asking and not what any of our foremen have been asking for some years'. The movement should come from the elbows, with the arms flat against the sides. It's a delicate gesture that belies the strain it puts on the chest muscles.

'Muscles?' someone asked.

'Flab, he means.'

'Oh, right.'

But Alan wasn't getting his point across. 'You're sticking your elbows out like chickens,' he said. 'We don't feel like Chicken Tonight.'

I sank into my seat. I knew that, should anyone ever coax me up to join this circle, it would definitely be me with the chicken wings. And there was no way I could let that happen. I squeezed the melodeon for all I was worth, which, since I'd only just got it, was not a great deal. I didn't know any of the tunes. Bert showed me a book of morris music.

'My bible,' he said.

It was a thick tome, and heavy too, filled to bursting with traditional dances. I cursed my wet nurse. Why had no one taught me these tunes in the crib? Why was I only finding out now, now that my brain had atrophied and my fingers turned to plasticine? How long would it take me to assimilate all this? Just looking down the pages there were at least four different versions of 'Shepherd's Hey' alone. How long would it be before I knew the difference between 'Old Woman Tossed Up' and 'Old Woman Tossed Up in a Blanket'? A blanket can make all the difference to an old woman. Would I confuse 'Bobbin-a-Joe' with 'Bumpus o' Stretton'? Or substitute 'Laudnum Bunches' for 'Lads-a-Bunchum'? Would I 'Go and Enlist for a Sailor' or get hung up on 'Ladies' Pleasure'? At this stage it could go either way and clearly I had a lot of work ahead of me. Would I eventually become 'Dearest Dicky' or would I remain forever the 'Blue-Eyed Stranger'.

There was a break and Gerald the bagman went through items of business. He'd received an email from a lady asking if they would perform a set at her wedding. Was anyone interested? There were mumbles. One suggested that they should do it, but only if the groom would come and practise the dances for six months. They were having problems getting new men into the side. Another said they'd do it, but only for money.

'Yeah. Ask for money,' came the consensus. 'At least £150.'

At least! Looking around at the heaving bodies, still gasping for air and steaming up the windows of the church hall, wilting the corners of jumble sale programmes, I considered £150 a bargain for their efforts. Then it was back to the practising, ending with 'Over the Hills and Far Away'.

We poured into the Sultan. Gerald told me it was a good pub. 'They're very tolerant.' When the men come in to 'do their mummers' they're met with friendly enthusiasm. Mummers?

'We did it in Roehampton once. Christ!' The clientele in the upper-class suburb had had no time for the morris and had yelled abuse. 'It's just ignorance,' Gerald said.

The lasting ignorance would be a source of regret to Cecil Sharp, were he still alive. Sharp wanted children to be taught folk songs and dances at school. He achieved some success with this too.

The Board of Education accepted morris dance into the curriculum for physical education. Sharp wanted children to absorb their roots early in life. The trouble is that teaching children something at school, making it another piece of homework, is about the best way to turn them off. For folk tradition to work it needs to be just that. 'Country dancing' was still in the primary curriculum when I was at school and was met by boys and girls alike with the kind of embarrassed derision normally reserved for our parents' choice of coat when picking us up from the school gates.

In 1909 the Shakespeare Memorial Theatre at Stratford-upon-

Avon held a series of folk song and dance competitions. Judging the music was Cecil Sharp. Judging the morris was Mary Neal. Neal used the occasion to try and patch things up with Sharp. Surely they could pool their resources. But Sharp would not cooperate. Neal believed it was madness to create a barrier – as long as young people were getting enjoyment there was no sense in beating them up over detail. Sharp countered witheringly that 'philanthropy and art have nothing in common, and to unite them spells disaster'. This from the man who wanted to teach the world to sing. What was really going on?

It's tempting to picture the despotic Sharp as a caricature chauvinist. He certainly believed the dances would become corrupt and 'fake' unless he had sole control over their teaching, and to that end he set up a school of morris dance with himself as director. But it may just as easily have been the fundamental abyss between his approach and that of Neal. She believed the morris was a living tradition that came from working-class people and rightfully belonged to her seamstresses, theirs to do with as they saw fit, to share among the unlettered in a free, liberal way. Sharp, by contrast, saw the dances as fossils, relics of a bygone age. Something to preserve in aspic, exactly as they were found.

More worryingly, he had been reading a book called *The Golden Bough*. Written by an anthropologist by the name of Sir James Frazer and published in 1890, *The Golden Bough* sought to link modern folklore with pre-Christian vegetation rites. It argued that the customs we saw today were merely the surviving fragments of heathen religious rites. Pagan rites. Ceremonies and rituals from a time when

– here Frazer made many assumptions – people worshipped corn, the sun, horses and other things that weren't Jesus. He argued that the theme of death and rebirth in Christianity had its root in the cycle of the seasons, the winter death of plant life and the spring fertility, the sprouting of crops and the yielding of harvest; that Christianity – indeed all modern religion – was simply a development of bestial ancient rites. Frazer had his own reasons for pushing this argument, but his influence went beyond his motives.

Under the spell of Frazer, Sharp came to see the dances as remnants of primitive religious ceremonies, linked 'in some occult way' to the fertilization of living things. He found proof for this theory wherever he looked for it. One village dance included the slaughter, cooking and eating of a lamb. Therefore it was a memory of pagan sacrifice. Sword dances mimicked a decapitation, which 'might' have been a sacrifice – originally. The sound of bells 'might' have been to chase away the devil. In the days before people simply liked the noise they made when they danced.

Sharp had previously supposed, with no real evidence, that 'morris' was a simple corruption of 'moorish' and that the crusaders had brought the dances back from North Africa. This theory is still espoused today, although Sharp himself rejected it after reading Frazer. Ultimately, through Frazer, Sharp came to the conclusion that the tradition was a masculine fertility rite. Sadly, outside of the three or four Cotswold villages that still practised the custom, no men actually wanted to dance it. Mary Neal and her girls were the only ones making any headway, teaching the dances to other women. Sharp argued that, given the religious nature of the dances

– *originally* – to replace men with women would upset the natural order. In Frazer, Sharp had found a way to marginalize Neal and her living tradition.

There followed a series of bitter exchanges between the two, in the pages of the press and further afield. Sharp poured scorn on Neal's dances in the *Morning Post* and *Vanity Fair*. In return, Neal sought to discredit him in the wider country, collecting her own dances and questioning Kimber's authenticity as a primary source. Certainly the Headington Quarry side had already died out once and had been revived by Kimber and his pals as a way of making some money. Who was to say that the dances Sharp was now notating so assiduously had any basis in history? The argument raged on and both were lecturing widely until, in 1911, the Shakespeare Memorial Theatre, won over by Sharp's arguments – and, in no small way, by his standing as a lettered man with friends in high places – dropped Neal from its teaching programme. Sharp had won. Neal gave up. The popular morris dance was dead. It was now the domain of esoteric hobbyists. Better, claimed Sharp, to appeal to a minority in the right way, than to the majority in the wrong way.

A few English villages – Chipping Campden, Headington, Abingdon and Bampton – continue their own unbroken pre-Sharp traditions, and some guard their dances and music jealously. But most of the morris sides we see today have repertoires comprised from Sharp's collections. And collect he did. From 1911 until the outbreak of the First World War he dedicated himself to the morris, that it might once again become part of English national culture. He often caught a team of dancers on the very fringes of their fading memory and coaxed the dances back to life. It's safe to say that, without Sharp, many of the traditional morris and sword dances of England would simply have disappeared. It is ironic and not a little sad that the man widely credited with the revival of the tradition is also partly responsible for its marginal status, ensuring that it remains – as his assistant once put it – a 'hobby for cranks'.

Looking around at the men, tucking into the pints of frothy ale dispensed by Alan and joking among themselves, I couldn't have imagined a less cranky scene or a more ordinary group of blokes, slightly flushed from an evening's exercise and enjoying a beer. It could have been any five-a-side team. Six-a-side in this case.

'I've always been a loner,' Alan told me. 'I never took part in team sports. I always played squash. But the morris has taught me the importance of working with other people as a unit.'

'You might find,' Tim added, 'if the lads are having a kick-around, that the morris will help you with the football.'

Alan had grown up with dancing. His parents had been country dancers too. He told me he'd learned the morris steps in the womb. I liked this. Perhaps Sharp's dream was slowly working after all. I say ordinary blokes, but it does in fact take a certain type of man to push through the prejudice and occupy a pub where people might not understand.

Morris sides meet in pubs. That's what they do. It's an inevitable facet of the culture. And they repair to the pub after practice for ale and singing. Songs like 'Poor old landlord can't get the morris out, can't get the morris out . . .' Sometimes they whip out their instruments and there's a session. They certainly prop up the bar, and most landlords who find themselves in favour with a morris side quickly learn to appreciate the voracious appetites of a dozen or so hearty drinkers. The relationship between the morris and the pub is as intrinsic as that between the music and the dance. You can't separate the two.

But that's just what the government was trying to do. The controversial Licensing Bill that was worming its way through the Commons classified all such bar-room singing as live enter- tainment, and as such it would be prohibited without a licence. Landlords wanting to put on events would have to apply and pay for permission. And if they didn't know they were going to have an event? Well, they couldn't possibly apply for a licence every day just in case the morris might drop in for a few bars of 'Sweet Jenny Jones'. In other words, the spontaneity and freedom of the morris tradition would be stifled.

I could see where the government was coming from . . . It was high time there was a tax on freedom of expression. For too long the people of England had been allowed to sing 'Auld Lang Syne' at New Year without paying anyone.

The wording of the bill was such that a loud, large-screen football match could be viewed in a pub without worry. But if the crowd of happy supporters should begin to chant a song, they would cause a breach of the act. Outlaws. If the morris came in and just one of them forgot himself and began humming: criminal.

The man on the other bunk with no front teeth and a spider-web face tattoo looks me up and down. 'What you in for, pretty boy?'

'Two bars of "Constant Billy". I didn't mean to, it just sticks in your head.'

There had been protests, and some concessions. Religious people would, following an amendment, be allowed to sing their songs of praise in a church or temple, but secular people singing folk songs would fall foul of the law. Anyone harbouring a piano in a public place – in a village hall, for example – would need a licence, as the piano would have the potential to be played. And we couldn't have that. Despite its gross unfairness the bill was advancing. The English Folk Dance and Song Society was campaigning furiously to have the wording changed. It really believed that if the bill were to become an act, an important part of English folk culture would be lost entirely. But progress was slow. The government refused to see why a spontaneous, unamplified session in the back room of a pub, among three mates, is not strictly a live entertainment event, and it also declined to see why on earth it should respect the tradition. The battle raged on.

I asked Tim about my chances of accompanying the side. Sharp had believed that – *originally* – the squire would have been some sort of high priest. I asked with all due respect. In between glugs of beer Tim told me straight.

'I mean, I don't mean to cast aspersions but, um, if it turned out you were *capable*, I mean, if you *could* do it, then perhaps you could, er, well, you might just stand behind the others and, um, well . . . Anyway, you're welcome to come down any Friday you like.'

And so I would. A challenge had been laid down. I *would* become capable or die trying. And while the beautiful people of London were out clubbing till the small hours in bra-tops and high heels, I would be strapped into my English melodeon practising 'Trunkles' and 'Shave the Donkey'. I would return to the Greensleeves morris. But next time I wasn't going to be caught out. I knew what I had to do. It was time to throw some shapes. I dialled the number.

Cecil Sharp House was deserted. An advert for a freelance uku-lele player flapped forlornly in the draft as I padded downstairs. I pushed open a pair of doors and found myself in a large empty room with a sprung wooden floor. The walls were decorated with antlered reindeer heads and John Russell, a spry, grey-haired figure in a Ben Sherman shirt, was talking to a couple of rather subdued-looking middle-aged women. He was pleased I had come.

'You rang, you rang,' he said. His words had a theatrical quality and his face seemed permanently on the verge of cheeky giggles. Every sentence contained a joke. The women greeted me shyly, like marmosets in a sanctuary. John got straight to the point.

'We're going to learn some basic steps. Face the wall, young Richard, and no monkey business.' I did what I was told.

Now . . .

I don't know how it happened, but the next thing I knew, I was dancing.

'That's what we call the "foot-up",' John was saying.

How on earth had he managed that? It was like the jovial doctor who nonchalantly asks you what you do for a living and before you can say *journalist* he's got a spike in your arm.

'Hang on,' I started. But it was no use. John was taking no prisoners. Almost against my will I found myself doubling up the foot-up with a foot-down, a loping backward hop. John diverted my attention with a story about his old morris side, the Beaux of London City, and, unbeknownst to me, had me dancing a caper by the end of it.

'You're doing very well, young Richard,' he said. 'It took me years to learn these steps.'

'I haven't learned them,' I protested. 'I just seem to be doing them.'

It's all a blur after that.

Other people came: three women in all, a bearded man called Mike and a young American girl. We all shuffled about uneasily. No one seemed in great shape. Mike couldn't dance 'Rigs o' Marlow' because of his knee. Sheila couldn't do stick dances because of her shoulder. And I couldn't do any of them because of an innate lack of talent. We assembled anyway, in facing rows of three. John threw a switch on his ageing tape recorder and the bobbing melodeon music began.

'. . . and hey!' John would call.

The hey is supposed to be a figure-of-eight movement, but in my hands it was more of a downward spiral.

'. . . and turn in!' John would call.

And I would turn out, leaping away to a destination of my

own choosing, only to be manhandled back onto the straight and narrow by Sheila or Mike.

'. . . and back to back!' John would call and I would, of course, be back to front.

'Don't worry,' they would say. 'You're doing very well.'

How could this be true? Flatterers. I knew my heys were awry. I knew my single capers lacked finesse. It's best I don't even revisit the hocklebacks. It's hard to get the hankies going at the same time as your foot-ups. Much like trying to think and talk at the same time, it isn't until you try it that you understand what goes into it. John suggested I tie the hankies onto my fingers, but I failed to see how this would help.

My own lack of coordination was compounded by Paula, my opposite number during 'Rigs o' Marlow', whose shyness meant she couldn't meet my eye. This stick dance from Headington Quarry was one of the very first noted by Cecil Sharp in 1899. The steps are easy, allegedly, but the devil's in the sticking. During the middle section you hold the stick in the middle and your opposite number beats either side of your knuckles, upwards and downwards, while hopping from foot to foot. This puts you in a mildly unenviable position to begin with, made worse by the fact that you are hopping too, in my case, wrongly. Add in the fact that your partner is actually looking away from the action and it's basically knuckle purdah.

Then it happened.

Somewhere in the middle of 'Rigs o' Marlow'.

Was it a momentary release of endorphins?

Suddenly I was both dancing and grinning.

'Look at you,' Sheila said.

'He's away,' said John.

Somehow, in the space of two hours, something strange had happened. Like taking your first faulty circles on a bike without stabilizers, suddenly the dances had become perfectly natural. Wobbly, I'll grant you, but fun. Not weird or strange or embarrassing but curiously liberating. And I was doing them — more or less — correctly.

I was only mildly afraid. What had happened to me? Had I started something that would build a momentum of its own? Where would it take me? Would I buy my own bells? Would there be no turning back?

The morris and the melodeon. English dances. There was something for me here. When I got home I strapped on my squeezebox and searched out the tunes I'd been dancing to. Just as the melodies made sense of the footwork, so the dances made sense of the tunes. I found them, after a while. I didn't know how long it would take before the music felt like my own, but I would give it some effort. I would try to assimilate.

6 | The Mountbatten Club

Noel is a softly spoken Irishman in a bow tie. Some of the other members have been telling me how Noel married his way into the largest moped-selling business in Leamington Spa and became a wealthy man. They have no idea what he earns but he certainly does all right. His house is so detached, they say, he has his own postcode. The comments contain traces of envy and admiration in equal parts. Most of the men have worked all their lives in factories around the West Midlands; England's industrial black-spot since the turn of the last century. They are more likely to have smelted down the metal to make the mopeds or bolted on the wheels. Still, whatever the differences between them, this is, above all, a group of friends.

'Sorry I'm late, Mr squire, sir.'

Noel arrives after the others, tells a dirty joke and reveals an eccentric fantasy involving binoculars which he makes me promise not to write down. There is laughter all round and the conversation turns to the various types of binocular available on the market today. The men compare binocular sizes. Ron favours a monocular. Pete is fifty today so he's just been to get the birthday round in.

A discreet nod between Pete and Ron, the founder member, decides that I should be included, and now I sup my beer gratefully.

I look round the table at the group. Seven or eight men, all hearty, but perhaps not all so hale any more. Most are over fifty and grey-haired. Some have the etiolated smoker's complexion. Others are ruddy and well fed. Some have retired. Whatever their social standing, the men all have one thing in common. They are all elected members of an exclusive group. There are many similar groups around the country. In Hampshire they are Johnny Jacks, in Cheshire they are soulers. In Lancashire and Yorkshire they are pace-eggers, in Gloucestershire they are Paper Boys and in Kent they are Hoodeners. They are known collectively as mummers. But what does that mean?

'Some people think we're the Masons,' Ron chuckles, 'and some think we're into satanic rites . . .' He leaves the comment to hang in the air, lights another cigarette and stares at me in a strange way.

The first time I heard the words 'mumming play' they were uttered by a teacher at school. She told me how the Marshfield Paper Boys rubbed soot on their faces and went by torchlight through the village streets at night in a 'traditional ritual' which dated 'back to pagan times'. The key phrases resonated in me. Pagan . . . Ritual . . . Cursed with an overactive imagination, and a fear of the different learned from my neighbours, I was ready to believe these ashen-faced, fire-loving, rag wearers were genuine necromancers who practised occult arts and collected bits of feather and animal bone which they crushed up into hallucinogens before going on a spree of human sacrifice, witchcraft and frantic dancing . . . I filed it in the back of my mind under 'Never Look Here'.

But a mummers' play is just a traditional English folk play, performed by ordinary working men in the street, square or marketplace. The range of venues has naturally changed with the times. Now it includes the foyer, the precinct and the Warner Village shopping and leisure complex. But although the tradition has kept pace with modern life, the one place you won't see any form of mummery is on a theatre stage. 'We are not London actors,' one play declares. Mumming was always just the locals putting on a traditional street show for money.

I knew this because I had been reading a little yellow pamphlet I had found at Cecil Sharp House called *Introducing the Folk Plays of England*. According to this, the players would not tour in the way theatre groups would. Because of this, the plays tended to remain rather obscure, parochial events. The groups of players are known by various names, from Blue Stots to Bull Guizers, but 'mummers' has become the common term for a group of folk players and 'mummers' play' has come to mean any traditional play. The word may possibly derive from 'mime' and 'miming', but that is where the connection ends; the plays involve speech and song and are far removed from the art of mime. In fact, it is safe to say that they are fairly well removed from any attempt at art.

The players dress in strange costumes: a flat cap and blackened face, a ragged man with a sword in each hand, a man in ribbons and rosettes with an incredibly tall hat, a man dressed as a ram, and no small amount of bearded she-males. A butcher, St George, a Turkish knight. The pamphlet was written by Ron Shuttleworth, 'author of *So You Want to Start Mumming*'. Shuttleworth had set down his qualifications: 'On paper I have none and any expertise comes from experience gathered over eighteen years with an all-year team called Coventry Mummers.'

Team? I was intrigued. Was there a mummers' league? I went home and searched for the Coventry Mummers on the Internet. Ron's pamphlet was published in 1984 – nearly twenty years before I read it. Perhaps the group had disbanded. But my luck was in. The Coventry Mummers were still going: available for hire at weddings, fêtes, christenings. Mr Shuttleworth, it turned out, had been a little modest. As holder of the Morris Ring Folk Plays Archive – or the Ron Shuttleworth Collection as it is starting to be known – Ron was in fact the world's leading authority on mumming, mummers and all forms of mummery. If anyone could answer my questions, I thought, he could.

I contacted Ron and he invited me up to Coventry. The Mummers met every week, at the Mountbatten Club, he told me. Sometimes they rehearsed, they usually discussed a bit of business, but mostly they just met up and had a drink. 'It's as much for the social side of it as anything,' Ron said. I was welcome to come up and watch. Would I like to stay the night? Would I need a meal? Or breakfast? If they got enough men on the night they would rehearse a play for me. He signed off with the word 'Wasael'. Not 'weasel' – 'wasael'. Pronounced *wassail*. It was a new word to me. A folk word. I began to get excited.

According to Ron, there are three basic types of English folk play, which recur in different places: the sword play, the wooing play and the hero-combat play. The most common is a combat play involving St George. Sometimes he has become King George. Elsewhere, the hero is Robin Hood and sometimes Bullguize – possibly a corruption of 'bold geezer'. The play is introduced by a presenter, who may or may not be Father Christmas. It depends. One scholar describes a mummers' play from Newbold where the characters are given as Father Christmas, St George, a Turkish Knight, Moll Finney, Humpty Jack, Beelzebub, and 'Big Head and Little Wit'.

After being introduced, the hero exchanges boasts with an adversary, namely Bold Slasher or the Turkish Knight. Bold Slasher is clearly evil:

BOLD SLASHER
I'll hack you and cut you as small as flies
And send you to the cookshop to make mince pies.

St George returns the boast and a fight ensues during which St George slays the evil knight. 'Oh mercy!' cries Father Christmas, who turns out to be Bold Slasher's dad. A doctor is called, who revives the adversary with a tincture. It is not always clear what qualification this quack has to treat the sick . . .

FATHER CHRISTMAS
How came you a doctor?

DOCTOR
By my travels

I've been to Italy, Titaly, France and Spain
And now I'm back to cure the diseases of England again

. . . but his treatment seems to work, for up gets Slasher and the team then attempts to solicit money from the audience, with help from various end-characters, such as the Devil. The mummers might play a bit of music at the beginning, and there may be one or two songs, but basically the play is extremely short, over in one ten-minute act.

The train to Coventry pushed on into Northamptonshire. To my right there were low-lying green hills. The setting sun was beginning to make silhouettes of the wooden tangle along the treeline and I spotted a couple of rabbits in a divot. In this light I found it easy to forget the divisions of land and electrical wires. I could picture St George and Bold Slasher having their fatal showdown on the open, twilit hills.

Ron Shuttleworth was born in Sheffield, but when he met Jean from Coventry he moved down to the Midlands. He went to work at the Ford plant in Solihull and stayed there, making cars, until he retired. Now he runs the Folk Plays Archive. It has been his life's work. He can now say that his collection holds more than any other that is publicly accessible. And if anyone can challenge this claim, or is following a like interest, he would be delighted to hear from them. 'Kindred spirits,' he acknowledges sadly on his flyer, 'are few.' His house is a modest semi- in a quiet part of suburban Coventry. A nice place, with net curtains in the bay window.

Ron answers the door, a short elderly man with a full head of white hair, a trim white beard and spectacles. He is wearing a neckerchief inside an open-necked shirt. He walks slowly, short of breath, and leads me into the front room, where there is a teapot and an open bottle of warm milk on the table. The room is sparsely furnished: an old armchair faces the television set, with its back to the room. A glass-fronted cabinet holds about a hundred books on folklore and British history. One is called *The Complete Encyclopaedia of Weapons*. The mantel holds a tower of unopened cigarette packets. On the dining table is a large pub ashtray and the whole room is filled with the warm, dark brown smell. As Ron chain-smokes, I listen to his story.

He joined in with the folk revival in the early sixties, he says, and went singing in Coventry pubs where folk sessions were held.

'I found that, as I had a loud voice, could hold a tune and remember the words, I was classed as a performer and I could go out and get paid to do this stuff. But after a while we started getting people who were far more competent than I was.' He chuckles, a guttural, smoky gurgle. When I join in he stops and looks at me oddly. I stop too.

He had come to mumming through the Camping Club, he says. During the sixties the club ran regular folk weekends. Eventually they span off. At one of the dance meetings someone was lurching about in a ram costume. It was the Derby Tup, he says, part of a folk play from the town and something of a mascot. The horned ram took young Ron's fancy and he tried to interest the group in looking at more plays. But they were sniffy about it. All they wanted to do was morris dance.

'I got fed up with the attitude. People outside the club were starting to hold proper weekend folk festivals. But when I suggested we join in and mingle with other people they said, oh no, we'd far rather hire a village hall and dance among ourselves. So I went with the folk revival and let them carry on with their little dances.'

In truth – though he might not have known it at the time – Ron owed his discovery to two men, Thomas Fairman Ordish and Alex Helm. Ordish was a nineteenth-century civil servant and a pillar of the Folklore Society. His extensive research into early theatre led him to believe that the traditional mumming plays were a direct continuation of Anglo-Saxon custom – along, he claimed, with hobby horses and May games. He gathered quite an extensive collection of mummers' plays and on his death Ordish's colleague, Helm, a teacher, was persuaded to edit the old collector's papers. The eventual publication of the play texts in the 1960s had much to do with their revival as a calendar custom.

So Ron started looking for local plays and 'ran into' his repertoire. The plays the Coventry Mummers do now over Christmas are local to the area. 'We play them for entertainment. They *are* traditional but we – well – modify them.' Ron laughs. When I join in, he stops and stares at me again.

I ask how he knows what costumes to wear. 'Well you don't,' he says. 'But we wanted to be noticed, so we went for big bold colours. St George has this tabard thing. We took that pattern right through the range with different colours, you see.'

'Is that traditional?' I ask.

'Eh? Well, I know we've had some flack from people who thought we were non-traditional. It's getting better. In the old days you used to get the dead hand from the *folklorists*.' Ron says the word in an upper-crust voice. 'Well, I read up on folklore,' he carries on wearily. 'People say there's significance in this or that. But I thought, we all mostly work in factories, it seems stupid to have all this rural kit. I worked for Rover, so I made all the weapons out of Birmabrite. We'd got another bloke who worked in a bright anodizing plant, so we went in there and passed the swords round, you know. People used their skills on them.'

Swords? Skills? I have worked in a Midlands car factory myself. I try to imagine turning up there and tinkering with my morris kit – or being taught a skill, for that matter. Times, I think to myself, must have changed. I ask how sharp the swords are.

'It's not dangerous,' Ron says. 'Once a bloke hit the top of my shield and it smacked forward, hit me in the teeth. I was spitting blood.' He laughs again, his deep, infectious wheezing. I can't help laughing with him. He stops, stares at me oddly and mumbles: 'Of course, many teams use wooden swords these days.'

I put it to Ron that mumming plays are linked to ancient fertility rites.

'Bollocks,' says Ron.

Indeed. This notion was germinated by James Frazer. In what seems to the modern scholar like a frenzy of random connections, the Victorian anthropologist compared ancient myth to the tribal rituals of Africa and Australia, and these to British folk

customs. Chronology and geography were no obstacle to Frazer as rain dances, tree worship and maypole shindigs were effortlessly fused, unencumbered by logical reason. Sir James concluded that folk customs had evolved from vegetation rites and published his ideas in *The Golden Bough*, the book that captivated the imagination of Cecil Sharp among many others. It caught the romantic mood of the moment, this notion that there once was a jolly old England where women worshipped hares and green men frolicked to the sound of the hurdy-gurdy, while virgins cavorted under the mistletoe and dark figures in animal skins beat on big drums.

Frazer, though highly unscientific in his assumptions, made a lasting impression on a romance literature scholar called Jessie Weston, who was subsequently unable to let go of the idea that the Arthurian Grail quests could be linked – by hook or by crook – to mummers' plays, the morris and those fertility cults.

It is to Frazer's flawed analysis that we owe films like *The Wicker Man*: its links between folk song, hobby horses, maypole ribbon-dances and pre-Christian sacrificial rites have no basis in fact. Even so, there are those who would argue strongly that the mummers' play, focusing as it does on death and rebirth, is necessarily a survival of some early vegetation ceremony and that it is naive to suggest otherwise. But the death and resurrection themes in the plays could just as easily have a Christian root. The fact that tradition places the plays at Easter and Christmas would support this, but Frazer was very keen to argue that Christianity itself was merely a development of paganism and that the resurrection of

Christ was only a new way of telling the oldest story: the life force renewing. 'No one really knows,' Ron says, 'but a lot of these so-called ancient customs are only traceable as far back as Frazer's book.'

So the mumming plays may not be fertility cults, but they are not theatre either. 'We had an *hactoor* once. We had to slap him.' Ron laughs, I join in automatically and get the look again.

I ask Ron if he has ever been on a theatre stage.

'Eh? I've been on a stage. You can't see any people beyond the footlights, it's just black. How can people perform in this vacuum?' He clears his throat and apologizes for using milk straight from the bottle for the tea.

'You don't bother so much when you're on your own,' he says.

Later, in the archive itself, one bookshelf catches my eye. 'Are all these books about folk plays?' I ask, and Ron seems to contract a little at the question.

'Those are Jean's books,' he says. 'She did a lot of research into Elizabethan Coventry when she was here.' There is a long silence. Coventry's medieval buildings, along with much of the city's charm, were crushed in the Second World War. All that remains of its pre-industrialized past is the tiny, narrow Spon Street, its black beams and whitewash a fleeting monument to a former market town. Now it is just another supermarket town. If you could erase the concrete, the paving slabs and ring roads, and wipe away the grease from all the burger takeaways, what would you see? Is there still land underneath, trying to breathe and renew?

'You've got to have an obsession to keep you going,' Ron says at length. He gestures towards his collection. 'I'm obsessed with this. That's what keeps me going.'

I look around the room. In another house it might be have been a dining room, there might have been a large table, place mats, doilies. There might have been a dresser with crockery and jugs, framed photographs. But here there are microfiche files and ledgers, ring binders, box files, envelopes and loose leaves, folder after folder filled with paper documents. Books, pamphlets, newspaper cuttings. Everything anybody has ever set down about English folk plays is here, documented, put away and available for reference, should anyone ever need it.

'I'm the one on my hands and knees in libraries,' Ron says, 'In all the dust and spiders.'

Ron drives us to meet the other mummers. I don't know what to expect. I notice Ron has brought a plastic case, like a first aid kit. When I look closer I see it is printed with a St George's cross, white on blue. As we are travelling, Ron returns to the subject of the theatre. Another thing that sets actors apart from mummers, he says, is the cult of the rehearsal.

'We take a very, very relaxed attitude to that.' He laughs again. I want to join in, but I know better this time. I want his eyes on the road. 'Sometimes we do. It all depends how many men we get,' he says. Yes, it is men only.

'Is that traditional?' I ask.

'I think it's deliberate,' Ron sighs. 'Anyone can join, theoretically, as long as they have a proposer, a seconder and a full set of votes.' He leans in to me slightly and lowers his voice. 'Actually, we do have a blackball situation at present.'

'Blackball?'

'Well, we're living in each other's pockets so much. You get enough back biting in life. There's one bloke I know would love to join the Mummers but one of the others just will not have him at any price.' Any Mummer can veto a new man, he explains.

'And what about women?' I ask. Ron sighs again.

'See, if you introduced women it would change it.' There is a small silence, then Ron says: 'Subtly, I'll grant you.'

We pull up at our destination and I follow Ron in. As the door swings shut behind me I get my first glimpse of the Mountbatten Club. Its name had led me to imagine the kind of club where gravy-stained old former politicians take port after a modest dinner of rolled duck, kedgeree and eggs Benedict in an oak-panelled salon once frequented by Somerset Maugham. But this is Coventry, and the Mountbatten is more the kind of place where working men throw darts and drink Double Diamond beneath the strip lighting, where the Formica flooring and plastic chairs glower in competing shades of red. It is also almost completely empty.

I like it instantly. There are a couple of mummers at the bar, who greet Ron as we approach. The barman has the kind of face from which all expression has long been lost. He seems friendly. I buy Ron a pint of cider and a couple more mummers drift in.

'Richard's come from London to see some mummers rehearse.'

'Well, you picked the wrong side then,' they laugh.

The staircase is pitch black and I keep from stumbling by fixing on the foot of the man in front of me. Just for an instant my imagination plays a trick on me and I wonder if this is not the moment that will be re-created on TV's *Crimewatch UK*, as the satanists lead me into the darkness, with their strange blue cases marked with magical symbols, containing who knows what?

Upstairs and bathed in yellow light, we sit around a large table. Other mummers arrive sporadically, complaining about the busted light bulb. They sit, tell jokes and laugh at each other. Once it is established that I am not trying to join, the men are open and friendly towards me. I ask them how they began performing folk plays. Most say they were interested in the folk scene but they couldn't play an instrument, sing or dance.

'This is about the only thing I can do . . .'

'And you don't even do *this* very well.' They all laugh. Noel says he joined to travel the world and have sex with a lot of different women. The squire takes control of the agenda: money matters, forthcoming bookings, a trip away. It is businesslike in a low-level way. Most of the mummers are paying scant attention, assenting or dissenting lackadaisically, telling jokes, getting rounds in. Ron opens his blue case. It has a few pieces of paper in it.

Noel's wife has just 'forced' him to 'buy her' a top-of-the-range caravan. Noel thinks it is safe to say it is the best caravan money can buy. There are a few murmurs and grumbles. Ron says it depends what she wants it for: 'Once you go over a certain price, all you're doing is what I call *putting on the style*.' Noel has no real answer to that.

The squire is trying to get the mummers to agree a date and venue for a trip away, with wives too. Various locations are mooted, but the Lake District proves the most popular as there will be things for the ladies to do there, they think. Ron suggests a good route from Coventry.

'Oh, I don't think I'd go that way . . .' says the squire.

This is a bad move. Ron takes offence, turns his back on the squire, who is also the group's newest member. 'Well, *you* may not,' Ron says. The squire quickly moves to diffuse Ron's anger. The others are quiet. At length Ron turns round again. As the others are talking I watch Ron. Every now and again he glares at no one in particular, the same way he looked at me back at his house. Suddenly I realize why. Every time he takes a pull on his cigarette, as the smoke fills his lungs, his eyes widen as though he has been affronted. I thought he was glaring at me but he was just enjoying a cigarette. And every time he made a joke, he rewarded himself with a good puff.

There is no other business, so the squire declares the meeting closed. Not that many are listening. Someone starts singing. The men, still at the table, gripping their pints, join in casually on the chorus:

> For we are jolly boys
> We'll do no harm
> Wherever we may go
> And we're coming out a-guising
> As you very well do know

I am surprised. The move to song seems so incongruous. None of the men fits the popular image of the folk enthusiast. Until now the Coventry Mummers could have been any group, any lottery syndicate or works social. But all of a sudden they are performing the ancient folk plays of England and I am fascinated. I feel stupid for being there, ignorant of it, with my notepad in my pocket like some latter day Cecil Sharp up from the metropolis, studying my own people as though I am different. But I'm hungry for answers. These are my plays, so why don't I know them? Why didn't anyone pass them on to me?

Oral tradition in my family amounted to 'One, two, buckle my shoe . . .' My infant school teacher, Mrs Cave, had been driven by a higher function. As my fellow pupils and I sat eating our crayons and fiddling with Stickle Bricks, Mrs Cave, like a fire alarm, would suddenly and without warning launch into a shrill chorus of 'Little Donkey' or 'Away in a Manger', to which we were supposed to sing along. Weekends provided no respite. At Sunday School I was taught how to sing 'If I were a fuzzy wuzzy bear, I'd thank you, Lord, for my fuzzy wuzzy hair'. The songs I learned in my early years all contained the word 'saviour'.

Or perhaps I had simply worked in the wrong factories. My first ever job was making chocolate in a giant Victorian red-brick plant near Bath. I had originally been given a production line job on Christmas selection packs, but I had helped out a recently divorced man called Andy who returned the favour by seconding me to an easy life on the chocolate-making floor. On my first day there I was brought before Bert, the foreman, a proud, didactic man in his sixties.

'You smoke?' he asked me. I was pleased at this, as he appeared to be welcoming me into his clique with the offer of a cigarette.

'Yes,' I answered. Bert wagged his finger.

'I don't. Never have. And if I catch you eating the work I'll be down on you loike a ton o' bricks.'

Bert, of course, had instantly sensed that I was not as other chocolate workers. I didn't have the full glass-and-a-half of local vernacular. My accent was not broad enough, my vocabulary was suspect. I was not to join that group.

Still, the job was easy and demanded little of my time. My particular function was to open a valve on a metal tank with a special tool and fill up a capacious wagon with the freshly liquefied 'work' that oozed out thickly from the tap. This took about half an hour, during which time I was free to do what I did best – stare out of the window and watch the dawn over the woods or hunt for herons fishing on the Avon. Once the wagon was full I was to transfer my sweet, sticky load to the giant pool of liquid brown, ten feet by twenty feet, at the far end of the shop floor, where it would be stirred by giant mechanical blades. There was a folktale there. It involved a man called Bob Smart and the giant mechanical blades. 'They never found him neither,' was usually how it ended. There was another tale about a consignment of embezzled wafers, a car boot and a night visit to Cheddar Gorge, which climaxed with the words, 'Bugger'd died, hadn't he?' No one brought in any swords for me to coat with chocolate and no one sang songs about

St George, but a man did once try to throw himself from the roof of the Murray Mint building.

I may have worked in the wrong factories, but the mummers don't reproach me for my ignorance, nor do they find me suspicious. They are pleased to have the interest.

One by one they get up and assemble at the far end of the room and begin their tup play, scripts in their hands. One man plays the tup and pretends to be under a blanket, crouching and using his hand as the snapping jaws of the beast. Ron was right, there is no attempt at theatre, no ornament, and there is something refreshing in that. It is rough, but not quite ready. The players stand a little awkwardly and in no particular place. Lines are fluffed all round. Bold Slasher does not wring his hands and cry, 'But what's my motivation?' No one has been reading up on Stanislavsky. As the mummers speak, I see Ron mouthing their lines to himself. When one of the men stumbles over his words, Ron gently lifts his eyes to heaven. He looks very happy. The happiest I've seen him so far. The troublesome tup is both slain and revived. Then the play is at an end. More drinks arrive somehow, we end up downstairs again and no one says 'Darling you were marvellous'. I realize that this is only a rehearsal. I should come and see a proper street performance.

'The one you want to come to,' someone tells me, 'is the Banbury hobby horse festival.'

'Hobby horse?'

'Oh yeah, they all go there, the morris lot and the mummers and that.'

Noel starts telling me about a great party that weekend. I am invited. Horses, morris men, mummers, tents. I say I will be there. Can I bring my wife? Noel's eyes light up.

'Oh yes, bring any girls you like,' he says.

Time is getting on and I need to catch my train home. I call a taxi.

'Cab from the Mountbatten Club,' I ask. The girl on the other end laughs.

'None of our drivers'll pick up from there,' she says.

'What? Why not?'

She laughs again. 'Sorry – they just don't, OK?'

I look around the club. There is a large silver tray full of triangular sandwiches on one of the tables. The mummers are helping themselves. The barman is grinning to himself, polishing a glass slowly with a towel. In one of the corners an old man is staring into space. It's hardly the St Paul's riots.

'I'll drive you to the station,' Ron offers. But it soon becomes clear that this isn't going to be any time soon. This is his night out. Why cut it short? Some of the men have gone home already. But the performance and the drinks have made the rest highly convivial. Noel is talking about young women again. Apparently I am to bring some 'spare girls' when we next meet. I am not sure if I know any girls of the type Noel is imagining. Ron, finally picking up his car keys, tells me it's all bluster. Noel used to be something of a ladies' man when he first joined.

'Groupies?' I ask as we get in the car.

Ron chuckles. 'But he's got himself a lovely wife now, though, and settled down.' He makes the mummers sound like a rock group. We drive through Coventry. At night, under the lights, it looks a beautiful place. You just have to know the right streets. 'If I had a wife like that – well . . .' Ron sighs, as I look out of the window. I have enjoyed my evening with the mummers.

'You'll come back and see us, won't you?' Ron asks as we approach the station. I say I will.

'You might have to remind me who you are.'

'Yes,' I say. 'Of course.'

Something has been nagging at me since I met Ron. He's clearly the driving force behind this particular group and he isn't getting any younger. I ask: 'Do you think we have an obligation to pass on our traditions?' Ron frowns.

'I don't know. Don't know if I can tell you that. We do it because we enjoy it. I suppose there is a sense of carrying on a tradition, yes.' There is a long silence. 'It would be nice to think it won't die out completely.'

'Do many young people join the group?' I ask.

'Sadly no,' Ron laughs. 'The troupe just gets older and older.'

The word 'troupe' makes me think of my great-grandfather Percy. He had not stayed in the warehouses and calico print shops of his Manchester upbringing. Instead, he had moved to London and formed an acrobatic troupe that played the music halls as the Three Delevines. They had travelled the world, performing a mix of acrobatics and music. I had only recently uncovered this story from my parents and was fascinated by it. It made sense to me. As none of my immediate family was musical I had always assumed there had never been such a tradition among us, and as I looked through Percy's old photographs of music hall turns dressed as devils on roller skates, people toting masks and banjos, I recognized the source of my own urge to perform. There is something about putting on a costume or a mask that allows you to live, however fleetingly, a little closer to your unfettered self. You forget ties, responsibilities and binocular sizes and enjoy a purer, freer experience. This is what the mummers get from their plays and they do it in the way that makes sense to them, away from the aggrandizing footlights of the stage and out on the streets where they live and work.

I step out into the night and the beer claims my senses. The station toilets are shut and I spend the twenty minutes before my train arrives thinking of Bold Slasher . . .

The motif of death and resurrection in the mummers' play is a conundrum. Our most famous traditional resurrection story concerns one Jesus of Nazareth. It's tempting to believe that this gives the mummers' play a Christian connotation, but the early folklorists argued just the opposite: that the play reflects instead the timeless truth of seasonal change. They believed that the process of regeneration, from the dead land of winter to the fertility of spring, was the ancient message that underpinned not only these plays but also Christianity itself. Where did they get this idea?

In a passage in *The Golden Bough* headed 'The Magic Spring', Frazer lays out the basis for the all-pervasive theory. So unsophisticated was 'primitive man' in his thinking, Frazer claims, that it did not occur to him that when the leaves fell off the trees for winter they would return of their own accord. The 'savage' thought, Frazer writes, that by mimicking in costume and paint the greenery he longed for, he would somehow communicate his need to the gods – that this act would become a magical rite, for which the gods would reward him with the blossoming of new buds. And when a morris man wears flowers in his hat, what we are seeing is a survival of this pagan greenery decoration. This is what the whole notion hangs on.

Influenced by Frazer, who had in fact sought to delegitimize religion by linking it with 'heathen' rites, the early folklorists believed that the plays were survivals of just such a ritual fertility cult – of an 'old religion' that came long before Christianity. But how true can this be? Before I can uproot the answers I feel I need to dig a little deeper in the earth. I need to get closer to the land.

I think I know where to go.

Drones

Chris Allen, lute maker, is gazing at his hands from behind his spectacles, manipulating an imaginary cat's cradle. 'When you're playing the lute you're like a trappist monk. You've got to be so solitary and introspective. It's very intense. I never thought I would want to do anything else.'

There is a pause while we both contemplate this. We are sitting, smoking in Chris's workshop, a peeling, rotting timber shack which, long before he acquired it and started making lutes, used to be the village post office. Some of the shelves still have prices inscribed on them, barely visible behind the rows of intricate wooden parts, tools, strings, rosin and books that line the walls. There is a cast-iron boiler in the middle of the floor, which gives off a dull glow as the winds outside lash through the vale. It's raining in sheets, and has been all day. I finger my cigarette and start to scan the surfaces for an ashtray. Every flat space is covered with sawdust, papers and thin slivers of untreated wood. A festival of kindling. The whole place would go up in a flash: the end of a career.

'But then, when I discovered the hurdy-gurdy and folk music,' Chris says suddenly, getting up, animated, 'it was the musical equivalent of going downtown, getting completely pissed and kicking shit out of the shop windows.' He grins, then notices me hovering with my cigarette. 'Oh, just use the floor,' he says, and grins again.

Hurdy-gurdy? I look at the instrument sitting precariously on one of Chris's chairs. It looks like a small boat, a carved figurehead at one end and an outboard motor at the other. The motor is actually a crank. The crank turns a wheel, the wheel vibrates the strings, four of which are drones, two of which are stopped by a row of keys which you play with one hand while cranking with the other, and four more simply sit there and resonate. Inside the keybox is a mass of wooden teeth, which strike the strings and create the notes. They're all finely adjustable. There's also a buzzing bridge. By jerking your wrist in the right way you can beat out a rhythm on the buzzes. A droning buzz.

'Sometimes I just sit out here on my own for hours listening to the drones,' says Chris. He grins. 'You know, moronically turning the handle.'

I bought one. Sod it, I thought. How hard can it be?

7 | Hull, Halifax and Hell

The rain came just after Wakefield. The sky darkened and the drizzle clung in beads on the Ridings shopping centre and on the windows of the Gap Kids store. By the time the train pulled out of Huddersfield and began to track the Colne Valley, the deluge was turning puddles to rivers and earth to mud. I was glad I had worn my flimsy deck shoes from Lowestoft. Down in the dale, as we passed through Slaithwaite and into Marsden, mill after mill squatted over the river, each dominating the water like a giant grey swan, the long dirty neck stretching up out of the mist. But the chimneys that had turned the houses soot black were quiet now. You could see right through the tall mill house windows, through the empty shells where the frames once rattled and all the trouble began. The train rolled on past a lot full of JCB diggers, through clumps of yellow gorse, washed-out cherry blossom and stone walls covered in moss.

There's a folktale here, an old legend about the first cuckoo of spring. The story goes that the people of Marsden noticed that the arrival of the cuckoo coincided with a change in the season, the onset of spring. They thought if they could only keep hold of the cuckoo, they would keep the spring for ever. So they started to build a tower around it. Brick by brick they surrounded the bird where it had landed on a rock. But at the last minute the cuckoo flew away. The tower, so the legend goes, 'were nobbut one course too low'. I'd have put a shoebox over it myself. But a fair had grown up around the legend of Marsden Cuckoo Day.

That was the story on the National Trust website, in any case. Something about it didn't ring true to me. I had come up to investigate, but I was also interested in this theme of death and rebirth, roots stirring under the spring soil. I wondered now what the moors could teach me. We like to speak of 'nature' as though of a realm divorced from man and woman. We watch the leaves fall in autumn, the tides ebb and flow on the seashore, and struggle to see our connection. We acknowledge the pull of the moon on the oceans, yet we dismiss astrology as superstition. Our doctors dispense expensive drugs, disparaging the natural remedies that have kept us alive for millennia. It is as though our instinct to survive and breed is something we dreamed up for ourselves. Nature it seems, is something we dominate – not the other way round.

My great-grandfather Percy, the acrobat, passed on his love of the stage to his son. Percy died in 1938, a year before his son fathered my mother. I never knew my grandfather or Percy. Yet somehow, magically, part of their tradition was passed through to me. But there is no real mystery. It is only the life force renewing itself. It happens everywhere. For example, my first pet was a woolly caterpillar, which I captured and kept in a sealed jam jar on my windowsill in the midsummer heatwave. When it fried to death I buried it under my parents' rosebush and cried so much that the next day it was miraculously reincarnated as a hamster.

As if for protection, the terraced houses of Marsden huddle around the red-brown clock tower of the Mechanics Hall, their sandy-coloured bricks long since turned black, their slate roofs glittering with the downpour. The hall itself is a testament to community spirit. It was funded and built in the nineteenth century by ordinary mill-workers who wanted to educate themselves out of oppression and poverty. Now it serves as a community centre.

Above it all, rising like a mountain out of the dale is Marsden Moor, a golden, rocky mass of heather brash and peat bogs on the edge of the Peak District. It surrounds and dwarfs the town, rolling off towards Saddleworth, High Peak and little-known places such as Old Woman, Netherthong and Gusset. With blanket bogs as deep as twenty-five feet in places, the moor contains some of the most bleak and challenging country in England.

Marsden station is built at the top of a small hill. When you get to the bottom you're in the centre of town. It's a compact place, centred around the old woollen mills. The River Colne is fed from a number of sources high on the moor they call Close Moss, and it tumbles down into the dale, coming to a head in Marsden. Two weirs take centre stage, where the river is flanked by shallow, rocky banks covered in bright green moss. As I passed, white ducks and mallards sat on the banks with their bills under their wings.

It was Friday afternoon, and I was booked in at a guest house called 'Water's Edge'. It wasn't hard to find. I rang the bell and

105   *Hull, Halifax and Hell*

a large red setter flew at me, breaking the calm with a piercing bark.

Are you, by chance, familiar with fight-or-flight syndrome? It's an instinctive process. When the brain senses danger, the bloodstream floods with adrenalin and your muscles tense up, readying you for whichever route you choose. Would I take on this mad dog? Or would I run like the wind? In the event, the choice was made for me. As the beast collided with my chest to administer, as it turned out, rather a lot of licks, I buckled and something in my left leg ripped. I said:

'Good dog. Ow!'

'Naughty Molly,' a child's voice chided in lilting West Riding tones. As my affectionate assailant was called off by a six-year-old, I limped inside and made my soft, southern hellos.

Water's Edge was a small, cheery guest house, run by a chatty, friendly woman called Kate. She had a happy voice, which cheered me up after my shaming confrontation with the animal kingdom. The bathroom and toilet had a sign up with a comedy Scot saying 'Och aye the loo'. In the hall there was a noticeboard with a newspaper article pinned to it. It was all about how Marsden had been used as a location for the medical drama serial *Where the Heart Is*, starring TV's Leslie Ash. Along with nearby Holmfirth and Slaithwaite – pronounced 'Slough-wet' – Marsden had also been used to set the scene for the sitcoms *Last of the Summer Wine* and *League of Gentlemen*. As ITV explained: 'Because it is an area of outstanding natural beauty, choosing a location was easy.' I have always loved the expression 'area of outstanding natural beauty', or ONB, as it is known to some. Having covered six-eighths of the land with concrete and forced animals into untimely extinction, we then give what is left marks out of ten for a good effort without our help. I sat down on my bed in the 'Pink Room' and examined my leg. As I suspected: no visible sign of injury, which meant I would get no value out of moaning. Actually, I wouldn't mind if the red setter became extinct.

A stoic limp around the town told me I had arrived too late for lunch at any of the pubs, but I found a chippy on the main drag. You have not had pie and chips and gravy until you have had it in Yorkshire. I could stand my fork up in the gravy, there was not a spot of grease on the chips and, to cap it all, there was very little on the menu for over £1. Not even the spam fritters, and I would have paid extra for them. Sated, I picked up a leaflet about the Cuckoo Day fair from the tourist office and hobbled back to Water's Edge to read it and restore my sodden flimsy deck shoes with the complimentary hair dryer.

The leaflet presented me with a number of options, one of which was listening to the town choir. I decided to go up the steep hill in the wet. So, at seven in the evening, I joined a group of walkers outside the Mechanics Hall for a 'medium themed stroll' up Marsden Moor to catch the cuckoo. There were three or four people in National Trust uniform to help me catch the cuckoo. None of them was wearing flimsy deck shoes, but one man had shown up in shorts.

'There's Marsden Moor,' said Alan, who was leading the walk. He pointed upwards at the dark, foreboding presence that loomed over us. 'Don't look at it too long.' Then we were off and up it. Alan strode ahead, pointing out interesting bandstands, ancient farmsteads and a green man carved into a gatepost, his face beset with oak leaves. He said something here about Celtic fertility gods but I didn't catch it. What I do know, though, is that the ornamental foliate heads we now call 'green men' originated in Europe in Christian times.

We followed after, a band of about ten, our cagoules rustling in the fresh moorland air until we were high above the mills and the houses were no more than specks. We negotiated a tiny, muddy path cut into the grassland and heather. Thanks to Molly the dog, I strode manfully with one leg only, dragging the other behind in the manner of a lame goat. When we reached the highest point, we came to a halt and Alan described a wide arc all around the town with his hand. The 5600-acre estate was now a National Trust property, he said. The Trust looked after everything, as far as the eye could see. There was a lot of work to do, reducing and correcting erosion from the elements, spreading heather over the bare peat to protect the habitat of the wild reed warblers, red grouse and meadow pipits that nest and feed there.

The estate was not just an ONB, but also an SSSI – a site of special scientific interest – because of these moorland birds. The legend was all about bringing in the warm spring weather, but the men from the Trust had been praying for these April showers. Forty acres had 'caught fire' on Monday and Alan's team had been forced to get up at dawn to beat it down. The fire would destroy not only the habitat of the birds but their chicks and eggs too, along with any newborn lambs the spring stork had brought.

Caught fire?

Alan elaborated. Kids had set it alight. There's not much to do around Marsden. 'It's a big property to maintain,' he added wistfully.

And expensive too. The National Trust works on a localized basis. You give money in Marsden and it stays in Marsden, to do Marsden's work.

'If you want to give at the end, that's fine,' Alan said.

We walked on. The moor was impressive, and it wasn't just the scale or the rugged sparseness of the heath. It was the lack of divisions. There were no hedges or fences, no walls to mark out territory or property. Just raw earth, rock and wild plants. I experienced an overwhelming sense of freedom, which I felt the urge to express. Had I not been in my flimsy deck shoes and walking with a marked limp, I dare say I would at that moment have strode off along the Pennine Way towards Toot Hill, Madwoman's Stones or Lost Lad, whooping as I went. But I didn't. Instead, I located a goose and went to pet it. This was a bad idea. The goose butted me repeatedly in the groin with its blunt orange bill and, in the rumpus that followed, it's safe to say the goose added considerably to Molly the dog's sterling work on my leg.

Meanwhile, Alan had gone into his routine. 'Centuries ago, when people were very superstitious and believed in all sorts of gods . . .' he began. He then told the cuckoo legend. He pointed to an anvil-shaped rock where the cuckoo was said to have landed.

There was no evidence of a tower. There was no evidence of a cuckoo either.

It was not unreasonable to expect a cuckoo. The meadow pipit is one of the most common 'hosts' for the predator. When the warmer weather brings the cuckoo up from the south, it seeks out the nesting pipit. The usurper waits until the female pipit has flown the nest to look for food, then in a flash the cuckoo is inside. She scoops out an egg and lays one of her own half-incubated Trojan Horses. Then she is gone. The cuckoo egg hatches ahead of the others and the blind baby cuckoo ruthlessly ejects the pipit eggs one by one, scooping them up onto its back and throwing them over the side. That was the theory anyway. As a fine mist of drizzle wet the bogs, the warm cuckoo weather was not strictly in evidence. If spring had sprung on Marsden Moor it was keeping it a secret.

From here, high on the hill, it was easy to get a sense of how the giant factory mills had tyrannized the area. I was stunned by the proximity of the home to the workplace, by the thought of the power and influence a successful Marsden mill-owner such as William Horsfall, who had built the mill I was looking at, would have wielded over his neighbours in the early nineteenth century. It's impossible to overstate the degree to which Horsfall was hated by his employees, and local legends illustrate his contempt for the suffering and poverty of those he exploited. But you have to look at his murder in political terms.

In 1812, when Horsfall breathed his last, England was a land bitterly divided under the Tory government of Spencer Perceval.

On one side of the line there were the aristocratic rich. In this year, when the waltz came in to fashion, Jane Austen was preparing to publish *Pride and Prejudice*, her scathing tale of upper-class largesse, love and social climbing in England's salons and country seats. It described a world in which one sneered at merchant oiks who were ghastly and vulgar enough to have earned their fortunes through trade, where women did not work but demurely played the *pianoforte* until the right sort of husband hove into view laden with venison, partridge, fine wines and invitations to a ball.

On the other side of the line there was everybody else. Gaunt with toil and hunger, the ordinary working people were lucky if they could get a bit of 'old milk' to take with their oatmeal gruel. Mostly, they would take it with nettles. The year of 1812 was the worst in a bad bunch and it is unsurprising that things came to a head then. But to get a sense of why, you have to rewind a little.

In 1793 England went to war with France. It was to be a long, drawn-out series of conflicts that would drag on until the Battle of Waterloo in 1815, crippling England's overseas trade in the process. The woollen industry, once England's crowning glory, went into a deep recession. Money was scarce and was made scarcer by the rising taxes the government imposed to fund the war. This alone would have caused a good measure of misery, but there was more.

The world of work itself was changing at a fast pace.

Until the end of the eighteenth century, weavers in Yorkshire had lived and worked in their own homes. These self-employed artisans owned their looms, performing every one of the multitude of operations that turn wool into cloth. They then took the finished pieces to market. Typically they would graze their animals – sheep for wool and cows for milk, perhaps a horse – on the commons. Some enterprising weavers with capital to invest set themselves up as clothiers, hiring other weavers to work for them.

But the clothiers became frustrated with the cottage industry framework. It cost them too much money to send a horse between weaver, cropper and cloth hall, so they built larger factories, bought machinery such as Arkwright's new spinning jenny, which did the weaving work of nineteen men, and brought their weavers and croppers in-house.

Then, in 1800, the Tories did something to the common land. They privatised it. Over the course of the next two decades, at a rate of a hundred and fifty acres a year, the ancient open fields were 'enclosed' by landlords. The common people were supposed to receive compensation for losing their grazing rights, but in truth this rarely happened. Weavers found they could no longer keep animals and support themselves. They had to get jobs. They accepted pitifully low pay and dangerously long hours, but at least they wouldn't starve.

Then came the famines. The years 1809 and 1811 brought exceptionally bad harvests, raising the price of a loaf of bread beyond the reach of a weaver on basic wages. And wages were hardly going to rise in the middle of a war-torn recession. Since few were grazing their own cattle any more, milk was in short supply too, and profiteering was rife. People who had for generations supported themselves simply could not afford to eat now that they were employees, and yet the option of self-employment had been effectively removed. Workers appealed to Parliament to protect their rights. The government would not condescend to legislate for trade matters. It believed that the social order was the only just regulator. That is to say, a man should know his place. So, instead, it took away what rights the workers had, just in case the peasants were under any illusion as to their standing in society.

As they bought more machines, the clothiers came to depend less and less on the skilled work of the weavers, especially that of the croppers. These men wielded massive shears for removing the fuzz and would finish a piece of cloth to a very high standard. Because of the immense strength needed to operate the shears, coupled with the delicate craft required to finish the cloth, the croppers were considered the cream of master craftsmen. The pride they took in their work was crucial to what was to follow when that pride was taken away.

The clothiers had found a new machine – Harding's shearing frame. To the average factory owner it was a boon. It did the work of ten skilled croppers and did it better. To the oppressed workers this final loss of dignity was the last straw. Those who were lucky enough to keep their jobs would be reduced to the status of unskilled machine operators. Most simply refused to use them. Others decided enough was enough. If Parliament would not protect them it was time to seek justice through direct action.

The croppers formed a clandestine alliance, bound by oaths of secrecy, vowing to overthrow the tyranny of the mill-owners and to improve the lot of the common man. At Longroyd Bridge in Marsden, in John Wood's cropping shop, in Leeds and in Halifax, the Yorkshire croppers united and smashed their frames.

The newspapers had long been carrying stories of militant lace-workers in Nottingham. These men, fearing that new machines would put them out of work, had simply broken them. They struck at night under cover of darkness, their faces blackened, their identities a closely guarded secret. Moreover, they held their bosses to ransom, demanding better wages and conditions. They burned mills and terrorized their owners. In printed broadsheets and open letters they set out their demands and signed them 'General Ludd', after the Leicester stocking-knitter Ned Ludd. He had become a legendary figure after apparently smashing his machine in a fit of pique. Now a movement was named after him.

News of these uprisings in Nottingham had reached the Yorkshire press, and in January 1812 the Yorkshire Luddites burned Oatlands Mill in Leeds. Their highly organized campaign of violence and destruction created a climate of tension and fear. They ransacked houses, seeking out frames, looting for weapons or collecting money to fund their campaigns. They broke into factories and destroyed the machines. Always at night. Always a surprise. Huge rewards were offered for their identities. But if sympathetic neighbours knew who the Luddites were they kept quiet. The Luddites were never betrayed.

Local magistrates, out of their depth, appealed to Parliament to legislate. The government reacted. To protect not the workers but the capitalists. Perceval made frame-breaking a capital offence, but the act only exacerbated the violence. The Luddites reasoned that it would be as well to be hanged for murder as for frame-breaking; it was Perceval who sealed Horsfall's fate. The hated clothier was held up on his way home by four Luddites with pistols.

The *Leeds Mercury* carried the story under the headline 'Atrocious Murder': 'They all four fired, and inflicted four wounds in the left side of their victim, who instantly fell from his horse, and the blood flowed from the wounds in torrents.' One of the men confessed in order to save his life; his three companions were tried and found guilty. They died martyrs, hanged at York.

On the way back down the moor I got chatting to a local woman called Sue. Born here in Marsden, she had moved away for work, but had been forced to come back to Yorkshire because it was 'too expensive to live anywhere else'. Trouble was, with all the attention the town was now getting from television exposure, house prices were rising here too. I asked her what it was like to live in Marsden. She said it was all right now because the town had got an art gallery and a posh pizza place on Peel Street. I asked her if her parents had celebrated Cuckoo Day when she was younger.

'Oh no. I don't remember that, no.'

The walk ended at the Riverhead Brewery Tap, where a 'folk evening' had been promised. The Riverhead is a brew-pub — a place that brews and serves its own beer. Most of the ales on offer were, appealingly, named after local reservoirs perched high on the moor. The higher up the moor, the stronger the beer. But I opted for the dark ale brewed specially for this weekend: Ruffled

Feathers. It was a rich, nutty ale with a touch of malt on the nose, some barley, lots of hops, plenty of water, a good sprinkling of yeast and sugar, some alcohol and a hint of cuckoo on the finish. Perfect. The trouble was, the folk band hadn't turned up. Alan was pacing up and down the upstairs room.

'We promised a folk evening,' he muttered. 'That's what we've got to deliver.' He addressed the room. 'Does anybody know any songs?'

Two middle-aged women who looked like twins said they could do some singing if he was desperate. As it happened, they had brought with them a thick book of handwritten song words, but they had not prepared themselves to be the main act.

'We thought we'd do a bit in between the others,' said Pam.

'We haven't brought our keyboard,' Judith said.

I could see what was happening. It was a precarious situation. Dither any longer and there would be no show at all. I could no longer remain an observer – this called for direct action. I came out with an expression I don't use very often:

'I'll get my banjo.'

'You fetch it out, lad,' an old man said.

When I got back, Judith and Pam were holding the room in raptures, singing in close harmony.

> When I were courtin' Mary Ann,
> T' owd squire, he says one day:
> 'I've got no bed for wedded fowks;
> Choose, wilt ta wed or stay?'

Avalon: waiting for the magic spring

Points west: sunset over Watchet beach

Gruff dancing: the fenland molly

© James O Jenkins/eyevine

Solid elm: the Dorset Ooser

Sacred sight: dawn at Cerne Abbas

Dick Brooker: he follows the Straw Bear

The rural idyll: creating tradition in Marsden

I couldn't gie up t' lass I loved,
To t' town we had to flee:
Frae Hull, an' Halifax, an' Hell,
Gooid Lord, deliver me.

I've wrowt Leeds an' Huthersfel',
An' addled honest brass;
I' Bradforth, Keighley, Rotherham,
I've kept my barns an' lass.
I've travelled all three Ridin's round,
And once I went to sea:
Frae forges, mills, an' coalin' boats,
Gooid Lord, deliver me!

You worked the looms, you kept a roof over your head. If you didn't like the conditions, well, you could move away. Or you could burn down the mill. Far from being nixed by the York hangings, Luddism spread. There were riots over power looms in Lancashire, the demise of a lace factory in Loughborough and a resumption of frame-breaking in Nottingham. Perceval himself was murdered in the same year as Horsfall. The last recorded Luddite incident occurred in 1830, fifteen years after the war ended. Farm workers destroyed new threshing machines. They achieved some small successes, and wages were raised a little, but ultimately the Luddites were on a hiding to nothing. They could not stop the technological revolution and it seemed that Parliament would support capitalism all the way. What was good for the merchant traders was good for taxes.

Armies of men were employed to apprehend or kill the Luddites, or protect their victims – all in vain. But if Perceval had acted to protect the rights of the common man to a fair wage and decent, safe conditions, this might have been a very short story.

As the Ruffled Feathers went down, more singers came out of the woodwork. Pam and Judith taught me some songs and I played along. I was glad the band had decided not to come. People were racking their brains and coming out with old songs they had half forgotten. Even me. A man called Pete arrived with a stick and a cravat and delivered some lovely old songs, albeit with his finger in his ear. Another man, with the help of rather a lot of Ruffled Feathers, got up, borrowed my banjo and made up a song on the spot about Tony Blair, George Bush and Saddam Hussein. It was a good song. A woman with a frame drum waited until we were all at an advanced stage of merriness before launching into a number that required a lot of actions. Pam and Judith sang to us about the 'pratty pratty flowers' of Holmfirth, their village.

I was jealous. I had never lived anywhere that had its own anthem. There was no special song from my home town, and nothing I had grown up with. And if there were, what would it be? 'The Cruddy Cruddy Crisps of Croydon'? The 'Cheesy Cheesy Wotsits of Wallington'? But in Marsden there was a palpable sense of pride in the area and what it stood for. I asked a woman what she thought tradition was. She told me: 'We like how we are.'

Pam and Judith weren't sisters at all, though they looked so similar. They had gone to the same school and had been singing together ever since. Everyone was telling me about things I should come back and see. There's a Slaithwaite legend about 'moonraking'. Some locals were trying to fish out some illegal booze from the canal where they had hidden it when they were challenged by the excisemen. They feigned drunkenness, pointed to the full moon's reflection in the water and said they were only 'raking for the moon'. The excisemen dismissed them as village idiots. Slaithwaite now celebrates this every year – as do the people of Bishops Cannings in Wiltshire, who tell the same story.

There was a host of other events I should see: the Saddleworth brass band contest, and something called the Longwood Thump. I had a long and meandering chat with a smiling elderly lady, who ended the conversation by telling me she was off to deliver the milk. I asked her if she remembered Cuckoo Day from when she was a child.

'Oh no, no. Can't say as I do.'

No. The problem was, no one could, and I was sure I'd heard that cuckoo story before, but about Borrowdale in Cumbria. In fact, I knew I had. The Borrowdale story went: 'If we'd nobbut laid another line o' stanes atop we'd 'a copped him.' That's not all. The same story is also attributed to Gotham in Nottingham. And Wing in Leicestershire. It's an old, old joke.

Alan had been compèring the evening in a stalwart sort of way, announcing each number and geeing up the other drinkers to applaud and cheer. He had done a good job. I asked him straight about the origins of Cuckoo Day.

'Well . . .' he said. There was a silence. 'We made it up.'

'Who? The National Trust?'

'Yep. About ten years ago.' A defensive tone crept into his voice. 'Well . . . all the other villages have got one. In Slaithwaite they have the moonraking and Holmfirth has the folk festival. Tomorrow we'll have the duck race. It's a pound to sponsor a duck.'

Tomorrow, the National Trust men would release a thousand numbered rubber ducks into the River Colne and race them over the weir. The first at the finish line would win a prize, but that wasn't important. What mattered was that every duck sponsored meant the National Trust had secured another pound for its meadow pipits and its reed warblers. Another quid to help put out the fire after the bratty kids of Holmfirth had gone on a hazing spree over the tops. And there's no better way to get people to spend money than to make it a tradition.

Like the January sales.

Saturday began with a hearty breakfast at Water's Edge. Outside, as if in answer to our call to the cuckoo, the sun had poked its head out of the overcast and was lighting up the stalls. There were women selling potted plants and a children's silver band in which everyone seemed to be playing the tenor horn. They were all wearing their school uniform, except the drummer, who had shades on.

Then there was the morris. I walked towards the sound of a melodeon, but on closer examination it wasn't the morris at all. It was the Saddleworth Clogging Garland Dancers: a group of five mature women and one bonny young maid dressed in floral print frocks, white pinnies and clogs. The tunes were familiar and I looked for the musician. But the dulcet tones were coming from a portable cassette player.

I watched as the women described complex patterns on the cobbled street, their wooden footwear clacking pleasantly as the tape wowed. I imagined this at least was a local tradition. But if it was it had died out long ago. This revival, based on the memory of someone's grandma, had been made up or adapted from morris and other country dances. The costume was a re-creation of Victorian mill-girls' dress and the buckled clogs were from Derbyshire. The women carried long poles bound round with ribbons and topped with floral garlands. These, back in the old days — you know,

originally — would have been the hoops of butter barrels and the flowers would have been picked wild, explained Hilary, one of the women. But the team used silk flowers now. 'It's too much trouble to do it every time.' Yeah, why bother?

A local morris side arrived, and there was a procession in which the country dance tunes mingled uneasily with the military aggression of the silver band and marching drummers. At its head was the cuckoo itself. In fact, it was a cardboard cut-out of a cuckoo, propped up in a wheelbarrow. The barrow was pulled by a jeep. The jeep had National Trust emblazoned on its flank.

Down by the weir, the Trust men had cordoned off areas of the bank with day-glo orange porta-fencing. To make things safe. On ordinary days kids could skip down to the waterside and drown unhindered, but no one was going to get wet in the Trust's name. Then the ducks were launched. Egged on by the masses that lined the river, spilling over its walls, chanting, cheering and dancing, one thousand yellow plastic ducks bobbed down the river, eddying wildly and snagging on twigs. Not all would reach the finish line, but each one would fund new seed, the spreading of brash, the protection of the bogs. Each one would help ensure the habitat of the meadow pipit, and so of the cuckoo, the herald of spring. As I made up the hill for the station I wished the Trust men luck. They deserved success. After all, these days you can't rely upon the land to regenerate itself. Why not perform a little ritual to help nature take its course? I didn't know it as I chugged back towards Huddersfield, but I was about to get a lot closer to the fertility cult.

8 | A Bunch of May

In the darkness, something goes off. A bell, an alarm . . . It rattles inside my head and I open my eyes. I am in a strange bed in a strange room. I pull the blankets away and stumble towards the noise. My left leg buckles and I remember I can hardly walk. I placed the alarm clock in this wooden recess before going to sleep, but in the small hours the cupboard simply acts as a demonic amplifier. I grasp the clock and thump it into silence. It is twenty past four in the morning of the first of May.

I steady myself against the jamb and enjoy the silence. Peace at last. Suddenly, a clap of thunder, close overhead, shakes the wooden house and the hollow sound rumbles deep inside me, like my hunger. Forks of wild electricity light up the room and I pull away the curtain to see a torrent illuminated in the flashes.

It's sheeting it down.

Bushes are dancing in the wind and all at once it dawns on me. I am going to catch my death – high on a hill, far from home, on the first official day of spring. In the light of this epiphany, I decide to go back to bed for ten minutes.

The plan was quite simple. Catch the 7.30 out of Waterloo,

alight at the Sherborne veterinary surgery and station (it's a compact town), ride eleven miles to the village of Cerne Abbas in a 'Beaver Cab' and lodge the night at 'Badger Hill'. Then simply rise at dawn and observe a heathen fertility ritual.

It sounds easy enough, but I find reality has presented one or two obstacles: namely, the unequal ratio of pissing rain to waterproof clothing, and a busted leg not unconnected with being attacked by a goose during a catch-the-cuckoo 'medium themed stroll' on the West Yorkshire moors. The bird was supposed to have brought the good weather. But already we're into May and no sign of a glorious day. How had I missed the spring? In London the signs are not as immediate as they are in the country. Caught up in the daily commute, it's easy to pass by Brook Green and mistake the first tentative crocus tips for a sprinkling of Cadbury's Mini Eggs dropped by a careless child. How can I be expected to look up from my feet and spot the buds when there is so much chewing gum and dog shit to avoid? How can we be expected to tune into the seasons when cable is showing repeats of *A Touch of Frost*? The bird should have told me. I curse the cuckoo and decide to dither for a further ten minutes.

A car glides slowly past the window, and a sixth sense tells me it is making for the Giant Viewpoint Car Park around the corner – the agreed meeting place. In truth, I'm starting to have second thoughts about my plan of meeting some strangers in a dark car park in the middle of the night. As if to emphasize my misgivings, a massive sheet of lightning flashes into the room, casting ghoulish shadows on the cavity wall.

4:40 a.m.

Beware of an oak

It draws the stroke

Avoid an ash

It courts the flash . . .

4:41 a.m.

Wonder what an ash tree looks like . . .

My stomach is still rumbling in sympathy with the thunder. Part of what lured me here was the promise of a cooked breakfast in the pub afterwards and a pint of the local brew to wash it down. Of course, there are some who believe the thunder will sour the beer. That would be my luck. In the fifteenth century, people thought thunder was the wrath of God and rang the church bells to make it go away. Others thought the lightning would ripen the corn. In any case, it is as well to have some thunder now, otherwise the swans' eggs would never hatch. As long as you don't point at the lightning, that is.

By ten to five the rain has finally calmed to a mild drizzle, so this is probably my best chance. I slip out into the early morning and breathe in the air. It smells of wet soil and creation. Despite the recent storm, the air is warm as I approach the Giant Viewpoint Car Park.

The Giant being proposed for viewing is known as the Cerne man. He is a 180-foot figure of a man, definitely a man, and he is carved in foot-wide trenches into the chalky side of the tallest, steepest hill in these parts. The drawing is rudimentary and graphic, consistent with ancient Romano-British art, but – appealingly – includes eyebrows. He is the largest of two human figures in southern England, his cousin being the Long Man of Wilmington in Sussex, and he carries an enormous knobbly club in one hand, just in case his virility is in any doubt. In fact, his virility is left in no doubt by the somewhat unambiguous 40-foot erect penis and scrotum combination standing proudly at his front. This being England, the phallus has earned its owner the sobriquet 'Rude Man'. Because in England it is very rude even to have a penis, let alone to draw one in chalk on a hillside.

The penis also makes our Giant a little unusual among the many figures carved into English hills, and has led more than a few to conclude that he is a pre-Christian fertility symbol. Why not? The origins of the Cerne Abbas Giant are not known, but are the subject of lively and ongoing debate. There is a popular belief that the figure represents the Graeco-Roman god Hercules. Others believe he can date back no further than the seventeenth century. There is certainly no mention of the Giant until 1694, when the churchwarden paid three shillings to have the figure recut. Other English hillside figures, such as the White Horse at Uffington, have medieval records. This alone does not prove that the Cerne man isn't older, but it is odd that the Church should have willingly paid to have it kept up if it was such a potent pagan symbol. The first survey of his dimensions was published in the *Gentleman's Magazine*, in 1764: 'This monstrous figure . . . appears almost erect.' Another survey, by a vicar called John

Hutchins in 1774, tastefully omitted to mention the Giant's colossus altogether.

I've been doing a bit of reading on the subject and my favourite source is the commentary provided at <www.sacredsites.com>, a website put together by Arizona-based pilgrimage enthusiast Martin Gray. Mr Gray holds that the Cerne Abbas Giant is a representation of the Celtic fertility god Cernunnos – a conclusion drawn entirely from the similarity of the two names – and that a sight line taken up the Giant's penis on May Day points directly at the sun as it rises over the hill. Presumably he means the first of May, not the bank holiday. Childless couples, Mr Gray maintains, 'still copulate' on the grass inside the Giant's penis in order to conceive. He says the site has lots of 'feminine energy', supplied by the 'pagan well' called Silver Well, to balance the masculine power of the Giant. He does not say how a well can be religious or otherwise, but nontheless Mr Gray's website has been awarded the distinction of Cosmic Website of the Week.

Mr Gray's attractive mix of fantasy and fact is a good example of the Chinese whisper process by which legends get passed around. And legends do get passed around because, as Doc Rowe put it to me, 'locals feel obliged to give the media what they want'. But forget Cernunnos, the locals called their deity Hele – in various spellings, it would seem. The French writer Gotselin (1058–98), tells of St Augustine's mission to Cerne – Cernel, as it was then – around 603 CE. When the crusading Christian arrived, according to the story, the locals drove him out, wearing fish and animal tails as a mark of disrespect. Gotselin refers to the Cerne people as 'demoniac' worshippers of 'Helia'. Other old written sources claim that Augustine actually destroyed the 'idol Heil, or Hegle' at Cerne and, in anger, he turned the tail-wearing gesture back on the people, creating a gruesome tailed race. Thus dominated and disfigured, the mutants are said to have seen the light and love of Christianity and teamed up with Jesus. They were happy and they knew it. Some versions of this story claim that Augustine himself caused the Silver Well to bubble forth from the ground at that very moment, using the medium of miracle – or witchcraft, depending on your viewpoint.

It is true that Christians claimed the natural spring for themselves. Aelmar, Earl of Cornwall, founded a Benedictine abbey at Cerne, whence the village acquired its suffix of Abbas, and built around the well, enclosing it for baptisms. The monastery is now in ruins but the well is still there, flowing in the abbey churchyard, sheltered by limes and flanked by wishing stones. For whatever reason, the Giant was never erased or destroyed by the monks, and more than a thousand years after Augustine's first mission one Bishop Pococke, on arriving in the parish, asked the locals what the Giant was called. They told him: 'Hele'.

Pronounced 'hale', as in 'wasael'? Or 'heal', as in New Age healing plates? Why not a god of health and fertility?

At the summit of Giant hill is an Iron Age earthworks, a square enclosure built out of the ground, which locals call the Trendle. The Giant's proximity to this lends weight to theories of his pagan antiquity. And it is to this ancient site that I am now headed. It is still black as night. I don't know about a sight line up the Giant's penis, but in this rain I'd be grateful to see more than six yards ahead.

Luckily, I turn the corner and see that the Giant Viewpoint Car Park is bathed in light from the headlamps of numerous cars and I can see a few figures milling around. At first I assume it is simply a dozen childless couples forming an orderly queue, but as the rag jackets come into focus I realize it is my crowd. Among those gathered is a smattering of curious locals, a pair of bemused tourists, a photographer working on a book about rural Britain and a chap from BBC Solent, with a video camera. The photographer is clearly not from around these parts and has forgotten to bring a coat. One of the men lends her a massive smock and her hands disappear inside its sleeves.

'Hello,' I say. 'I'm here to meet Alan Cheeseman.'

'That's me,' says an enormous man with a toothy smile. Alan is the bagman of the Wessex Morris Men, a forty-six-year-old side formed as an offshoot of the White Horse morris. It is the Wessex Morris Men who are about to perform this dawn ritual. Part of Alan's job as bagman is to lug the 'Ooser' – a carved wooden giant's head, with bull horns – up the hill. Most morris sides have an animal, usually a horse, which takes part in the dances. The Wessex Men have the Ooser. One of the men looks at me, looks at his watch and shakes his head.

'You're mad,' he says. 'At least we've got an excuse.'

The rain stops.

'That was lucky,' I say.

'It never rains on the morris,' says another man.

'Yeah – if it does we just go in the pub,' someone responds.

There is a hint of light over the Giant Viewpoint Car Park so we start off into the dark wood. I follow Alan. He is a large man but he is clearly struggling with the Ooser, which he transfers uneasily from arm to arm. 'It's made of solid elm,' he explains. I wonder what an elm tree looks like. I still have no real idea of what is going to happen, but I remember something Ron Shuttleworth told me in Coventry. He said: 'A lot of these customs, or whatever you call them – you'd think they would be more spectacular than they are. Some tourists can be quite disappointed.'

And I wonder: is that what I am? A tourist? A voyeur, waiting for something wacky and bonkers to happen, so I can get my money's worth? But I don't feel that way. It is starting to go much deeper. I want to join in. It is beginning to feel like my own. I have been waiting for this feeling. Hoping. Although I don't know quite what to expect at the top, walking up the hill now feels perfectly natural.

The morris have set a brisk pace up the hill and the first thing I notice is how steep it is. The second thing I notice is how slippery the ground is, after the rain. The third thing I notice is how cold mud feels against my nose. Still, I get up and soldier on. I try not to think of all those old English superstitions about stumbling. We come out of the wood and I see some figures higher up the hill, picked out in black against the deep blue sky. It's an attractive, mystical sight. There is a compelling stillness about the dawn, and we can just about make out the valley below and the downs beyond, their fields of oilseed rape a strange, pale green in the early light. The journalist from BBC Solent says he has been meaning to come along for years.

'Mind you, I nearly stayed in bed when I saw the weather.'

'Unthinkable,' I say.

Another local legend has it that an invading Danish giant was caught napping on the hill and beheaded in his sleep. The villagers drew a white outline around his body to show where he met his fatal doom, like a scene from *Giant Hill Street Blues*. Another bit of folklore suggests that a woman who wants to conceive should spend a night alone on the Giant's penis. It occurs to me that a better way to conceive might be to spend a night in company.

Finally we are at the summit and into the Trendle. The gale up here is whistling and the BBC man is frantically adjusting his dials. The two musicians stand to one side and compete over squeezebox volume.

'He'll probably pick mine up all right,' the man with the black accordion says confidently.

'I shouldn't think so,' retorts the man with the red melodeon.

In any case, they are off, with a tune called 'The Lollipop Man'.

Alan dons the Ooser and a six-man side begins to dance. When I say he dons it, I'm being a little glib. At length, he gets the beast above his head and its sackcloth covers his body. He then sways about in a ghostly fashion, caused mainly by the wind and the need not to fall. Still, this gives him an unearthly, lurching gait and the Ooser — a ghastly horned silhouette against the dawn sky — looks fantastic. The men dance around and before him, sticks in hand. They are performing Cotswold morris dances of the type noted by Cecil Sharp, and high atop this hill, with the Ooser wobbling ominously, they look impressive and the music takes on a plaintive, primal quality. Primal, yes . . . The morris makes a whole lot more sense up here and I realize that my presence, and that of the others, is irrelevant. They would do this with or without an audience.

I have yet to catch a glimpse of Hele himself, and it is getting light now, so I head for the edge of the hill. When I say I head for the edge, I mean I fall over it, helped by a gust of wind. I then slide down the wet grass and chalky slurry until I come to a halt in a heap, halfway down the hill. I try to stand up and my foot slides from under me, not for the first time. Again I fall face-forward onto the mud.

My leg hurts, so I rest motionless against the hill for a short time. Perhaps it is the early morning air, but I suddenly feel oddly removed from events. My vision takes on a surreal, filmic quality, as though I'm watching myself from afar. I take a moment to find perspective before deciding I don't want it. I let the strangeness of my situation wash over me and try to experience it without context. I try to forget why I came and instead to see things superficially, as others might should they suddenly tune in. I want to understand what might prompt a group of people to carve a man into the hillside, so I try to let the landscape shape my perception. Looking down, a hundred and twenty feet below, I can just make out the formless clumps of hawthorn and a dim glittering I take to be the River Cerne. Above me the gorse patches are straining against the wind. Across the valley I see the dark mounds of the downs. In the daylight they will shine yellow with oilseed rape flowers. Now they look like sleeping monsters. The effect is to shrink me in my own mind. I feel trivial among the elements: a tiny part of something massive and unknowable, with the power to shake trees, make rain, give life. I feel no different from a hare or a mouse and certainly no more powerful. When the elements threaten man, his instinct is to assert himself and dominate. What could be more assertive than conceiving a colossal warrior, club in hand, his manhood standing proud, and hewing him directly into nature?

I lie for half a minute, perhaps more, to regain my breath before dragging myself slowly up the hill. At length I reach a neat strip of white chalk and gravel, one of the Giant's ribs, I think. Then another. Yes, I am on Hele himself. I wonder if he'll heal my leg. The sun is casting an eerie blue light onto the grass when I see the horns. They rise over the hill, out of the field, into the morning light. I blink and look again, as if seeing the Ooser for the first time. The horns are followed by a pair of eyes, monstrous and huge, set into a giant head of grinning teeth and animal hair. Six pairs of hands reach up to the creature, which bobs and dances in the dawn. If I didn't know it was the morris, what would I think? Would I believe I had truly stumbled upon a pagan fertility rite. Have I, in fact, done just that?

I drag myself closer. All the parts are here: sunrise on the first of May, an ancient site at the top of a hill, a chalk god hewn into the earth, a masked creature in sackcloth. Around him, in a ring, dances a group of men in black and white, dwarfed by his size, long sticks in their hands. As they raise their sticks up to the horned giant I ask myself, could this really be an act of religious deference? Is this really a surviving relic of pre-Chrstian worship? I take a deep breath and limp back towards the small crowd, determined at last to get some answers.

I find a spare man and ask him straight.

'So this goes back a fair way then?'

'Yerst. About 1972 we started it, when the bank holiday came in.'

'Ah.' Not exactly pre-Roman is it, 1972?

I try another gambit. 'I've heard it's a fertility rite.'

'Eh? Oh. Well. See, the villagers used to have their maypole up here. Yerst, they'd come up here and have their maypole dancing, so maybe that's how it's got confused.'

'Ah. Confused, yes.' I know I am.

The maypole. It would seem to be the quintessential English folk icon, but what does it mean? Is it the totem of pagan tree-worship or simply the twig of Victorian whimsy? Modern folklorists believe maypoles appeared during the fourteenth century, but many of the references to maypoles in early history have been helpfully supplied by those who wanted them banned: the kind of seething moralists who still write indignant letters to the *Telegraph*. From their tirades against low fun and frolics we learn that the selection and erection of maypoles, along with their decoration, was for many hundreds of years an important part of English community life and formed a focal point for May Day celebrations. The maypoles were not restricted to rural communities and were just as common in towns and cities, including London.

But, how they upset the pious and the temperate. The maypole at Cornhill in London was taken down in 1517 after apprentices rioted around it. It seems odd now that such a flowery, effete sort of stick should have acquired such a wild and dangerous reputation. There is no evidence to support the idea that the maypole was a phallic symbol. Folklorists have searched for evidence and come to the conclusion that a big log was simply a good place to hang garlands and flowers. But it was considered evil by many. The Protestant writer Philip Stubbes, in his *Anatomie of Abuses* (1583), describes the maypole as a 'stynckyng idoll' that is 'covered all over with flowers and hearbes, bounde rounde aboute with stringes, from the top to the bottome, and sometyme painted with variable colours'. Variable colours? What's wrong with plain? This has to stop. Where's my quill?

To: Ye Editor

Sir,

Variable colours and stynckyng hearbes are indicative of the kynde of sliding moral values that will bringe this once proude countrye to ruine. What next, pray – sunne-dried 'tomottoes' or somme suche ungodly foreign mucke? Are we to descende once moore into the kynde of gaudye barbarism from whyche the Goode Lorde hath once saved us? *Amen.* I have personally nevere seene any Maye faires or riots, lyvynge as I do a quiet and pious life in a Tudor-looke dwellinge heere in ye suburbes, but they must be stopped all the same. Down with all maye pooles and all their ilke. And let us be delyvered unto the blysse of non-variable colours, through Jesus Christ our Lorde. *Amen.*

Yours & c.

Royston Doyston (Rev.)

Chaire of ye Residents' Committee

The Rectory

Tunbridge Wells.

That's better.

In fact, to some seventeenth-century writers maypoles became a metaphor for the 'good old days' of tolerant England, while all around them the actual poles were being pulled down, banned and suppressed by reactionary clergymen (see above) and regional government. Why?

The public order 'offence'.

If maypoles were a focus for social revelry, they also became a pawn for those who wanted tighter social control. When Cromwell and his Puritan Protectorate came to power in the 1640s and went on a banning spree, maypoles were the first up against the wall. At the Restoration of the monarchy in 1660, maypoles flourished once more and enjoyed good times until the Industrial Revolution of the nineteenth century, when they began their decline.

Back on the hillside, the Wessex Morris Men and I are also on the decline. The dancing is over, the Ooser has been lowered and it is time to make for the Cerne Valley to bring in the May and eat of the fruit of the land. I discover two ibuprofen and codeine tablets in my pocket and eat of them joyfully.

Down at the Giant Viewpoint Car Park, the morris are breaking twigs of hawthorn from a large bush and holding them in bunches. When they all have a bunch of may in each hand, the men gather behind Alan, 'in' the Ooser, and the two musicians lead the march into the village. The procession is oddly dignified. The men fall into formation and march past hedgerows and banks of bluebells and stitchwort towards the old thatched cottages and half-timber town houses of Cerne Abbas village, flowers and foliage in their hats. Suddenly everything fits into place.

> A bunch of may we bear about
> Before the door it stands
> It is but a sprout, it's all budded out
> It's the work of God's own hand.

We are leading the May festivities. We are bringing in the May. Someone has to. Yes, really it feels as though someone should. It doesn't feel remotely daft. Not when you can smell the raw soil, invigorated by the rain, stirring dull roots . . .

We come to a halt in the square opposite the Red Lion pub.

It is seven in the morning. I expect the windows to open up and to hear the goodly cheers of the locals. Buxom maids will surely lean out in their bodices and wink in a come-hither way. In the event, the response is more modest. A group of about four has gathered in front of the pub. They wear anoraks, carry plastic bags and stare with impassive, mirthless faces in the light drizzle.

Bringing in the May – 'going a-maying' – is a custom as old, perhaps, as the Giant itself. Certainly the custom of going into the woods, collecting flowers and greenery, and adorning houses to welcome in the season was well-established in the thirteenth century when the Bishop of Lincoln chastised clergymen for taking part. Protestant naysayers and social reformers such as Philip Stubbes claimed virgins were routinely defiled as part of the maying frolics. Although historians question the basis of such claims, the receipt of a 'green gown' from lying down on the wet May grass has been documented by the poet Robert Herrick. Like maypoles, bringing in the May was banned under Cromwell's Commonwealth, and, like the maypoles, it enjoyed its first revival at the Restoration. It continued unchallenged until the early part of the nineteenth century. Then, and on into the twentieth century, the practice evolved into a children's visiting custom. Children would make a spring garland, visit houses and ask for money.

> So wake up you, wake up pretty maid
> And take the may bush in
> For it will be gone ere tomorrow morn
> And you will have none within.

The men dance outside the pub for about an hour and I get chatting to Dave, who looks to be in his early thirties, standing out this particular dance with his girlfriend, Lizzie. I ask how he became interested in the morris. Dave tells me that, living in Shaftesbury, he never got out much, but not for want of trying. The nightlife was dead. One night a mate 'dragged' him to a morris meeting for something to do.

'I thought, yeah right. But then we went in the pub after and got some ales in and got singing and I thought, oh yeah I could get into this.' He grins. There is a pause.

Lizzie reminds him: '*And* you got a girlfriend.'

'Yeah. I got a girlfriend.'

I ask him why he thinks more young people don't join.

'In't cool, is it?' he replies. 'But then you grow up a bit and get over your embarrassment. Take it for what it is.'

It is now eight o'clock. Suddenly the portals of the Red Lion open. The musicians are first in, the Ooser and others follow, still dancing. Inside, tables have been laid for breakfast. The barkeep is clearly working grudgingly. The landlord is asleep on his feet. After our hillside exertions, the smell of the fried bacon, egg and sausage is like the scent of ambrosia.

The barmaid tells me I should have booked in advance.

'Oh. Not to worry,' I say. 'I'll settle for a pint of Palmers Bridport Bitter, from the only thatched brewery in England, please. I hear it has a bitter hoppy taste with some malt and a bitter aftertaste.' She looks at me without smiling and tells me I can only have beer with a breakfast. After she has gone out of the room I order a pint from

the landlord, which he serves up, frothy and warm, in a glass with a handle. As it goes down I get chatting to a morris man called Tony, who is leaning on the bar.

'Some say your dance is linked to ancient fertility rites,' I say. Tony looks into his beer and, after due consideration, says: 'I think that's a load of bollocks.' I think of Ron Shuttleworth and when I laugh Tony says: 'Well, it might be, I suppose. I quite like not knowing. Some people think you have to get to the bottom of everything. I like the mystique.'

This is the crux of it. It doesn't matter what the origins are.

There doesn't have to be a link between the morris and the Ooser and the Trendle and the Giant. It doesn't matter if this is what people did before Christianity or not. What matters is that they are doing it now. They do it because they enjoy it and because it feels right. In this pub, the atmosphere of conviviality is justification enough. Take it or leave it. If the Wessex Men didn't bring in the May, who would? Tony Blair? Would it be New May?

Around us, the morris are finishing off their breakfast with a couple of songs.

'Yeah, we've got all sorts here,' says Tony, who used to be the squire. 'Teachers, architects, a policeman.' It is as though he is telling me a secret, and it occurs to me that a person could have a professional, working relationship with a chap, see him every day, and never suspect him of morris activity. That is because there is nothing remotely odd about the morris.

The Palmers has had the required effect, so I get another one in for us both. It emerges that Tony and I both own banjos, so sensing a kindred spirit he invites me up to his cottage in nearby Holwell for a session. I say I'll look in on my way home.

Outside the pub the morning air is crisp and hopeful. It smells of leaves and wet soil and, with two pints of warm English beer inside me, I limp happily back to Badger Hill. My landlady, Patricia, is just serving up breakfast. It's nine o'clock and I feel ready to start the day. In fact, I feel so good I wonder why I don't begin every day with a dawn fertility dance.

May Day was not a holiday for four thousand police officers in London. All police leave was cancelled as the entire Metropolitan force was deployed to combat possible rioters. For May Day is now a holiday in honour of organized labour. Modern celebrations, including marches by the Trades Union Congress, Amnesty International, the International Union of Sex Workers and the Communist Party, have taken place traditionally in London and other European cities for some years.

In recent times, militant anti-globalists have capitalized on the congregation of left-wing sympathizers on May Day to launch attacks on global capital. Multinational companies such as McDonald's and Nike have been targeted with violence. The police have responded with riot squads. In the previous year it had kicked off late in the day; peaceful protesters were controversially penned in with the violent few by police walls on all sides. A total of fifty-four arrests were made for public order offences.

Police warned the oil company Shell and ABS AG, the largest Swiss bank, that rioters would target their headquarters. UBS bosses told staff to 'keep a low profile'. On Bond Street, luxury goods and fashion retailers Dunhill, Gucci and Prada, along with a raft of mobile phone shops, boarded up their windows. Outside Dolce & Gabbana, a small group of anti-fur protesters made their point quietly while the shop remained boarded up. In Parliament Square, statues were fenced off with wooden boards to stop protesters climbing.

Of course, London has a long-established tradition of riotous assemblies on May Day. The post-Restoration London May Fair was notorious for public order offences, the revelry often lasting a full two weeks. In 1686 it was forcibly transferred from Haymarket to the area now known as Mayfair, but was eventually suppressed and the land built upon.

Those who now organize the anti-capitalist protests on May Day have sought to establish an unbroken tradition of anti-state uprising from the imagined torchlit 'pagan' festivals of yesteryear – namely Beltane – to the trade-union-led marches of today. They identify the word 'pagan' with a desire to challenge Church and state. The <ourmayday.org> website has published a rather tenuous history of the 'ancient origins' of May Day which seeks to give so-called pagan validation to the workers' struggle to overthrow capital: 'As trade societies evolved from guilds, to friendly societies and eventually into unions, the craft traditions remained strong,' it orates.

It sounds plausible enough – the People's Fair – but the history is full of errors and liberally mixes fact with romantic fantasy, like half-remembered scenes from *The Wicker Man*. It talks of the ancient election of a 'May Queen', but the May Queen, now a popular part of holiday celebrations, was entirely a Victorian invention. The authors also talk of lovers entwining each other in the ribbons around the maypole. But the ribbon dances we now associate with maypoles were again a Victorian addition. The old maypoles might have used ribbons to bind the greenery together, but they were never used in dances.

This history is a perfect example of Merrie Englandism at work: the confection becomes the accepted form of tradition. Fiction becomes history. It is socially dangerous. The Victorians did a frightening thing with the May games. They appropriated them, outlawed the bawdy elements and forced the sanitized, ersatz 'culture' back onto the masses. These are your roots, they said: see the lovely ribbons, see the May Queen. Now do the dance. This is what England ought to be, they said. It was a form of social control and it is ironic that a group of anti-state polemicists, so vigorously opposed to governmental diktat, have bought so heavily into the Victorian reformers' lies.

It doesn't matter how May Day used to be. The details have been lost to all but the academic historian, but what survives is the firm conviction that this holiday is ours, that it belongs to the people. May Day has survived countless attempts at suppression and has evolved. It is a living tradition with roots as deep as you want to dig. Whether for you the day is about bringing in the hawthorn bushes or about standing up in solidarity with your fellow workers, the message is the same. The urge to go wild on May Day is as old as the hills, as potent as the hare in the corn.

In the event this particular May Day passed off quietly in London – although, having scaremongered for days about riots, the papers and wires were undecided on the scale of disorder. The *Guardian* reported twenty-eight arrests for public order offences. Another paper claimed there were thirty-two arrests, one for possession of a weapon. Some reported minor clashes in the evening, while other papers filed early and missed them.

Despite the lack of a riot, one plucky paper had a go at a story: 'Police Condemn May Day Minority'. It quoted a Deputy

Commissioner Royston (I may have changed his name), who said it was 'unacceptable' that a 'small number' of people felt they didn't need to obey his instructions. Bless.

But enough of the papers. I had more important things to do.

The time had finally come for me to dress as a horse.

9 | Cock Horse

Had someone suggested to me, even a month before that carefree June weekend, that I would end up struggling in a hot sack, far from home, I would have called the police. In fact, looking back, it is a wonder no one *was* arrested. Good times and burlap, you may think, can never go together. But that's where you would be wrong. The world is simply a better place when you're a horsey.

June was drawing to a close. The weather was warm and sunny, and London's mired streets were seasonally lush with greenery. A solitary Monster Munch packet was shimmering like a silver leaf in next-door's mimosa as I gazed out of the window, anxious to be away. The Coventry Mummers had invited me to see them perform in Banbury as they took part in something called a hobby horse festival. I didn't know much about it, except that it involved dressing up as a horse. I thought I could handle that. The requirements seemed simple. I called the organizer, Simon Pipe. He wasn't home.

'We usually get one like you,' Simon's wife Ant Pipe, said when I told her about my book. 'What do you do for a living?' There was no sense lying.

'I'm a journalist.' Oddly, this was a plus point.

'So is Simon. In radio. He works bloody long hours as a matter of fact so are you going to camp in our back garden? It's all the same to us.'

I said I didn't want to put her to any trouble . . . This is English for 'Yes, please'.

'Well stay at the campsite then.'

'Oh, right . . .'

'Fine. We'll put a tent up for you, you can muck in with the children. Come and find us in the Bell tomorrow.' Click.

I packed a cat mask I had borrowed from my ten-year-old niece and caught a direct train to Banbury. From there I cycled the three miles to the village of Adderbury, where the festival was to begin. The sun had been shining all day and now, as evening drew in, it was casting a rosy glow over the Oxfordshire hedgerows. In one field the wind caught the corn in a long wave, as though an invisible horse ran through it. On second glance, though, I couldn't be sure it was really corn. But, cycling into the village with my banjo on my back, I felt curiously vigorous. This is what life is all about, I said to myself. Freewheeling downhill past crops you cannot name, carrying a widely despised instrument and throwing yourself on the mercy of strangers who dress up as horses.

> Horses, always horses! How the horse dominated the mind of the early races . . . You were a lord if you had a horse. Far back, far

back in our dark soul the horse prances. He is a dominant symbol: he gives us Lordship: he is the beginning even of our godhead in the flesh. And as a symbol he roams the dark underworld meadows of the soul. He stamps and threshes in the dark fields of your soul and mine. The sons of God who came down and knew the daughters of man and begot the great Titans, they had 'the members of Horses' says Enoch.

So D. H. Lawrence mused romantically on the horse, and its member, in his *Apocalypse*. When the world ended and the four riders galloped in, when the world was screaming and running for cover, Lawrence would be looking at horse apparatus. But he is right about man's preoccupation with the animal. Long ago, not eight miles from here, a red horse was once cut into the Warwickshire hillside, at Tysoe. Most likely the work of Angles who settled the Stour Valley in 600 CE, the red clay beast watched over the Banbury–Stratford road for millennia, until finally ploughed over and lost in a new forest in the 'Age of Enlightenment'.

Adderbury was ethereal. To the city dweller, the country always seems preternatural. 'Which way's the Bell?' I asked a man at the village green. He pointed down the road, past a row of red stone terraced houses, with a look that said, I know your type. Coming here from London with your horsey ways.

In fact, the first written record of the term 'hobby horse' in England does come from London. It appears in the churchwarden's accounts for St Andrew Hubbard in 1460: 'To Mayers child for dawnsyng wt ye hobye hors'. The record was collected, along with most else concerning the mysterious hobby horse tradition, by a Dr E. C. Cawte.

Cawte, who reckons on a Scandinavian root (the Danes were pretending to be goats long before we caught on), describes two main varieties of pretending to be a horse. The tourney horse is the oldest form. You stand inside a frame with a head at the front and a tail at the back, while a skirt covers your legs. You are both horse and rider. The mast horse, while more primitive in style, is actually no more than two hundred years old. The horse head is attached to a pole concealed within a sack. The user bends double inside the sack and grips the pole. Often these have a pair of snapping jaws, operated by a bit of string inside. All this I found out later. Right then I had absolutely no idea what I was getting into.

I found the pub and went in. It was poky and everyone looked at me. I had been hoping to sneak in and quietly assimilate.

'Ah!' cried a large, bearded Brian Blessed lookalike dressed in a neckerchief, waistcoat and sailor's cap, his pewter tankard held aloft. 'That's either a banjo or a frying pan!'

'It's a frying pan,' I experimented.

'Let's hope it sounds better than a banjo.' Roars of laughter. The man had an enormous bunch of keys, with fob, on his belt. From another part of the pub I heard someone telling an anti-banjo joke.

'I heard there's going to be music later,' I said.

'Yerst, yerst – and singing, singing. Why? You're not going to play the frying pan are you?'

'I might. Actually, I'm here to meet Ant and Simon.'

No one seemed to be dressed as a horse.

'Yerst, well, they've gorn. Left me in charge. They'll be back later.'

So I bought a drink and settled into the back room. A session began. 'Here's a lovely little song,' boomed Brian Blessed, 'called "Peggy and the Cake". It's in D and you know it.' Had he really said 'Peggy and the Cake'? It sounded like it. To my surprise, people all around me joined in on the chorus.

> Rib tiggy hey and a rib-eye steak
> For Peggy and her cake.

Or something. The beer was taking effect. The man next to me peered into my open bag and spotted the animal mask I had brought with me. He caught my eye and gave me the slow nod. The same nod of complicity I had received from the ticket clerk on my way to Whittlesey. A group of people next to me suddenly produced melodeons and began playing them. 'This one's in D and you know it.' The atmosphere was convivial and eventually I relaxed. One man sang 'My Grandfather's Clock' and kept forgetting the words. The others helped him out. No one seemed to be bothered about singing well or not, so I felt at home.

Even so, it took me a couple more pints before I dared pick up the banjo. I plucked out a song I had learned from a record, called 'Rosemary Lane', which I reckoned might be English. It's a song about a maid who sleeps with a sailor to keep warm and ends up pregnant. It was in A and nobody knew it.

Last orders came and went.

At last I found Ant and Simon. Simon was a youthful-looking, tensely energetic man with ginger hair, freckles and prominent features. Ant looked perfectly sensible.

'Yes, we spotted you,' Ant said. 'Come on then.'

It was a cold, clear night outside. A tall man appeared and spoke with a soft Gloucester accent.

'I'm Steve. I'll put your gear in my car.' Steve, Ant and Simon took off in convoy, down a dark, unnamed country road and I pedalled furiously after the diminishing tail lights until finally we pulled up at an enormous oak tree. Simon's cottage was opposite. The range was still glowing inside the kitchen as we drank fruit tea and Ant told me how she and Simon had met. He had advertised in Bristol's *Venue* magazine for a morris dancing partner. She had ignored the ad at first. But over time she had realized it described her. So she called him. 'Of course, when you start going out, you stop dancing,' she said.

Around and about, on the floor, on tables and old chairs, were parts of horses. Oval frames and tails. Big heads, little heads, skirts, manes, ribbons and bells. Unfinished heads made from socks with ping-pong balls glued on for eyes. A rag dress of tiny proportions.

'Look out for Molly in the morning,' Ant said. 'She's our four-year-old. She's excited about the tent so she'll probably wake you up.' Simon appeared with a miner's head-torch, which he gave to me, without explanation. None was needed. I strapped it to my head, switched it on and walked solemnly across the grass towards the small ridge tent that was glowing in the moonlight. During the night I heard the quick, small movements of animals, and little cries.

I awoke to the sound of tiny footsteps outside the tent and a child singing:

> Ride a cock horse to Banbury cross
> To see a fine lady who rides a fine horse
> With rings on her fingers and bells on her toes
> She shall have music wherever she goes.

It was a fine summer morning. As the sun beat down on the conservatory I joined Molly and her sisters Rosie, aged seven, and Flora, aged one, for a breakfast of Rice Krispies in Tupperware bowls.

In the car on the way into Banbury, Simon told me how he had come to the hobby horse through the morris. He had joined various morris sides but had come to realize he wanted more out of the tradition than the copying of some old dance that had been noted down, possibly incorrectly, by Cecil Sharp. Sadly there had been no room for creativity in his morris team. Then he had moved out here and formed his own experimental side. He called it the Outside Capering Crew. He wanted more theatre, more showmanship in the dancing. 'Our dance is edgy and hard-driven, but that's because it was designed to be theatre. Traditional dance is often fantastically dull.' Simon had been in local radio for some time and spoke in measured sound bites.

We came into Banbury, past the cross. Not the original. The Puritan MP Sir Anthony Cope pulled that down in the sixteenth century. The Protestant extremists also tore down the maypole:

that was dirty dancing and tolerance was not part of their brief. The current 'cross' – more of a 'straight' than a cross – was finally erected during Victoria's reign.

The 'Cock Horse' rhyme is a red herring, Simon was saying. There was never a tradition of hobby horsing in Banbury. But the connection had been too good for him to resist. Why didn't the town capitalize on this to draw interest? Simon saw the lack of tradition as an advantage. 'You're not on anyone's territory.' Most morris sides had a horse and many other people dressed as animals for their own reasons. This would be their festival. Meanwhile the event would promote Banbury and please its traders. The local press, however, had not supported it these last three years and as a result the event had been slow to take off. 'People don't feel the same bond to their place. They don't feel the same urge to participate,' Simon said. 'It's not gelling in Banbury.'

Outside the tiny St Mary's primary school, the festival-goers were thronging. A good few, adults and children, were dressed as horses already. Others were changing. Underneath their horse costumes many were dressed in morris regalia, all in white with ribbons, rosettes and bells. Others were in rag jackets. There were lots of people from the pub. They had seemed quite normal the night before.

Brian Blessed, whose real name was Mark Lawson, was there in top hat and rustic peasant costume with his horse and a strapping she-male. They were the Whitstable Hoodeners, a revival team from Kent. Kent is home to a unique mast horse tradition which died out around the turn of the last century and was revived

155   *Cock Horse*

in the sixties. Their horse was very old. It had a mirror on its head.

'Ah well, you see, that's a magic mirror,' said Mark. 'It wards orf the evil eye.' According to the collected lore, horses have been seen traditionally as vulnerable to attack by supernatural forces, such as witches. Paradoxically, a horse's skull is often thought to have been used to protect houses against just such spooks. Either way, the horse was seen as a force for good.

Steve took me to one side and spoke gently.

'I've never seen Coppin from the outside.'

'Coppin?'

'My horse.'

'Oh . . .' Steve's horse was a hoodeners-style mast horse. That is to say, Coppin was a rude burlap sack wrapped around a pole, on the end of which was a wooden head. But what a head. His ears were made from the backs of a pair of leather shoes. His eyes were wonky. He had leather lips, a tongue and an expression of barely restrained mania. He was the Goofy of sack horses. I loved him.

'I was wondering if you would like to . . .'

'Get in the sack?'

I did not need to be asked twice. But first it was time for Steve's animal behaviour workshop.

'The first thing is to know your character,' Steve told the people, who were munching on early-morning doughnuts in the tiny classroom. 'Are you going to be a nice horse or a naughty horse? Are you gentle, or are you cheeky?' People were listening carefully, rubbing chins. The man who got his words wrong in the pub was there, dressed as a beautiful, snapping horse in black cotton and gloss-painted wood, called Trigger. The man was Robert Chisman, member of the Illustrious Order of Fools and Beasts. His ten-year-old son, Chris, was with him. Chris had his own horse, called Trotter.

'It's important to keep the illusion,' Steve was saying. 'When you take your horse costume off, do it around the corner, out of sight.' When you were successful the public would actually interact with the horse head, and not yours, which would be hidden in your sack. It was a wonderful phenomenon, he said.

'Think of the sounds you can make.' You could snap your jaws or stamp your feet. It was important to learn your repertoire of movements. How did a horse say 'come and play'? And how did it say 'stay off, I bite'? Above all, you should work out your routine. How would you interact with people as they walked by, to turn the situation into comedy? If you passed a bus stop, would your horse join the queue or pretend to hitch-hike?

I held Coppin and stroked his leather ears. I asked myself what sort of horse I would be when I put him on. Would I be cheeky? There were some spectacular horses in the room, a bull, and a stag called Eric. Some were very elaborate tourney horses, some had papier mâché heads. But I was drawn to Trigger, Trotter and their keepers. Robert put his arm around his son and hugged him proudly. Robert was also a member of the Trigg Morris in Cornwall. Chris wasn't. That was the problem. The Trigg team would not let the boy take part in their dances, even though he was desperate to join his dad. So each year Robert drove Chris three hundred miles from Polperro to Banbury so Chris could take part with Trotter. Chris looked like his dad, a soft, kind face with buck teeth. Trotter had a thin face with evil eyes.

Steve was advising the group on how to deal with troublemakers. Chris was listening intently, nodding vigorously. Sometimes people would call you names and laugh at you, Steve said. Sometimes they would come up behind you and push you. Sometimes they might grab hold of you. Kids mainly. They didn't see the person, only the horse. You had to expect it. Had anyone actually been attacked or ridiculed? Chris had an imploring look on his face. He was a small boy for his age. He was leaning on his dad, shyly. It was all right for people like Steve. He was at least six feet tall. He was a grown-up too. At that age a man's shoulders are broad enough to carry the odd jibe or raised eyebrow. At that age you have your scars already.

'Just walk away from trouble,' Steve was saying. 'Never fight back. And remember, animal disguise is no excuse for bad behaviour.' He raised his eyebrows sadly. 'Because we have had one or two police incidents in the past. Remember there's a fine line between amusement and harassment.'

Once outside, we got into our horses and I had a jumping competition with Chris, aka Trotter. Steve was pleased I had agreed to get inside Coppin. It gave him a chance to see how the animal looked in action. I found out what sort of horse I was: a lame one with a loping gait, although my leg injury seemed to be on the mend. Steve opened a pink plastic pencil case and slid out a three-

160   *The Magic Spring*

hole pipe. From a black bag he produced a tabor drum. As I loped along under the burlap, he played the pipe and tabor. I followed the piper. It was hot under the burlap and I couldn't really see.

'Mind the road,' Steve said suddenly.

We were in procession, on our way to begin the wholesale occupation of Banbury. There was the Whitstable Hooden Horse, the Red 'Oss from Adderbury, Simon's Crew with their four tourney horses, and the horse from Bristol with its over-large head. There was the Bloxham Morris with a giant grey elephant, Wickham Morris with their red dragon, Eustasia the Unicorn, and the Fine Lady (a man) 'on' Blanche the White Horse. There was Vibria the dragon and the impressive tent-shaped bull, Taureau de Perols. Klang was another dragon, Nelson was a stag, and Leominster Morris had a ram. Loose groups had been arranged, and we all carried blue collection boxes. We were making for the centre of town, and as we passed through the Castle Quay shopping centre I loped into Dixons and bought some micro-cassettes for my Dictaphone. The boy at the till said it was the first time he'd sold micro-cassettes to a horse.

Cassettes or no, I had hardly had time to talk to Simon so far. I hoped I would soon, as I still did not know what was going on. Perhaps I didn't need to. I loped up to some children. Steve advised me to get down to their level so as not to scare them. They eyed me warily but their mother was welcoming. She patted my wooden nose. Steve gave them some sweets. Had I not been dressed as a horse, the whole scenario might have seemed very different.

We amused the townspeople as I loped through the market,

up and down the pedestrianized walkway, while Steve played the pipe and tabor. All I had to do was point the head at people and they stared back at it. They pulled faces at it. I pulled the string and snapped Coppin's jaws. The people jumped. I would creep up on old ladies sitting on benches and point Coppin's head over their shoulder.

'Don't look now, Edie.'

'Wassat dear? Oh God!'

It was easy to make people laugh when you were a horse. People were surprisingly good-natured about it too. As a horse you could do so much. You could challenge burly looking men and their mates laughed at them. They did not square up to you because you were a horse. You could go down on one knee in front of beautiful women and their husbands would laugh because you were a horse. People let me closer to them than they would have let a man.

Children stroked my wooden head. I bowed it coyly. Some tried to feed my wooden head sweets and fizzy drinks. As I gained horse confidence I rubbed my wooden head up against big, matronly women, like a cat looking for affection. Old men in flat caps stared into my lopsided eyes and tickled my leather ears. People cradled my wooden head in their arms and stroked it. I snapped my jaws experimentally and was scolded indulgently. I was accepted into every group I approached. I loved being a horse. Being a horse gave me things I could never get as a human.

'Sometimes I go out on my own as Coppin,' Steve was telling me. 'Just into town.'

I saw Trotter. Chris held his pole bolt upright and ran in

little steps. The horse with the evil eye nearly doubled the boy in height. As Trotter, Chris was no longer a shy child. He was a wry, sardonic horse with a majestic golden mane and a superior expression. He pulled tricks on people. He interacted without fear. One day he would be a grown-up like his dad and his shoulders would be broad enough. Until then there was Trotter. Trotter was charming and funny. An alter-ego. He looked fantastic, a tall black stallion.

As I reached the bandstand I became aware of a religious zealot with a microphone, preaching a kind of unstable, frightened mutation of Christianity. As he screeched hellfire and damnation into his public address system, his wife incanted behind him and fiddled with her fingers. I loped up to him. He denounced me.

'You beasts with your cloven hoofs,' he cried. 'And your filthy pagan religion. Oh, you can dance and make fools of yourselves. With your stupid little jingle bells. But when the music is over and the mask comes off . . . ' I think the rest went 'blah blah blah', but I missed it as I was too busy gathering up more animals to dance in a ring around him. It's not that I hadn't been denounced by Christians before – I had – but never as an out-and-out Satanist. I thought it would be fun to play the role. We had a good time and so, in his way, did the manic street preacher as we gave validity to his fear. But what was he afraid of? His preaching was not an expression of faith. A true Christian has nothing to fear from a man dressed as a horse. It seemed his outburst was an expression of his lack of faith, his fear of death, magic and the unknown. Before him were no more and no less than three or four daft blokes who were nearly ready for a lunchtime pint. The pagan monsters were of his own imagining. Weren't they? Like Sir Gawain challenged by the Green Knight, he had abandoned faith in God and placed his faith in the supernatural, placed himself at the mercy of his own demons. This wasn't Christianity, it was the inverse of faith. No wonder he was screeching.

But much as I loved being a horsey, it was getting awfully hot under the burlap in the midday sun. Steve and I disappeared round the back of Barclays to swap roles. I took off the horse and blinked in the sunlight. It felt odd to be outside the sack. I felt vulnerable and visible. Steve put Coppin on and I noticed properly for the first time that the two of us were vastly different sizes. Where Coppin had engulfed me, it sat atop Steve like a crude equine pashmina. As soon as the sack was on him he was off. With great, thumping steps he ran at the shoppers, the bells on his ankles ringing out. A big man in a small sack. People shrieked.

I caught sight of Simon and the Outside Capering Crew. They were capering outside Mothercare, doing a frantic jig around some long, white bacca pipes. Their musician, Lawrence Wright, held his melodeon to him like a lost sailor might hold a last bottle of rum and stared off into infinity as he pulled on the bellows. Simon and his three dancers ran at each other, shouting 'Look out, I'm coming in' and 'Aaaarrgghh'. It was compelling and edgy – a far cry from traditional Cotswold morris dancing. I was fascinated. A large crowd gathered.

Down the road, opposite Debenhams, the Abbots Bromley Horn Dancers were doing their age-old thing. In truth, it is not a

dance at all but a quiet stroll. The eight-man team dresses in faux-
medieval costume designed by Victorians and six of them carry
a pair of horns each, set into a wooden reindeer head. There is
also a bowman who mimes firing at a hobby horse, while a lone
musician plays something that sounds like an end-of-the-pier
number. In spite of appearances, the Abbots Bromley dance attracts
a great deal of awe. This is because it is an ancient and unique
custom, the earliest record of which is from 1686, although there
is some evidence to suggest that it pre-dates the Civil War. The
horns themselves have been carbon-dated to around 1065. It is also

the oldest unbroken tourney horse tradition, and in the folk world, old is great. No one really knows what it is all about and the way the current dancers perform it, grinning sheepishly as they walk the steps, shows that they have a healthy and happy sense of the absurd. They're proud of their tradition but treat it affectionately and lightly, bantering among themselves.

We massed for a hearty lunch of lasagne in the Reindeer, a fine old pub in Banbury centre, and I asked Steve about his life. He told me how he had given up the rat race and the oil industry to work on his sculptures and with local schools, giving workshops on folk art. He had helped many of the people at this year's festival to make their animals. He had made the four beautiful tourney horses for the Crew. He was smiling but he had an elegiac air. Suddenly I overheard the words 'Coventry Mummers'.

'Are they here?' I asked someone.

'Propping up the bar of course . . .'

I made my way into the main room and got myself a pint of Hook Norton, the local finest. The Whitstable Hoodeners had obviously already had a few. They were performing their play in full kit and the horse was snapping at the punters. Watching intently, smoking seriously, was Ron Shuttleworth. I knew he could put it all in perspective for me.

'Cecil Sharp went to Ilmington on his bike and made friends with a morris musician called Sam Bennett,' Ron told me. 'Now, Sam didn't get on with the Ilmington Morris, in fact they had kicked him out, but he did well out of Cecil Sharp. Flew all over at the expense of the Society, playing his fiddle.' Ron took a drag on his cigarette and gave me the stare. Sharp had been keen to establish a link between the morris and the hobby horse. Bennett, keen to keep the scholar's patronage, had told him to come back in a month when he would show him something. Sharp did and, lo and behold, Bennett had suddenly produced a horse. 'We reckon he'd gone in his shed with the *Racing Post* and some glue, because no one had ever seen this 'oss before. Then Cecil wrote it down and gave Bennett his half-crown or whatever. Thank 'ee kindly, sir. You know what I mean?'

It felt good to see Ron again, but it took us another pint before the Coventry Mummers managed to muster themselves and head out into town for their next performance. I followed them, keen to see how the show would look in full costume. They set up by some benches and, with scant regard for an audience, began to declaim. People stopped instantly and soon a crowd had gathered.

Of course, Ron had been right. It all came together in performance. The tup, with its Birmabrite horns, was excellent. The bearded lady, sublime.

'What's next?' asked a mummer.

'Some kind of massed group,' said Ron, studying the festival schedule.

'God, we're not in any massed group, are we?' asked another mummer.

'No, no,' Ron assured him, and they slunk off.

In other parts of town the animals were at large. Every corner turned revealed another creature. You might see a pair of antlers peeping round a corner. You might stop to watch a dancer and find Trotter had crept up on you. A ram might pop into the caff for a latte. We were everywhere. The animals had taken over the town.

That evening, back at the Bell in Adderbury, we tucked into a barbecue supper in the garden. The sun was still hot and there was a smell of cut grass. I sat with Simon, Ant and Brian, one of the dancers from the Outside Capering Crew.

'Let's have a wide-ranging conversation,' Simon suggested. I put a micro-cassette in my Dictaphone and told Simon I wouldn't try to make him seem weird.

'But it *is* weird,' he protested. 'I think people like to celebrate their weirdness. I'm very serious about what I do but I acknowledge that a lot of it is pretty bonkers.'

'Yes but you *are* weird,' said Brian. 'The rest of us are fairly normal.'

'I'm not remotely eccentric,' Simon protested. 'But I do lots of things nobody else does. Oddnesses are wonderful. It's good to dress as a horse.'

Brian conceded that point. 'In a costume you can do things about which you would normally be hesitant, and you pick up a lot of personality from the costume. It's marvellous. Isn't that wonderful?'

Apart from the Kent Hoodeners, the best-known hobby horse custom takes place at Padstow, in Cornwall. Its origins are not clear but it is recorded from about 1803. Now it is a massive event involving the whole town. Hundreds of revellers dress in traditional white and red and parade with the (nowadays two rival) Osses, and the relatively obscure coastal town of Padstow, near the popular resort of Newquay, has become known internationally. Simon hoped Banbury would become as big.

'Padstow's big now,' Simon said. 'But two hundred years ago it was just three blokes, wasn't it? We're in a new age now. It's not about doing it in your local village any more. We could do this anywhere. People can travel now and we have communication, email, the Internet. If we didn't get on with the town council we'd just go somewhere else.' He was relaxed about the fact that his festival was not traditional.

'There's an absolute distinction between history and tradition,' said Brian. 'What we do is traditional, but we are not tied to the re-creation of something from history. It's a living tradition.'

'This is a morris village,' Simon said, talking about Adderbury. 'The tradition here goes back two hundred years and there's a feeling: don't mess about with it. But in any group of people, in time you are going to get one who is creative and they *have* to change it. I'm one of those and that is part of the natural forces at work.'

Natural forces? Like the mare in the corn? I told Simon I had enjoyed being a horse. Could anyone be one? 'Sometimes the morris give it to beginners,' he said, 'and sometimes they actually recognize that here is a man with a magic gift.'

Inside the pub Lawrence was bent double over his melodeon and he played into the night. I caught sight of the chap who had given me the nod the night before. He was dressed in a jacket made of green leaves. 'Here,' I said, 'I got denounced earlier on today by a street evangelist.' The man chuckled. 'Poor bloke,' I chirruped on, 'he really thought we were pagans.' The green man looked at me for a moment, smiled and said, 'We are.'

If Saturday had a liberating, free-form feel to it, then come Sunday, come the balance. The so-called Town Mayor's Day begins with a mayoral procession from the town centre to the park. The beasts, horses and morris men join them in an uneasy combination of pomp and anti-pomp. The sun is still blazing and the local dignitaries are accompanied by a marching band which drowns out the morris musicians. Following after the procession, the town's children run with their own little horses. Molly is there, dressed in her rags, looking like some kind of leaf sprite. Rosie has dressed up as Harry Potter and walks astride a unicorn.

As the officials file into church, to the theme tune from TV's *Van der Valk* done on snare drums and glockenspiel, the beasts cheekily stand aside and give them the royal wave. Eric the stag bows obsequiously before the mayor. Animals in the road are holding up the traffic and Trotter, aka Chris, has put his head through the passenger window of a trapped car. Steve, in Coppin, is standing behind a police constable in the middle of the road. He taps him on the shoulder. When the policeman turns, he jumps a mile and Coppin runs off, bells jangling, long legs gangling. When I catch up with him he is nursing a broken jaw.

'It's the hinge,' Steve says, stroking Coppin's wooden head. The horse's mouth is hanging open. 'I'm just going to nip to B&Q.'

Most of the animals hang around outside the church. They

don't join in with the Christian service. This, however, might say more about present-day attitudes to the Church than it does about pre-Christian religious roots for the horse. The folklorist Violet Alford, in *The Hobby Horse and Other Animal Masks*, argues, not entirely unpredictably, that the horse custom is a survival of our old friend the 'primitive' fertility ritual. Frazer in *The Golden Bough* describes a harvest-end custom that 'is or used to be observed' in Hertfordshire and Shropshire, where the peasants imbued an imagined 'corn spirit in the form of a mare' with power over the fertility of crops and wished it around the local farms for good luck. Some, particularly the Kent Hoodeners, whose mast horse custom is only recorded as far back as 1807, have sought to use this as proof of pagan ritual roots. But the idea is simply not supported by the available evidence – even the questionable evidence within *The Golden Bough* itself, for Frazer also describes similar customs in which the corn spirit is variously imagined as a wolf, dog, hare, fox, cock, goose, quail, cat, goat, cow, bull or pig. Folklorists have yet to spot a hobby quail. It is more than likely that the corn spirit and the hobby horse are unconnected. In fact, modern scholars say the hobby horse has always been part of the establishment, often seen at court, regularly used by the Church to collect money – always a pillar of the Christian community rather than the centrepiece to some sinister and frantic heathen rite. Only now does the horse seem to have been marginalized.

I am feeling far from satisfied with the pagan versus Christian arguments, but I can't put my finger on why. The folklorists say that, although the hobby horse, the man-horse, clearly pre-dates

LIMERICK
COUNTY LIBRARY

Christianity, there is no evidence to link it with specific rituals. But that doesn't disprove the idea. It simply fails to prove it. The jury is out, but I can't resist asking the Reverend Steve Fletcher, the vicar of Adderbury, what he makes of it. 'Well, this is where Christianity began,' he smiles beatifically, admiring the animals. 'Look around our church and you'll find all types of beasts, green men, gargoyles and the like, carved into the stone and set in the windows. Christianity came out of all of this, like Christmas.' In other words, he believes that Christianity simply perfected its pagan prototypes.

People like to believe that a custom has ancient roots, perhaps because it lends *gravitas* to daftness, or perhaps because the romantic idea of the mystical unknown is just too seductive. But things do not invent themselves. All things credited to 'tradition' were created by a person, whose identity has simply been lost. So, in two hundred years, when visitors to Banbury marvel at ye funny olde hobby horse weekend and speculate that it marked some primitive twenty-first-century rite, such as the worshipping of ye retail spirit in the form of ye summer three-for-two promotion, let me set down now that it was deliberately cobbled together one day from various other customs, with a liberal sprinkling of stagecraft and papier mâché, by an affable radio broadcaster called Simon Pipe and his chums, because it was fun and it made the children happy.

After lunch we move to People's Park, where there is a large arena laid out and stalls have been set up. There is a mini beer tent selling Hook Norton. Sandy Glover, the town crier, who is slurring appealingly into a microphone, has had some of the Hook

Norton already. The sun is hot again today and I can feel my face burning.

The festival organizers are split over the Town Mayor's Day. Some want to do away with it and keep the hobby horse event for themselves. But Simon recognizes the importance of including the wider community. The councillors are sitting primly behind a trestle table in their Sunday best, dispensing rosettes and cups to winners. Molly takes the fancy dress prize as 'Molly the Mad Morris Dancer'. Some majorettes appear, twirl things and leave. The marching band appears again. The children are dressed in stiff, military uniforms, their little faces taut. One stern boy is giving orders.

'Yeah, if it means we have to do some things their way, then fine,' Simon says. 'I'm happy with that. I mean, just look at this venue.' He waves expansively across the park. I see a green field full of horses.

Drones

Mike Gilpin is narrowing his eyes. I've come out here to the tiny village of Swaffham Bulbeck in Cambridgeshire to get some tuition. I'd rung Chris Allen in a panic, saying I was having some trouble with the hurdy-gurdy. You know, just getting it in tune. He gave me the number.

Not too many people play the hurdy-gurdy. Still fewer are qualified to give tuition. Mike was my nearest teacher. First a train to Cambridge, then a long bus ride to Swaffham. Then up a country road, past the village shop and pub, come to a field. There's Mike's cottage. Mike also makes hurdy-gurdies. It's his full-time job. They cost a lot of money.

He was good. He soon had me dominating the beast and, over a cigarette, I told him how the drones of the hurdy-gurdy appealed to me. He nodded slowly.

You see, I'd been thinking about where I grew up. As a teenager, sometimes at night I would hear a low hum. Sometimes it got suffocating. At first I thought it was my ears. I went to the doctor. Nothing. I started to think it was in my head. Then I saw the local news one night on TV. There was a report on 'the hum'. Some thought it was a secret military operation. There was a company in the city that did work for the Ministry of Defence. Others thought it was geographical.

The city was built in a natural basin. Clouds accumulated over the sprawl. Things hung. The atmosphere was heavy. People filled up with catarrh and coughed. The hum was probably mucus-related. Still others believed it pointed to mystical forces. Ley lines could be involved, plus UFOs. No one had an answer. It was a non-story in a slow news week. And yet it went on, droning. The hum.

'It's not for everyone, though, is it?' I said.

'What's that?'

'The sound of a drone. It's like bagpipes. A lot of people find it oppressive.'

So now Mike is narrowing his eyes. He lets out a puff of smoke.

'Some people are just scared of getting close to what they need,' he says, and raises his eyebrows.

10 | Shin-Kicking in June

The BBC London News was abuzz with urgent reports. 'There's a flag-flying frenzy sweeping the south-east,' it burbled. May – formerly the Merry Month of May – was about to give way to June and the summer heatwave was in full bake. It was also the Queen's Golden Jubilee weekend and the capital was awash with both colour and an odd, eerie patriotism. Every city window that didn't bear a Union Jack in honour of the Queen flew the St George's Cross, in the hope that it might coax England to win the World Cup. I was only half-watching the TV. The reporter cut live to a flag merchant who offered this advice to viewers in the Greater London region: 'What we're saying to people is, get your flag or flags now – er, from us – because even if you don't want to join in, you can always use them for curtains or blinds.'

I peered out of the window. The frames were too hot to touch and the gamy smell of the rubbish cans was drifting on what little breeze there was. This alone would have been enough to propel me at speed towards the station, had it not been for the added promise of having my legs attacked in public.

For the transition from May to June is also the traditional time for the little-known 'Cotswold Olimpicks', or Robert Dover's Games. High up on Dover's Hill above Chipping Campden, Gloucestershire locals battle it out in a range of singular sports, the highlight of which is a bout of competitive ankle-mauling. Afterwards, the crowd marches back to the town in a torchlit procession. I was drawn more to the torchlit procession than the games. The idea spoke to me of ancient times and ancient rites, and I needed to know more.

Once I had negotiated my bike onto the train, the guard refused to let me open the window because there was air conditioning. Of course, the air conditioning didn't work.

'That's because people like you keep opening the windows,' the guard smiled wanly, leaking moisture from his face as if to spite me. So we all sweltered, our clothes sticking to our skins like cellophane in the rain.

It's a joyfully short trip to from London to Moreton-in-Marsh. Freed from the Chiltern Railways mobile sauna, I sat for a minute on a grassy bank at the edge of the road, letting the breeze cool me and taking in the row of terraced sandstone cottages that led into town. The map said I was on the site of an early settlement. There was nothing in the land to corroborate this, just a field full of buttercups and daisies, but I believed it. At first I was struck by the silence, but gradually the details sharpened around me and I tuned in to the sound of grasshoppers rasping and the air in the trees. I made off up the road to Draycott, following a narrow runnel flanked by ivy-stricken oaks. At their bases grew cuckoo flower, cow parsley, dog rose and yarrow.

I will pick the green yarrow
That my figure be fuller
I shall wound every man
But no man shall harm me.

I took a right turn, watched only by an inscrutable dappled stallion with his head over a gate. Looking about me at the countryside, as always in this situation, I found it easy to imagine the same places, hundreds, thousands of years before, when people lived by the land. When comfrey was 'knitbone' and speedwell was 'bluebird's eye'. When plants meant potions, and horses were gods. I passed a field full of sleeping foals. Perhaps this trip would take me closer.

As I glided up Dorn Hill the ticking of my bike chain surprised a pair of rabbits playing in the road. They disappeared into the bank, leaving a quivering may branch to give away their entrance point. I peered through the hawthorn, but saw nothing within the wood but the dregs of last month's bluebells. They looked heavy and dull. I thought about picking a clump and pressing them in my notebook, but luckily I remembered just in time that it was illegal under Schedule 8 of the Wildlife and Countryside Act of 1981. Phew.

The hill was steep but the climb felt worth the effort as I freewheeled down the other side, through the village of Draycott, thinking of Cecil Sharp on his bike in the West Country. While noting a song from some gypsies, he had taken a photograph of the singer. Later, when the picture had been developed, he tried to find them again in order to repay them by giving the woman the photograph of herself. The nomads had moved on but Sharp didn't give up, he followed their trail for miles and miles down into Devon, on his bike. For an asthmatic, that's an impressive show. When he eventually found them he was overjoyed, and so were they. A little while later I saw my first thatched roof as my wheels ticked into Broad Campden.

I was staying at a guest house called 'Primrose Cottage', run by a retired couple called Sandra and Peter Snelling. I came to a halt at a wooden bench under a cherry tree and knocked. The front lawn was immaculate and hollyhocks were growing up the old eighteenth-century brickwork. The row of cottages would have been tied originally to the Norman chapel across the road, but now they were private houses. Peter and Sandra had found each other late in life and had a glow of contentment about them. They greeted me with a glass of orange squash and an individually wrapped branded cake slice. I was pleased to be at Primrose Cottage.

On the scale of picturesque hamlets, Broad Campden sat roughly at the zenith, just next to Camberwick Green. All the shortbread-tin houses were there, and I recognized a few buildings from my favourite place mat. Broad Campden was the sleepy hamlet for which the words 'quintessentially English' had been created. It was spotlessly clean and heartbreakingly beautiful – but almost too knowing in its desirability. The monks and journeymen had gone now. Many old barns, cottages and outhouses, once functional rural hovels, had been converted for high-end habitation by affluent salarypersons, their walls cleaned, herbaceous borders created, lawns watered and confident topiary established. The old walnut tree on the knoll had been replaced by a cherry, for its blossom.

But the affluent salarypersons who had got there and converted their barns first now wanted to stop more people like themselves from moving into the village, and had used the power of local law to stop them. The essential country character must be preserved, they said, just as it is.

Around the corner I slipped into the Baker's Arms and got a pint of Hook Norton and a lasagne from a dour fellow with an air of defeat. Although the games traditionally centred on nearby Chipping Campden, about five minutes away by bike, the quiet country pub had been persuaded to provide sponsorship.

Chipping Campden itself was a festival of showy patriotism. All the shop windows had little Jubilee displays, with doily-heavy tributes to Her Majesty. The old wool town spread out from a broad high street lined with ancient stone buildings, its covered market-place now boasting a National Trust plaque. The place was as quiet as a hayloft, but the demographics made themselves plain at once with the presence of a continental bakery and organic conserve emporium.

'Oh, it's an affluent area, all right,' the woman in the book-shop told me. 'Most of them have moved here from the cities, or commute.'

There were a few hours before the games began at eight. I decided a commute of my own might be in order, so I tied up my bike and strolled up to Dover's Hill to meet my contact.

Dover's Hill was a horseshoe ridge from which the wold fell away sharply into the Vale of Evesham, like a grassy waterfall. It gave a stunning view across the flat plains of the Avon and the Severn to Worcester, Coventry and something called Clee. At the foot of the bank the ground levelled off into a natural theatre, in which a woman halfway up a cardboard castle was struggling to dominate some bunting. A short walk away there loomed a haystack the size of a bungalow, bound around with interlocking branches, dry as tinder and hot to the touch. And at the top of the ridge there was a squat trailer decked out in loudhailers. Bob Wilson, chair of the Dover's Games Committee, was pacing about it, a gaunt, white-haired man in red trousers.

'Came to Campden in 1964,' he told me, puffing on a Rothmans in the sun. 'Retired in ninety-one. Used to run the Red Lion pub in fact.'

'But you don't run it now?'

'Good Lord, no.' He smiled enigmatically. 'I went to sea for seven years.'

Bob told me how the games had been started by another incomer to the area. Captain Robert Dover was a Cambridge alumnus and a barrister, recently qualified when he moved to the Cotswolds from London in 1611. He was widely credited and lauded by his contemporaries as having instigated the games, with a royal charter from James I. In fact, I knew some of this, as I had been reading a book by the local historian Francis Burns called *Heigh for Cotswold*. In it, Burns notes that the torchlight procession was added as late as 1967. I was disappointed in this, but not surprised.

Dover was by all accounts something of a celebrity. A book of poems called *Annalia Dubrensia*, published in 1636, was a compendium of immodest praise for Robert Dover written by his poet and lawyer cronies plus assorted gentry and relatives. Illustrious names abounded and Burns claims that, in their references to the ancient Greek 'Olimpicks', the writers succeeded in distinguishing the event from the rural whimsy of folk traditions and bringing the games to the attention of high and fashionable society. Certainly, the barrister and his showpiece were known to William Shakespeare – the playwright alludes to the games in *The Merry Wives of Windsor* – and to Ben Jonson, who contributed to the *Annalia Dubrensia*. Dover was also a long-standing friend of the influential courtier Endymion Porter, and he clearly carried enough weight at court to secure permission for the Games and to draw the community around him. A modern parallel might be if Cherie Blair moved to Dibley and started a donkey derby.

In any event, the Cotswold Olimpicks became a fixture. Such popular country sports as 'handling the pike' (perhaps a fish-holding contest), 'spurning the bar' (I'm guessing a bout of competitive pub-ignoring), dog racing and hare chasing carried on annually, along with running, jumping, dancing, tumbling and, er, chess, until the Civil War, when they abruptly ceased.

Were they stamped out by the Puritans? Imagine how that confrontation might have gone: 'In the name of the Commonwealth, step away from the chessboard and hand over your small wooden pieces.' Certainly, events such as Dover's Games became pawns in the political struggle. Royalty and royalists approved of sports (huntin', shootin', pub-ignorin') and encouraged them. The Puritans denounced all games, believing they led to immorality, debauchery and drunkenness: three good reasons for keeping them. They also suspected that many public events held around religious festivals – in this case Whitsuntide – were the relics of pagan religious activity and therefore evil. Frazer, it seems, was not the first to espouse the theory. Historians suggest Dover was simply the 'reviver or reviser' of long-held hilltop japes at Whitsuntide. If this is the case then the flaming torches may go back further than anyone knows.

In their *Annalia Dubrensia* the poets made their anti-Puritan position clear, while critics of the games suggested in the media that Dover had used the event to further the ends of the Catholic Church. It was a time of religious intolerance and political unrest. When the Civil War finally broke out in 1642, Dover's Hill, for a number of geographical and practical reasons, found itself at the centre of many military campaigns. Historians say this is the real reason for the demise of Dover's Games. Dover himself died an anonymous figure ten years later, having moved away.

The sun was beginning to set over the Malvern Hills. A balmy peace settled over the site, punctuated by the strange, short echoes of summer as the traders set up their stalls. Bob and I sat on a lone ridge-top bench overlooking the Vale.

At the Restoration of the monarchy in 1660, Dover's Games were reinstated and ran again unbroken for a further 192 years, though not without some criticism. In 1708 the poet William Somerville wrote a kind of gently mocking verse describing the debauchery and disorder of the games. In 1736 a minister from Stow-on-the-Wold warned his flock against 'the evil and pernicious consequences' of Whitsun fairs and 'Dovers Meetings'. In 1773 Richard Graves published a satirical novel called *The Spiritual Quixote*, in which a Methodist minister railed against the 'heathenish assembly . . . called Dover's meeting'.

In the early part of the nineteenth century the games enjoyed something of a resurgence, with the thrilling addition of 'jingling' to the menu of arcane sporting events. A man adorned with bells was obliged to jape about in a ring and avoid being attacked – a bit like morris dancing today. Prizes included 'a good pair of shoes to be jumped for in bags by men' and 'elegant favours to be danced for'. As well as the shin-kicking there was backswords, a brutal sport where a man had to draw blood from his opponent's head with a stick, plus other 'manly diversions not to be described within the limits of a bill'.

But the games had started to attract more people than the venue could handle. Historians have found accounts of con artists, brigands and thieves from the nearby industrial towns causing havoc, robbing the food stalls and brawling. This raised the ire of the local rector and Justice of the Peace, Canon George Drinkwater Bourne. He claimed the area had become overrun and 'demoralized'. Police accounts to the contrary have since been found, but at the time Drinkwater Bourne had his way: the hill was made private land – 'enclosed' – and the games again shuddered to a halt in 1852.

Although the Industrial Revolution brought a far-reaching

disdain for old-fashioned ways, Dover's Games were not forgotten. But for a hundred years – while railways were laid, bridges, mills and factories were built, and country folk spurned the melodeon for the phonograph, the morris for the music hall – the Cotswold Olimpicks lay dormant.

'Then, in 1951, we had this committee,' said Bob, 'and we thought, well, what can we do?'

Our conversation was interrupted by a call to Bob's mobile phone. It was BBC 7, the digital TV channel, requesting an interview with ten-year-old Harriet. The girl was standing by.

'Mum, I think I need some Rescue Remedy,' she said, a faint tremor in her voice.

'Don't be silly, it's only TV. You've done it before.'

'Yes, but this is *live*.'

When I was ten my experience of live TV interviews was limited to asking my dog if it had enjoyed *Hong Kong Phooey*. It was a one-way sort of deal. But this was for real and Bob was remonstrating with the presenter.

'We're not in Stratford-upon-Avon. You've got that wrong for a start. We're in Chipping Campden, have been since 1612.'

I decided to give Harriet some space and wandered across the field. People were beginning to arrive and mill about the stalls. A fairground organ cranked up a polka as a giant Sherman tank chugged into position. Some girls were trying to climb the 'unclimbable ladder' and a smell of frying onions was heavy on the air. People were making unpleasant faces through a horse collar. Gurning. Suddenly a confusion of noise broke the calm. I whirled

round and came face to face with the Cheltenham 'Scots' pipers in full kilt.

Now here is an unusual English tradition: pretending to be a Scot. Unusually for a hearing person, I like bagpipes. But here's a secret: they don't have to sound like that. England has some lovely bagpipe traditions of its own, not the least of which concerns the sweet, soulful Northumbrian smallpipes. By contrast, the Scottish bagpipe is the Cilla Black of reed instruments. The thing simply cannot carry a tune. Yet it has, by a combination of overexposure, monarchic devotion and apathy, nonetheless wheedled its way into the position of national treasure. Piping is at least traditional at the games, as recorded by the poet Michael Drayton in his 1612 oeuvre *Poly-Olbion*. If only it had been clay piping.

Fleeing, I found myself at a Punch and Judy show, a beautiful striped tent which the puppeteer had thoughtfully set up right next to his Ford Escort. 'It's very hard tonight without the microphone, boys and girls,' he was shouting. The childen watched on, awed.

I saw a man in a top hat carry a bladder into a Portaloo. Clearly the morris were out. In older times, only one team was allowed to dance and rival sides competed for the privilege. But two local sides now held court. The Chipping Campden men were a sprightly team with not a few youngsters among their number, notably their horse. This beast was a lad called Rob, who lumbered about in a diverting manner and was occasionally beaten with a bladder. The dancers from nearby Ilmington looked as though a spot of personal, possibly medical, revival wouldn't go amiss. Most boasted the kind of proud gentleman's physique gained by a lifetime's devotion to fine cask ales, and one was smoking a fag. But the Ilmington men still won in my book for having rigged themselves out in dark, broad-gauged corduroy on this fine summer's day.

I saw an elderly man with a long, straggly beard and a straw hat covered in flowers. Under his weather-beaten grey coat he was wearing a T-shirt that said, 'I Follow the Straw Bear'. It was Dick Brooker and he was smoking liquorice roll-ups. He said he was photographing all the British calendar customs. He was going to put all his photos into a slide show.

'Have you met Doc Rowe?' I asked.

'That's funny. I keep hearing about him.'

I tried to think of a way to get the pair together. They would make an invincible team. They could create the most extensive catalogue of British silliness in the world: the Dick and Doc Collection. Dick sat watching the dancers through wide-rimmed tortoiseshell glasses. He cut an elegiac figure, both distant and engaged.

'Oh, I've been all round,' he smiled, faintly. 'Of course, it's easier now I've got a van.' Something about the way he said it told me he was living in it.

The ridge was now packed with spectators and the loudhailers were blaring, too loud for comfort. Down in the dip there were children's races around the hill, a kind of competitive jigsaw puzzle, and a man shouting into a microphone. Next to him, dancing and bobbing like a happy little chipmunk, was a small grinning woman.

It was TV's Michaela Strachan. The bubbly former Pete Waterman acolyte was filming the whole thing for a little-watched daytime show, and her cameraman kept asking people to 'win again for the camera'. This process was making things drag on a bit. I was getting impatient for the shin-kicking and so was the man with the microphone. The light was beginning to fail.

'If you want to be in the shin-kicking, now's your last chance for the cameras,' he kept calling forlornly, but no one showed. May was fading away before our eyes. At this rate we would be shin-kicking in June.

At last, an entrant appeared. A balding man with an unappealing sneer. As he sat stuffing straw inexpertly into his trousers, Strachan pounced and stuck a microphone to his chops.

'So, er, are you *really* going in for it?' she interviewed. The man barely looked up and grunted a one-word response, which was followed by a long, awkward silence as Michaela grinned, still bopping to imaginary disco beats, and the camera rolled.

A rival shin-kicker was found. This newcomer was clearly more experienced and had a superior straw-stuffing technique. His legs looked like giant marshmallows. The two donned white coats and gripped each other by the lapels. The rules were simple. You held your opponent and tried to wrestle him to the floor by

means of kicking his feet from under him. Folks round these parts called it 'underplay'. The bald man soon had the sneer wiped off his face.

'Awwwww, vicious, vicious, vicious, vicious!' Screamed the man with the microphone as the rival mashed the bald man's legs with a breathtaking lack of mercy. 'Kick 'im, kick 'im, kick 'im, kick 'im!' The announcer appeared to be working himself up to some kind of unsavoury climax and the crowd was yelping with delight. 'Oohh, oohh, oohh! Awww, go on, kick 'im! Have 'im!'

It wasn't what I had envisaged at all. I had imagined a polite affair where gentlemen in top hats stood upright at arm's length and took turns simply to kick each other's ankle, perhaps to the tune of 'Oh What a Piece of Work Is Man' or 'Jerusalem'. But this was proper wrestling. The bald man was floored in seconds, picked up and floored again. He struck me as an outsider, like me, who had thought it might be a good wheeze to go in for the shin-kicking. For a laugh. He had been proven wrong and I quickly learned from his error, leaving him to twitch like a floored daddy-long-legs on my behalf.

Bob appeared.

'Of course, they didn't used to have straw for protection,' he whispered conspiratorially. 'Not in the old days. Locals used to beat their ankles with a hammer to toughen them up.'

I was troubled by the presence of the TV crew. I wondered why the committee and the competitors were so willing to fake and fudge things for the cameras. 'I suppose all this publicity must do wonders for local tourism,' I began.

'Absolutely not.' Bob was so quick and emphatic that it was clear he had been posed the question before. 'It's a local custom for local people. Young farmers and that. It's a country event. We couldn't fit tourists in here as well and we wouldn't want them.'

Some historians and folklorists don't agree. One has claimed that there was a concerted bid to pull in tourism to the area around the end of the nineteenth century, with the deliberate organization of fêtes, parades, and 'olde English' games. If this is true, the residents of Chipping Campden are keeping quiet about it. But I couldn't be doing with that now. Not with the shin-kicking to divert me.

More men had come to attack each other. The light finally failed and the organized brutalities carried on into the night. A boy turned to a girl and boasted: 'I would definitely have gone in for it if there were more kids.' The competition was finally won by an Evesham lad called Ian. I asked him how he felt.

'Pretty good,' he said, rubbing his ankle.

Down at the pyre, a man dressed as an ancient Greek was posing in his toga. The fire was about to be lit and the crowds quickly moved in. I bought a torch from a stall for £2 and held it aloft as the kindling was set ablaze. The stack went up in seconds and the heat burned our faces. Then the fireworks began. Hundreds of them, making colours and shapes in the night sky like drops of petrol in a lake.

We think of bonfires as a winter custom, but fire in May is nothing new. Records from as early as 900 CE show that Ireland had long celebrated a Celtic feast known as Beltane in that month. Druids, we are told by those who observed, would light two fires and drive cattle between them, incanting as they did so, to protect the beasts from blights before sending them out to pasture. This is the festival the anti-capitalists claimed was the real – original – root of May Day. Beltane happened in Scotland too and the Isle of Man, where gorse bushes were lit instead of bonfires. Wales knew May Day fires until the early nineteenth century, and in England May fires were lit in Cumbria until late in the eighteenth century. They are also recorded at the other extreme of the country, in Devon and Cornwall, during the same period. This might imply a sort of universal 'old religion', a Celtic pagan faith. But the fires might just as easily have been lit for different reasons.

That said, this was not a May Day fire. That time had long gone and we were only a few hours away from June. There are, however, reliable records of midsummer fires stretching back to pre-Christian times. In Buckfastleigh in Devon, locals torched a cartwheel and sent it down a hill in hopes of a good harvest. Although the custom was not recorded until the nineteenth century, a strikingly similar event happened in Aquitaine in France in the fourth century, when the local pagans apparently offered up the burnt embers to a sky god.

But this was Chipping Campden, Jubilee weekend. Pagan or not, there was something very basic and alluring about this particular fire. And we had no need of a fire – it had been the hottest day in a hot spell. What we needed was water. Our cheeks were burning, but still we stayed, young and old, enraptured by

the flames. Eventually I lit my torch and turned back into town. There were thousands of little beacons bobbing and snaking down the hill towards Campden, and the crowd walked in semi-silence. Many of the children were wearing inflatable cowboy hats. We passed a police car.

'What do we do when we see a police car?' a father asked his son.

'Torch it.'

'That's right, lad,' the man said.

But they didn't. No one was lawless and rambunctious. No one was dressed in animal skins and no one was beating drums or dancing in an especially heathen manner. Nevertheless, there was a palpable sense of reverence as we converged on the town, flames in hand. I felt that, if we chose to, we could rise up as one and accomplish anything. Smash the state, overthrow Parliament. Loot all the ciabatta from the bakery. But we didn't.

Along the high street, four-foot oil drums belched three-foot flames into the air and everyone threw their torches inside, to be devoured, consumed and safely extinguished by council officials. Tomorrow there would be a funfair, floats and displays as the Scuttlebrook Queen and her attendants were crowned. But tonight the fairground workers were still working on the rides, bolting metal against metal, fixing lighting gantries and loudspeakers. The waltzers and dodgems hogged the narrow streets, cramming their ironwork between the little houses, their gaudy carts peering into windows and knocking at doors.

Times move on. Dover's Hill was acquired by the National Trust in 1929, effectively removing the barrier to a revival of the Games. Even so, the latest phase did not fall into its stride until the mid-sixties, possibly influenced by the wider folk revival. But, like so many customs, what matters is not how it all began, but how it evolves and persists. There was something in the Cotswold Olimpicks that was worth conserving. Was it the sport, the commerce or the perceived value of distinguished roots? The good-natured band of upper-class patrons and committee members listed in the programme – Lady King's Norton, Brigadier D. J. Atkinson *et al.* – had stayed the same. But the con artists and robbers had gone, the drunken carousers had gone. The crowds on the hill were well behaved, with only the sober torchlit walk to link this sterile, well-organized event with the ancient pagan festivities of our imaginings.

I was parched. The games had been not only alcohol-free but also water-free. No one was selling any drinks on Dover's Hill and as I squeezed myself into the Volunteer, now three feet deep at the bar, I appreciated the cunning. With only half an hour now before last orders I pitied the Baker's Arms back at Broad Campden, which would be unlikely to see any post-games return on its sponsorship. I got three pints in just in case I never made it back to the bar. Paul from the Ilmington morris took out a wooden melodeon and a session struck up with a fiddler. Tim, the Chipping Campden fool, put away his bladder and joined in on guitar.

'That's all right,' he said. 'I don't mind being called a fool.'

'We call him worse,' someone said.

Dick arrived with his own beat-up melodeon. I had forgotten to bring mine so I sat enjoying the music, wishing I could play. Paul played an Irish tune, 'The Black Velvet Band' and everyone joined in. 'In a sweet little town they call Belfast . . .'

'Foreign muck,' Dick said.

When they threw us out of the Volunteer, the streets were ablaze and a band was playing.

When I got home there was a message on my answering machine. It was from a film-maker I knew called Reg, asking me to meet him. He wanted to discuss a film project he thought I might be interested in. I found him gatecrashing an upper-class Jubilee party in London's self-regarding Cleaver Square.

'Hello, we're gatecrashers,' he introduced himself to the stall-holders. 'Could we trouble you for a glass of wine and a hot dog.'

'How delightful,' the reply came. 'Wholegrain mustard or Dijon?'

As the first drops of warm rain fell on our paper plates, Reg outlined his film idea. I had my doubts about working with a film crew at this stage of my travels and I only half-listened. I was thinking about Her Majesty's Jubilee. I had pedalled across London to be here, through disused gasworks, rotting estates and shit-stained back alleys. The pubs were deserted and the streets were dead. This was the one and only Jubilee party I saw. Here in the tree-lined square, on the freshly raked gravel, among the royalists of the upper classes.

Under a small awning, four very old men played Dixieland jazz. In front of them a writhing woman in tight Lycra deftly fellated a burning torch to the old-time beat. She was surrounded by a ring of middle-aged men in pressed chinos, their wives shooting disapproving looks at the heathen dancing.

'Oh, all right,' I said to Reg. 'I'm game – what's the plan?'

11 | Crab Fair Blues

It was night as we sped toward Ambleside, and Lake Windermere was an eerie void falling away to our left. You could make out the dark mass of the fell looming above. The moon was casting bars of light onto the water. 'Look,' I whispered. The others glanced briefly then turned back to stare at the white lines as they rushed into our headlights. I had worried it would be like this.

September, the end of the apple harvest, and I had been persuaded to follow a film crew up to Egremont in Cumbria for the annual Crab Fair. They say the fair, with its Lakeland sports, is one of the oldest unbroken traditions in England. An apple cart drives through the town dispensing its bounty into the crowds. There is Cumberland wrestling, dog racing, and feats of skill and strength. Oh, and gurning.

The World Gurning Championship, to be precise. A prize is given to the person who can make the most unappealing face through a horse collar. You may have seen it on *That's Life*. That was what the film crew was going for. They were due to be joined by Richard and Judy, who were billed to broadcast an episode of their show live from Egremont Market Hall. It had sounded like fun at first, but as the seven-hour journey had worn on I found myself returning to something Ron Shuttleworth had told me in Coventry. A cameraman had been too pushy with the Padstow Hobby Horse one year, he had said, and the bloke had found himself in the dock, camera and all. Film-makers, you see, are only concerned with what they can get people to do on camera. If you didn't do it to camera, you might as well not have done it at all. That's what Ron said. I remembered Michaela Strachan and her crew at the shin-kicking in Chipping Campden. They stood in the way, blocking everyone's view, and in the end had the people fake it anyway, because the real thing didn't look quite right. Television demanded a lot for the two minutes of publicity it offered. 'People who are serious about their traditions can find it a bit arrogant,' Ron had warned. And here we were hurtling north-west at midnight, with a camera in the boot.

But when I smelt the clean, cool air through the open window, I forgot such worries. It was enough to be among the moonlit fells. Things would turn out right. The film-maker, Reg, turned to me.

'Did I tell you, Richard and Judy have pulled out?'

'No. Why?'

'They've gone to the south coast to look at a squid. The committee's really pissed off.'

'A squid? I'd say Egremont was spared.'

'No but they really needed the publicity – since their sponsor pulled out.'

'Sponsor?'

'Ben & Jerry's.'

Ben & Jerry's, the multimillion-dollar American ice-cream brand, had sponsored England's oldest harvest festival. There was a pause while I digested this. Then Reg said: 'But guess who's coming instead?'

'I don't know.' I tried to think of someone equally suitable to promote the goodness of natural produce. 'Edwina Currie? Nestlé?'

'Michaela Strachan.'

'No . . .'

'Yeah. And apparently she's going to compete.'

'In the ferret roulette?'

'In the gurning, obviously.'

'Of course, the gurning.'

It was going to be a long weekend.

Egremont, nr. Sellafield, Cumbria. Population: 2000. Exports, current: technetium 99, a radioactive waste product of the reprocessing of magnox nuclear fuel. Destination: Irish Sea. Exports, discontinued: haematite iron ore, mined; apples. Principal employer: British Nuclear Fuels Ltd, Sellafield. Unemployment: high. Windows mostly boarded up with: chipboard. Colour of pebbledash in Orgill estate: grey. Ruined twelfth-century castles: one. Exploitation of same for tourist trade: nil. Number of polystyrene trays with dried chips and curdled gravy, empty Superkings packets and pages from local paper drifting like ghosts in the wind on castle grounds: 1297 approx.

The pages from the paper told of nearby towns and villages:

Whitehaven ('Bus Driver Beaten Up'; 'Attack Victim Left with Nails Stuck in Head'; '. . . a Sellafield worker was found drunk in charge of his seven-year-old son after downing a bottle of vodka following a vicious assault on his wife . . .'); Cockermouth ('Teenager Stabbed for Giving a Lift'); Aspatria ('Man Blows Up Fox on Garage Air-line'), Cleator Moor ('Food Factory Closure Shock').

What was more, the *Carlisle News and Star* was onto the squid story. 'Richard and Judy's Snub for Crab Fair', it screamed. The fair, already 'in financial dire straits', was facing 'yet another setback after it was revealed that TV duo Richard and Judy would not be making an appearance at the event'. Committee secretary Alan Clements was 'gutted'. The report said the visit would have given the event some 'much-needed' publicity to go with the £1000 donated by BNFL. 'The worst bit is that they weren't even good enough to ring us and tell us,' Clements was quoted as saying. 'I have been secretary for nine years and obviously sometimes people let you down, you get used to it. But I have never known anyone with such a blatant disregard for the people of Egremont and the organizers of the fair. I am disgusted.' With reason. It seems Richard and Judy's producers had demanded exclusive access, meaning Clements had turned other TV crews away. I turned the page. Another local headline ran: 'Bones Found in Garage Are Child's'.

I visited the castle alone. Immortalized in verse by William Wordsworth, Egremont Castle, or what is left of it, sits on a grassy mound above the River Ehen. Moat ditches, now grown over with soft, mossy grass, surround it. William de Meschines built it close to a Norman site in the early part of the twelfth century. But its roots are far older. The Danes invaded this part of the country towards the end of the first century and built a fort at Egremont. By the sixteenth century, de Meschines's castle had decayed. In the moat I found a good tree with a mass of foliage at its base and climbed it. In the corner of my eye I was dimly aware of three children playing on a rope swing, hanging from a branch. The sun was out and the sky was blue, but there was a chill wind. It felt like the first day of autumn. The trees had yet to turn. The leaves rustled, as if to say we are still here, hanging on. A stone came out of nowhere and narrowly missed my ear. It hit the branch with a crack.

I looked at the swing, which hung motionless. Then to my left.

Nothing.

The kids had disappeared. I looked at my feet. The leaves were still rustling.

Rustling, perhaps, a little too much. And there, amid the oak leaves, I saw two tiny eyes sparkling. They saw me. There was a crash of twigs as a milk bottle came hurtling through the tree, on course for my face, followed by the sudden flight of three eight-year-old girls up the hill.

'Do you think he's gay?' one asked in a stage whisper.

I met the others in a pub called the Wheatsheaf, hoping to get a taste of the local brew. There were no real ales so I ordered cider. The barmaid took my order, looked me up and down and put the radio on. A mid-Atlantic voice droned out: 'Gaydar Radio, bringing you all the sexiest boys in pop, 24-7 . . .' Clearly I was not from around here. I asked about the evening's events, carefully omitting any reference to Richard and Judy.

'Oh aye,' the woman said, 'there'll be wheelbarra' races later. You'd best get up by the Kwik Save for a good view.'

Reg had climbed on top of the phone box outside the supermarket and was crouching there like a monkey, filming. Susan, his girlfriend, was holding his tripod. This is what his camera might have seen: the people of Egremont were drifting out onto the street, the women in their skimpiest tops, the shaven-headed lads in their best shirts. The women folded their arms against the bite in the evening air, and everyone waited. People loped around, smoking. Some were eating candyfloss.

As dusk crept in I heard the sound of a fair organ. The summer seemed impossibly far away. The light faded and then came the wheelbarrows, filled with grinning boys in costumes, pushed by panting local heroes. They had to down a half-pint of lager at every pub. The pubs had tables out. Some fell, some soldiered on, their wigs askew, their shirts wet with beer. When it was over the people drifted home or on to the pubs. Groups of young lads stood outside the Red Lion and the Black Bull, pints in hand. I went to a quiet pub called the Blue Bell and sat, with a lasagne, under an ancient framed newspaper article: 'The Red Men of Cumbria'. These were the miners, red from the iron ore.

'Do people still mine here?' I asked the landlady. She shook her head and wiped a glass.

'Biggest employer round here is Sellafield. If that place ever closed down this place would be like a ghost town.' She let the suggestion hang in the air then added, 'Or *more* like a ghost town. I had a shock when I moved here from Manchester, I can tell you.' She laughed. 'Downshifting, they call it.'

Reg and Susan arrived and I put away my notebook. At the facing table there was a group of people laughing, and one of the girls spoke up.

'Are you writing a review of the pub?'

'Not really,' I began. 'I'm writing a . . .'

'We're making a film about gurning – for Alan Clements,' Reg finished.

'Oh yeah, we saw *you* on top of the phone box.'

For Alan? Reg, it seemed, had persuaded the committee secretary he wanted a promotional film.

Reg looked at me and said quickly, 'I've told him it's just about the gurning . . .'

'Oh, well, if it's for Alan . . .' I heard someone say.

'You can interview us,' the first girl said, lighting a cigarette, 'about me mam. She's the world champion. Or, she's *been* the world champion, twenty-seven times. I can have her in here in two minutes. Seriously.' She reached for her mobile. 'Mam, I'm down the Blue Bell getting interviewed.' She was Brenda Woods, twenty-year-old daughter of Anne and Alex, former champion gurners. She was out with Tracey and Lee, having a drink. When the camera came out they began their act.

That night we watched a video of the Richard and Judy show. They had linked live to an aquarium on the south coast where 'Solomon the talented squid' was pulling food out of a bottle and eating it. That was his talent: finding food and eating it. His keeper at the aquarium was called Jo Trout. The show was full of awkward silences.

It got late. Reg and Susan wanted an early start the next day for the Crab Fair proper.

'The greasy pole is going up at seven,' Reg told me. 'We should get there early and help them put it up, you know – get in with them.'

Get in with them?

'Yeah,' said Susan. 'It's important not to patronize them.'

In the event we were late. The pole was up and glistening with lard by the time we reached the Wheatsheaf, on the marketplace, just opposite the Blue Bell. The leg of lamb at the top had been donated by S. A. & J. L. Wilson, family butchers. The sky was clear and there was an autumnal nip in the air. I picked a fuchsia from a bush and ran it between my fingers. The committee members were in the pub, dressed in their yellow sweatshirts. They were having an early-morning pint before getting started on the long day. There was no sign of Michaela yet.

Bob, the landlord, told me how local historians, interested in the roots of the fair, had deliberately revived certain customs and added them in after reading about them in old books.

'That's how I found out it all used to start off in the Wheatsheaf,' he said proudly. Then he frowned at me. 'Where were you last night?'

'The Blue Bell.'

'Wash your mouth out,' Bob said.

According to the local historians, Egremont's Crab Fair dates from the medieval period. When harvest was over, the serfs would offer up produce as tokens of goodwill when they paid their dues to the manor. A celebration grew out of the custom and in 1267 King Henry III granted a royal charter to Thomas de Multon, Lord of the Barony of Egremont, for an annual fair. The charter, now in the British Museum, specifies that the fair should take place over three days in September, to tie in with an existing Christian festival: the 'eve, the day of and the morrow after the Nativity of St Mary the Virgin'. These were originally 7, 8 and 9 September. However, the eleven-day shift following the adoption of the Gregorian calendar in 1752 pushed the Egremont fair back to 18, 19 and 20 September. Another provision of the charter was that the townspeople could sell ale without a licence.

'Here's hoping it won't get too rowdy,' Bob was saying.

'Do you get a lot of trouble?' I asked uneasily.

'Well, you get lads that've been drinking all day and that. It can go off sometimes. We've had a few windows get smashed in now and then.'

My mind started to wander. Egremont was a beautiful town in many ways. The squat terraced houses were romantic with their coloured lintels. The marketplace, busy now with stalls, seemed to hold some of its medieval character, especially with the greasy pole. The people were open and talkative, but the boarded-up windows, the snooker hall that looked like a crack den, the rudimentary chairs and tables in the pubs: they all told another story. An acid cloud seemed to hang over the town. Suddenly it looked like rain. I huddled in the doorway of the Wheatsheaf. Six men were trying to scale the greasy pole, standing on each other's shoulders under the dark sky. They buckled and fell.

'You can back down if it's a lass, like,' Bob was saying. 'There's no shame in that, 'cause you don't hit a lass. But not two lads. Nah, you couldn't back down then.'

I asked him about the gurning. 'Aye, well,' he said, 'you've got to understand, a lot of these round here have got a head start.'

For the three days of the fair, the historians write, the serfs of the Barony of Egremont would forget their tribulations and throw themselves into sports, games and carousing. But Egremont was not always a poor place. By 1800 the town was booming. Flax mills had built up along the Ehen, along with tanneries, corn and sailcloth mills. The first mineshaft was sunk in 1898. Records exist of nineteenth-century fairs. They tell of a thirty-foot larded pole. The prize at the top then was a hat. Its greasy captor would wear it about town as a trophy. Later, the townsmen started using a side of mutton. If no one won it, the meat would be divided among the poor. I wondered how far today's leg of lamb would stretch. The parade of the apple cart would mark the opening of the games. The local children would run after the cart and scramble for scattered crab apples.

We had a few hours before the parade – time enough to visit Bobby Spiers, honorary life member of the Crab Fair committee. Reg wanted to film Bobby's memories. Between 1939 and 1945 the fair was put on ice in honour of the townsmen away at war.

Bobby had been involved ever since the fair had been revived. Now, aged seventy-four, he had retired. It was time to let younger men take over. Bobby's wife was uneasy about us. 'He's not going on camera,' she said. 'He's just recovering from an operation; he's not fit to go on camera. You can have a chat with him but you're not to film him.' Reg was irritated.

Bobby appeared. Reg asked if he minded being filmed.

'I've said they're not to,' Mrs Spiers said. But Bobby nodded and Reg set up his camera.

Most of Bobby's memories, it turned out, were of personnel changes within the committee. He reeled off the names, which meant more to him than they could to us. 'I never knew my grand-da was *treasurer*,' he was smiling, his eyes far away. Susan, holding the big, woolly microphone, turned to me so Bobby could not see her and yawned conspiratorially. They couldn't get him onto the gurning. Reg was fidgeting behind his camera as the videotape wound on and on, but Bobby was happy. His was a company house, he said. He had worked in the pit office until it had closed. The mining company had gone into receivership and he had moved to a chemicals company. He ended up as an accountant.

'My friend had been there all along and he'd done well for himself. He said, "If only you'd joined with me, Bobby, look where I am now."'

Bobby told how Egremont had tried to establish itself as a venue for Lakeland sports to rival Ambleside and Grasmere. But it had never drawn the really big crowds. They were still hoping. The problem was money. He told how horse and dog events had been added over the years as people with different interests joined the committee. He spoke of his early memories of chasing the apple cart. 'The kids used to fly out like bombers,' he said. He showed me records of the sports, lists of who had won the wrestling in this year or that, and some old photos. Winning the wrestling, now that was something you could take a pride in. But there were some around town who made a meal of being champion gurners. 'I mean, gurning?' Bobby said, dismissively. Where was the pride in being the champion of that? Reg suddenly awoke, as if from a reverie. Bobby described one competitor. 'He was never a top-class act until he got his new face, as he puts it. He talks about it as if it were an art.' The word around town was that Peter Jackman had had his teeth out specially. 'But let's face it, you don't take out a good set of teeth. Or if you do, you really are a fanatic, aren't you?'

Finally Bobby had begun to talk about the gurning, and Reg relaxed. From his smile I sensed that all that had gone before would be cut.

Bobby laid his photographs out on the kitchen table. He used to have more, he said, but you lend them out and they never come back. A friend used to have a lot of old documents in his shed, but they had been stolen. He showed us black-and-white pictures of great gurners of history, grimacing through the traditional braffin. Bobby had them in a folder. The camera sucked them up, one by one. On the step, as we left, Bobby's wife said she thought she could hear a fair organ far away.

Back in town it was time for the parade of the apple cart. Bobby had warned against getting too close. 'It's mayhem,' he had said. 'Don't get anywhere near it.' Teenagers lob the apples back at you, he had told us. 'There was one inside the truck once with a brand new camcorder, caught an apple smack on the lens. That was the end of that.'

All of a sudden the 'cart' appeared around the corner and moved down the main street. In fact, it was a lorry, bearing the legend 'O'Connor Fencing'. Alan Clements and other committee members were in the back, in their yellow sweatshirts, throwing out the apples. They looked a bit large for crab apples. This was because they were giant cooking apples bought from the supermarket. They smacked the tarmac and were trodden on, spilling juice and pips. A small crowd of children caroused after the truck, leaping, catching. Inside the truck was Reg, filming them and grinning. What would his camera have seen? A neat square of activity, flying apples, laughing children in Adidas shell suits, a blur of motion. But it would have missed the otherwise empty street. I stopped following the truck and watched it recede, leaving a trail of apple debris on the white lines and tarmac.

On the pavement, by the bank, a women's morris side had assembled in apologetic fashion. A lone musician diddled on a piano accordion as the women went through the motions, roundly ignored by pedestrians who walked through the circle, bumping into the women, and queued for the cashpoint. The morris seemed woefully out of place here. There wasn't a trace of whimsy about the Crab Fair. No one was wearing ribbons and no one was trying to pretend the parade of the apple cart was a remnant of some ancient luck-giving fertility ritual, although, as with the wassailing of apple trees in Somerset, it could easily be. I found this highly refreshing.

The sun came out and I passed the afternoon up on the hill, watching the wrestling. It was not unlike the shin-kicking of the Cotswolds, but more refined, less vicious. When the better man threw his opponent he would lift him up to shake his hand. It was an art, a craft, rendered absurd by the fact that the burly champs were all wearing pants outside their trousers. The commentator was getting steadily more loquacious as he sipped from a glass. 'Whoops, nasty, that,' I heard him say, as someone's bulk hit the field with a thump. 'An old man, with an even older trick. Nicely done.'

In another enclosure the Amazing Magnus, a stocky man of mature years, had wrapped a rope around his neck and was encouraging local strongmen to pull him apart. They failed and the crowd cheered. 'Don't try this at home, children,' he advised. In the programme, Alan Clements had written that there would be greater audience participation this year, to help spread the scarce sponsorship. This was a bit of spin and what it translated as was fewer acts. Magnus was it. What they really needed was a new sponsor and to attract one they would need some top-class PR. Now that Richard and Judy had pulled out, Michaela was the fair's last hope. Would the Bristol-based former *Hit Man and Her* presenter be the oxygen of publicity, breathing new life into old customs?

Further away some children were coaxing their ferrets through lengths of plastic tube. They held the rodents by the neck and they hung there, immobile, their whiskers catching the breeze. Hard by the wrestling arena the terrier races had begun. The men and boys had the dogs in a wooden cage with a sliding front. They wagged a fake rabbit in front of the mesh and the hounds, driven to distraction, rammed their heads against the wire. Suddenly the barrier slid up and the dogs were out. The rabbit shot away, wound up on a length of rope, the dogs slavering after it. The commentator was tottering in his anorak, glass in one hand, microphone in the other.

'And it's a brown-un first, a brown-un second, a black-un third and t'other one last,' he cried. There was a pleasant, village fête atmosphere. People were selling hot dogs and burgers, swimming in seas of oil. Reg appeared.

'Have you seen this?' I pointed over the hedge. A few miles away, beyond the clumps of gorse spotted with yellow flowers, the land fell away to the Irish Sea. It was as though a great, white aperture had opened up. You could make out the foam of the surf. Inland, the fells rolled away towards Durham, bleak and beautiful against the blue sky. Then, over the gates and across the fields came greyhounds. Sleek and purposeful, they homed in on their owners, who egged them on to win with strange cries. Only last year the fields and fells had been closed to the public. The outbreak of foot and mouth disease had all but closed England's Lake District down. Livestock were burned and tourists stayed away. Businesses failed. Crops failed. People could only stare out of the windows at the vast expanse of wild open land, poisoned and out of bounds. To the south, the dark smear of BNFL Sellafield squatted guiltily on the shore. Elegant plumes of soft white smoke stretched up to the sky like fingers and caressed the patches of fluffy cumulus.

'Sorry, am I missing something?' Reg said.

Down at the Market Hall the brass band was chugging through a version of 'I Closed My Eyes' from *Joseph and the Amazing Technicolor Dreamcoat*. I took a seat in the second row, and it wasn't long before the Woods clan arrived. Brenda was excited and kept grinning at me.

'Are you going to go in for it then?' she asked.

'I might,' I said. 'I've been working on a gurn.'

'Is it the one you're doing now?'

'Ha ha.'

Tracey was pleased because her husband had won some money on the horses. Anne and Alex were quiet, concentrating, hoping for a win. They sat in a row, drinking luminous alcopops through straws. The smoke from their cigarettes made gentle clouds above the bells of the brass instruments.

The room started to fill up. There must have been five hundred people and the DJ, a young lad, played 'Dirty Old Town', the song Ewan MacColl had written about Salford. The sound was deafening. 'Egremont people,' he shouted into the microphone, bursting not a few elderly eardrums. 'Egremont town! This is your night. Come on, get buzzing.' Kids ran around. The bar got busy. The programme said it was time for the junior talent contest. Groups of

© Rosy Burke Design, Banbury

Horse necessities: making friends in Banbury

Parched: Midsummer fire in the Cotswolds

October Plenty: Harvest home or over-shopping?

Triumph: The morris at Trafalgar Square

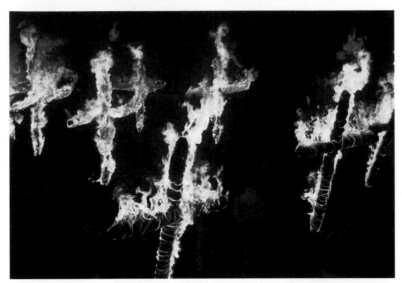

'Onward Christian soldiers . . .'

The Cliffe at Lewes

Reclaimed land: Glastonbury Tor

little girls performed immaculately choreographed copies of girl-band numbers and sang along, karaoke-style, in strident tones. A small, brave boy with a shaven head, combat trousers and a baggy Calvin Klein T-shirt marched on, sang a verse of 'D' Ye Ken John Peel', froze, then walked off again. There were more groups of girls, and then I suddenly recognized one cavorting cherub. It was the child that had thrown the bottle at my head. Elsewhere on stage, the Egremont Crab Fair Queen, a teenager with blonde ringlets, sat on the stage throughout, chewing.

The traditional Lakeland hunting songs were cancelled. Anyone likely to give a tally-ho was down in London, joining four hundred thousand others on the Countryside Alliance march, protesting at what they called the prime minister's urbanization of Britain, protesting against anti-hunt feeling in Westminster and a lack of support for country ways. Some things don't change. The Crab Fair hosted cockfights and bear-baiting until 1835 when the Cruelty to Animals Act outlawed them.

Cameras started to appear. Reg was there, along with others. They stood in front of the Woods family, blocking their view. They didn't seem to mind. They were bobbing in their seats to the music, sisters and friends on laps, as the DJ turned up the volume still louder. The gurning events had been sponsored by Carillion Rail, a track-laying firm that employed 'a good few locally' and also recognized 'the importance of local traditions' to its many employees. On stage, someone had stuck about a hundred A4 print-outs of the Carillion logo onto a fabric screen — the backdrop to the filmed action. One or two had fallen off.

The junior gurning heats passed mainly without incident. Frankly, their young hearts weren't in it. But then came the women's contest. Suddenly there was a commotion, and Brenda squeaked. Michaela had appeared. Her perky beauty shone out in the Market Hall and she grinned like a bleached chipmunk holding a lamp. Brenda rushed up to have her T-shirt signed. Michaela, the consummate professional, had time for everyone and, yes, she was definitely going to gurn. She had only two serious opponents in the contest. Anne Woods, the local favourite, was a dead cert, and Reg's girlfriend, Susan, had been getting tips off Peter Jackman. Susan was up first. She mounted the stage and came through with a highly impressive face. First the cheeks puffed out like a bullfrog, then her nose and lips imploded, as though someone had pulled them by a string from behind. Reg was grinning proudly, camera trained. Next, Anne Woods took the stage. The crowd went wild. This one had the whole community behind her. It looked like a landslide. Her face came through the braffin, the lower lip went up, the forehead came down. 'Oh yes,' cried the DJ, 'Anne Woods, what a result.'

Next up was TV's Michaela Strachan. The chirpy presenter took the braffin. The crowd was deafening. But, oh, what a disappointing gurn. Basically, she went cross-eyed. Never mind, the cameramen were ecstatic. Reg was squinting into his viewfinder. Bjorn the cameraman was treading on people and swivelling his tripod to get a good shot.

'Wasn't very good, was she?' said a woman behind me, tapping me on the shoulder. 'You going in for it then?'

'I might,' I said. 'I've been working on a face – tell me what you think.'

I gurned.

'Oh aye, put your name down,' said the woman, whose name was Debbie. 'You just need someone to egg you on.' But I was getting nervous. I had never gurned in public before. What if I stuck like it? The disco was pounding now, and so was my head. The heat was oppressive and the music so loud it felt like gunfire. People were stripping off. As I went to the bar, a big-breasted woman had cornered another woman and was wobbling her breasts in her face. 'Fuck's sake, gerroff,' a muffled voice came.

Finally my turn came. I gurned. Alan Clements was there, guiding me. 'One for the cameras, one for the crowd and one for the judges,' he said as he pointed me this way and that. 'Egremont town!' the DJ was crying. 'Yes!'

But I wasn't in the same league as the locals. As their faces mutated in front of me like radioactive accidents I knew I had no chance. I didn't even make it through the qualifying heats. A man next to me asked what I was writing. I told him and he said I should get down to Merseyside.

'That's where I'm from. Well . . . I grew up here in Egremont but I moved away like, for work.'

'Do a lot of people move away?' I asked. His dry smile told me I had asked a stupid question.

'Oh aye,' he said.

On stage the DJ was apoplectic with excitement. 'Egremont people!' He was crying into his microphone. 'Egremont town!

© James O Jenkins/eyevine

216   *The Magic Spring*

Forget the neighbours for once. Just get buzzing, I don't care if it's only for one night, make some noise, Egremont people.'

Jackman gurned. The crowd was in a frenzy. But, teeth or no teeth, Jackman's face had nothing on old man Mattinson. 'You're an Egremont man,' the DJ shouted. 'Get up here.' Mattinson's was a class act and he took the stage coolly in a tweed suit, like Cleggy in *Last of the Summer Wine*. And what a masterpiece! It was like looking at a Picasso that had been left out in the rain. No wonder he had won ten years in a row.

But the reigning champ was his own son Tommy. Looking at the younger man it was hard to see where the face was going to come from. There was no telltale sign, no especial ugliness: a presentable young man by all accounts. But, by God, when he came through the braffin it was like watching the devil himself. The whole of his upper lip articulated to create a villainous cavity. Eyes narrowed to pig-like slits and something white shone deep within the void – was it a tooth, or part of the nasal passage? It was hard to say. He looked like a Pompeii casualty. I was deeply shocked.

The disco pumped as the women's winners were announced. In third place was . . . Susan. The crowd cheered and she claimed her rosette. In second place was – wait for it – Anne Woods.

The crowd gasped. There was a shocked hush.

What?

Second?

In the row in front of me, Anne Woods went very pale. Brenda stopped jigging her little sister up and down on her knee.

'Egremont people,' said the DJ. 'I think you know what's going to happen.'

They did. But they didn't like it. As Michaela bounded on stage to claim first prize Anne Woods burst into tears and everything went into slow motion. Brenda was at her feet, consoling. People leaned in from the crowd.

'You was robbed,' someone called.

'It was a fix.'

But Anne hung her head. Now Brenda was crying too, wiping her eyes on the T-shirt Michaela had signed. Suddenly she looked as young as her years. Reg zoomed in for a close-up.

On stage Michaela was dancing with Alan Clements to a rave version of 'The Camptown Races'. Cameras were everywhere. An executive from Carillion Rail came on stage. 'I've been really impressed with what I've seen,' he said. 'And I'm a Whitehaven man, born and bred. Although I moved away . . .'

'But why does it have to be just tonight?' the DJ was crying into his microphone. 'This is how Egremont should be every night. Oh this is how Egremont should be. And it's all down to the members of the committee.'

The next day, the first fruits of Alan's PR appeared. The *Staffordshire Sentinel* ran a muted 153-word report, 'Michaela Strachan Wins Gurning Contest'. 'Ms Strachan, 36,' the report said, 'has vowed to return next year to defend her title.' This was not strictly true. The DJ had put her on the spot with a microphone in her face and, trapped like one of her interviewees, she had been given no choice but to agree. She grinned helplessly, while the disco pounded. Two days after that, the *Bristol Evening Post*, Michaela's local paper, printed a modest half-column story: 'TV Star Proves She's Not Just a Pretty Face'. My report makes three.

12 | John Barleycorn

My primary school was called Christchurch. It was not a place of objective secular learning. Mornings would begin with thirty minutes of Anglican worship, accompanied by the hunched figure of Mrs Ogborne at the piano. Every Thursday an irascible man called Gibbons would lead us in hymn practice. Gibbons was generally on a slow boil at these times and could be swiftly goaded into a state of emotional meltdown by the incorrect phrasing of a verse, or by the mischievous placing of unholy emphasis on words like 'naked'.

A favourite of mine was an old round that began, 'Every man 'neath his vine and fig tree'. If pronounced 'fug', the penultimate syllable could actually cause a bulbous vein to rise on Gibbons's forehead each time it came around. 'If I come down there,' he would cry out, his knuckles whitening with rage as they gripped the lectern, 'there will be tears.'

Despite everyone's best intentions the songs meant nothing to me, and Gibbons's unstable stewardship did little to endear to me his hobby of making a joyful noise unto the Lord. Bored by his anger, I would find other ways to amuse myself. Over the course of a long spring term I discovered that the songbooks were bound in a composite cardboard, the printed layer of which could be peeled off and chewed, leaving the soft, fleshy paper beneath ripe for colouring with felt-tips. This, however, left the question of what to do with the ball of masticated pulp. The solution came one Thursday during 'vine and fig tree', when the plosive syllable gave me the perfect opportunity to bear fruit of my own, albeit launched on a trajectory calculated to collide with Gibbons's bulbous vein. 'One boy is singing *flub* tree,' he screamed. 'And if I ever find out who it is, *heaven help him.*'

So it was with some sense of relief that I would welcome the divine intervention of the local vicar, one Reverend Dimoline. On occasions of special Christian significance this Angel of the Lord would banish Gibbons into the wilderness and give us an inspirational sermon from the stage blocks. Dimoline was a sincere and cultivated gentleman who had lived a life of travel and adventure. A glazed look coming into his eyes, the holy man would stare off at the climbing apparatus and deliver his oration.

'When I was stationed in Burma I became separated from my unit in the treacherous heat of the Irrawaddy jungle,' he would begin. And I was away. My mind would wander, lulled on a tide of soft English cadences, transported by images of tigers thrashing in mangrove swamps and screeching marmosets in flight until, at length, the cleric's voice would slow to a long, pregnant pause that woke me from the warmth of my reverie. 'And that is why our own saviour, the Lord Jesus Christ, gave us the thermostat,' he would conclude. 'Dear God, we give our thanks for the gift of shelter, for the gift of warmth, and for the gifts of science and, er, the thermostat. Help us to appreciate these gifts, through Jesus Christ our Lord. *Amen.*'

I'm willing to believe that the blinding significance of each Christian festival was deftly unveiled somewhere between the road to Mandalay and 'those brave men who tarmac our motorways', but at such epiphanies I was still away with the monkeys, busily eating my hymn book. I tried to busk it. Christmas gave itself away in the form of the Nativity play, i.e. people come to give you presents. Easter was a cinch too: 'Cult Leader Becomes the Walking Undead'. No, the one whose meaning always eluded me was Harvest. As the only festival at which I didn't get anything but had to give stuff away, Harvest was in my bad books from the start. There was something else too, but I couldn't put my finger on it.

The religious men told us to prepare a basket of food. For my part, this activity would be left until the night before the church service when, put on the spot by my laziness, my mother would ransack the dusty nether reaches of the kitchen cupboard for spare produce, which I would throw into an ice-cream tub decorated with bits of paper and a lot of Sellotape. The next day, marching in single file, we would deliver our offerings to the local church and leave them for the benefit of 'the poor'. They never said who the poor were, but I imagined they would have to be pretty inventive to fashion a meal out of a tin of Co-Op beef broth, three lumps of crystallized ginger and a United bar. Plus, I'd eaten the United on the way there.

All of this came back to me in waves as I sat in a pew in the church of St Martin-in-the-Fields, listening to the vicar give a sermon. It was late October and I had been drawn to central London by the promise of pearly kings and queens congregating en masse for a Harvest service. Caught up in the jostling crowd of camcorders and money-belts pushing for a glimpse of sequin, I had ended up in church before I knew where I was.

St Martin's lies just off Trafalgar Square, a few yards south of Leicester Square Tube station. When Christian tourists come to London, they end up at St Martin's. It's an ever-shifting, multinational congregation and the church keeps itself and its charitable works afloat via its crypt which offers the visiting public highly priced brass rubbing, wholesome refreshments and godly goods – miniature torches that say 'I've seen the light' – all in the kind of dingy, sepulchral gloaming that speaks of monastic devotion. The church had been modestly decked with small, ornamental sheaves of corn and arrangements of seasonal flowers, bought from a florist and displayed with an immaculate sense of chastity.

'Why do we call it St Martin-in-the-Fields?' the Reverend had begun. 'This particular church is only two hundred years old. It was never in the fields. Yet it remains a basic human instinct to give the fruit of the land to God.' I looked around. God had harvested little from the pearlies. The donations of food were meant for London's homeless and I couldn't help but think that, were I bedding down in the urine and used needles of the underpass at Tottenham Court Road, I might have other priorities than to get outside of a tin of Happy Shopper haricot beans in brine. But beggars can't be choosers. When poor relief was first set up, at

the time of the Luddite uprisings, the income-challenged were
lucky to get bread. The vicar thanked the Lord for the orchard
and the mine. He also thanked Him for 'packaging and the things
we get from supermarkets'. I briefly imagined the Creator, using
only divine light, proudly fashioning the first tube of Shake 'n' Vac
and unleashing it unto Tesco in a shower of glittering particles,
before the vicar's voice, as Dimoline's had so many years before,
lulled me into a state of reverie. I awoke from my reminiscences in
time to sing, 'We plough the fields and scatter the good seed on
the land . . .'

Outside, the pearly monarchs were standing around in their best buttons, waiting to be photographed, a bit like our real monarchs. Dick Brooker was there with his instamatic, snapping away. Each parish of London has a pearly king or queen, although it's not an exclusively cockney club. A small boy's coat bore the sequinned legend 'Pearly King of Stevenage'. They certainly looked arresting, but I didn't understand the Victorian hats. There is really no mystery, though. The pearly king of the City of London and his wife told me that the tradition had begun in 1875 when a young rat-catcher called Henry Croft fell in with a grizzled bunch of street traders, the costermongers. Croft was interested in raising money for the poor, the homeless and orphaned, and took inspiration from the costermongers' flashy white-buttoned clothes, which they wore to attract attention. He took it one step further and covered himself from head to toe. He then asked the costermongers for help, and the tradition began. 'That's a really beautiful story,' said an American girl who had been videoing the conversation over my shoulder.

An opportunity to find out more about Harvest came a few days later, when Doc Rowe invited me to attend an event in Southwark called October Plenty. The festivities were due to begin on the South Bank of the Thames, outside the Globe Theatre, the modern replica of Shakespeare's Elizabethan playhouse. I was interested to attend a city event, as for the larger part of the nineteenth and twentieth centuries folklorists had focused their studies and collections exclusively on rural customs. Urban behaviour was not interesting to the early collectors, and certainly Cecil Sharp and his acolytes had had no mind to note the songs of the urban poor, only the music of rural peasants. This focus had done much to spread the notion that the English countryside was a timeless, unified place with a common character where the remains of pre-Christian rites were acted out by unquestioning yokels bound by dumb tradition – rather than an ever-changing landscape made up of simultaneous and conflicting trends, where traditions grew and changed along with the people.

When I arrived, a group of actors wearing the costumes of an imagined peasantry were performing morris dances to a fiddler dressed as a bear. It was a brisk, chill day and I envied the bear her fur as I stamped my feet against the cold. The dancers invited onlookers to join in – something you wouldn't catch the real morris doing. The crowd was only too happy to take part.

'Look how happy everyone is,' a woman behind me said. 'People are smiling.'

'Yeah. Probably because it's free,' a man replied.

London.

Suddenly there was a commotion of drums and I looked to see a green man, decked in foliage and bark and heading a slow procession, coming towards us. On his head he wore a wicker basket which brimmed with flowers, bright fruit and berries. He trailed ivy as he walked. The green man was followed by a woman dressed as Bold Slasher, her Turk's hat bound around with corn and barley. Bringing up the rear was a rustic cart carrying a giant effigy.

227   John Barleycorn

The ten-foot woman was made entirely from comestible produce fixed to a calico drape on a crude frame. Her nose was an aubergine and she had two rosy apples for eyes. Her mouth and eyebrows were fashioned from long red chillies, while her breasts were two ripe, round pumpkins set against purple cabbage leaves. She was covered in sprouts and had a very interesting navel made from a crusty spiral loaf. I started to get hungry and looked longingly at her delicate fingers – baguettes to you and me. A bagel-bedecked hobby horse capered past.

There followed a brief ceremony inside the Globe, where the

actors offered up the fruit of the land to God. In this case it was a corn dolly, presented to the theatre director. Then it was off to the Borough market and we processed through the narrow Southwark streets following the rhythmic sound of the melodeons. I fell in step and it occurred to me that, had I been raised in Hamelin, the pied piper would have had me away without too much effort. In fact, any old piper would have done, I wouldn't have cared if he wasn't pied. I was busy asking myself yet again why no one had ever taught me such music when I was a child when, in a flash, I recognized a jaunty melody. The morris call the tune 'Monck's March' but I had been taught it by Gibbons as 'George Fox'. The Christian songwriter Sydney Carter had added his own words about the leather-clad founder of the Quaker movement to the old English tune.

Another interesting Quaker was Sir Edward Tylor, the Victorian man of letters who kick-started the new discipline of anthropology, the science of humankind. Tylor was a lapsed Protestant Christian who had found much to admire in the work of a German scholar called Wilhelm Mannhardt. Intellectual and artistic Germany in the mid-nineteenth century had moved into what is now called its Romantic period, a defining characteristic of which had been the search for a unified national cultural identity. Educated men had looked to the German countryside for inspiration, in a search for the perceived wisdom of the noble savage, and Mannhardt had collected and documented masses of rural customs. As rural customs, they did focus somewhat on the essential rural activity of harvesting sustenance from the land, rather than the urban activity of eating parts of it and throwing the waste into the street. Mannhardt, using a leap of creative imagination inspired by Darwin's new theory of evolution, concluded that the rural customs were not complete, current and whole, but were fossils: relics from a time before Christianity, when a less evolved people worshipped vegetable spirits.

Back in England, Tylor was enjoying this idea. It allowed him to justify his contempt for the ritual of orthodox Christianity. In his seminal works of anthropology he developed what has become known as the theory of survivals. This is the belief that folklore is a remnant of a previous stage of human evolution and so can be used to reconstruct that earlier time. Tylor believed folk customs were relics of pre-Christian, or pagan, vegetation rites. He had a great influence on another lapsed Christian, our friend Sir James Frazer, who brought the same idea to a wide readership through *The Golden Bough*. Frazer's family had been members of the Free Church of Scotland. Like most radical Protestant organizations, this church had a profound distrust of ritual and tended to denounce it – as I had been denounced by the evangelist in Banbury for the sin of wearing bells. Frazer and Tylor shared a deep revulsion for the 'barbarian' rituals they discussed. They believed that, just as prehistoric fishes had grown legs and crawled out of the murky water, 'pernicious' savages in animal skins had evolved into liberal metropolitan intellectuals in stiff collars, like them.

Historians now say that Frazer's main objective in *The Golden Bough* was to discredit Christianity and religion in general. The survivals theory allowed him to do this to a wide audience. *The*

Golden Bough sold like hot cakes and is still in print. It is impossible to overestimate the scale of its influence, but despite his own feelings, Frazer's work did not inspire a similar revulsion for primitives in his readership – rather the reverse. All this talk of spirits and animal skins was an appealing mix. Paganism was in.

The folklorists of the time picked up the survivals theory and ran with it. Tylor and Frazer used the theory to lambaste the Church, but it could be used by others, too, to further their own agendas. Mary Neal finally gave up her fight for control of the morris revival when Cecil Sharp persuaded her that she had upset the natural balance of the universe by substituting women for men. At length, she came to agree that the dances she so loved were in fact relics of a pagan male fertility cult, and she even apologized for her 'error'. The pull of this theory of origins was so strong and so persuasive that even today in the twenty-first century – more than thirty years after the fanciful nonsense was first pulled apart and disproved by a stream of scholars – you can still look up, say, the Ripley Morris on its website and read: 'Morris dancing is a pagan fertility dance.' The media of today enjoys this theory too, but, like a lot of things we read in the papers, it's been sexed-up.

The Borough market was offering hot cider and organic produce from around the world, albeit at London prices. I procured a pint of lumpen scrumpy and a chewy kebab. The rain-damp concrete area beneath London Bridge soon filled up with our throng and, having laid down straw, the musicians gave a rendition of 'The Death of John Barleycorn'.

There was three men came out of the west,
Their fortunes for to try,
And these three men made a solemn vow,
John Barleycorn should die.
They ploughed, they sowed, they harrowed him in,
Throwed clods upon his head,
And these three men made a solemn vow,
John Barleycorn was dead.

Then they let him lie for a very long time
Till the rain from heaven did fall,
Then little Sir John sprung up his head,
And soon amazed them all.
They let him stand till midsummer
Till he looked both pale and wan,
And little Sir John he growed a long beard
And so became a man.

They hired men with the scythes so sharp
To cut him off at the knee,
They rolled him and tied him by the waist,
And served him most barbarously.
They hired men with the sharp pitchforks
Who pricked him to the heart,
And the loader he served him worse than that,
For he bound him to the cart.

They wheeled him round and round the field
Till they came unto a barn,
And there they made a solemn mow
Of poor John Barleycorn.
They hired men with the crab-tree sticks
To cut him skin from bone,
And the miller he served him worse than that,
For he ground him between two stones.

Here's little Sir John in a nut-brown bowl,
And brandy in a glass;
And little Sir John in the nut-brown bowl
Proved the stronger man at last.
And the huntsman he can't hunt the fox,
Nor so loudly blow his horn,
And the tinker he can't mend kettles or pots
Without a little of Barleycorn.

I caught sight of Doc, filming and asked him the meaning of the song.

'John Barleycorn is the crop,' he said. 'When he's killed, it's the farmers cutting the barley down with scythes. But then he's reincarnated as real ale.' He smirked and added: 'It's the corn spirit, see.'

Corn spirit my eye, and if anyone knew it, Doc did. 'John Barleycorn' was first printed on a seventeenth-century broadside, a kind of printed flysheet sold on the street which could contain anything from a political diatribe to a poem. Many songs were published in this way, well into the late nineteenth century. There is no mention of John Barleycorn before this publication, although it is often 'said to be much older'. The song would have to go back a very long way to precede Christianity. 'John Barleycorn' neatly demonstrates the idea the Victorian and Edwardian scholars held that rural folk were entirely literal in their outlook and were of a single, homogeneous class. If the peasants described the corn as a man, then surely it followed, the intellectuals reasoned, that these unsophisticated labourers truly believed that he was one. A corn god called John. Hell, it sounds likely, doesn't it? But, in fact, it took a lot of imagination to believe this, against the evidence, rather than to accept that country people were capable of using literary devices such as irony and the pathetic fallacy. The reason for this, I feel, was not academic rigour but prejudice. The early folklorists wanted so badly to believe that country folk represented a human substratum that, should they on their travels stumble upon a countryman who was well read, they tended to ignore him. On the other hand, the broadsides ensured widespread dissemination, so there was always the possibility that the country-style ballad had in fact been written in London, Oxford, York or Bristol by a literate intellectual.

The actors had launched into a mummers-style street drama, but after an hour of rubbing my hands against the October bite as they acted out *The Marriage of Wit and Wisdom*, I saw with increasing clarity the difference between actors and mummers. Actors live to be on stage. Once they have an audience, wherever it is, there is no stopping them. Mummers, by contrast, would prefer to be in the pub. Fifteen minutes is stretching things beyond the call of duty and, frankly, keeping them from 'a little of the barleycorn'.

After the play had drawn to a close, a woman carrying an impressive collection of empty plastic carrier bags snapped at me for smoking and I stole away to talk to Bold Slasher. The corn-bedecked Turk turned out to be Sonia Ritter, artistic director of The Lions Part, the theatre company that had staged the October Plenty event.

'We're all urban people,' Sonia told me. 'We want to do something that brings us back in contact with the land. We're interested in ecology and in protecting our environment. As actors, what can we do? Well, we can adapt these old traditions; these are things that are going on all over Europe and other places, where people have retained their ethnic customs.'

I asked her why she thought the English had not. She blamed Protestant religion and its intolerance of idols and ritual. 'Many traditions had to be revived after the Civil War.'

Yes, but the Civil War was quite a while ago now. History shows there is another reason, in which urban life has played a vital role. In 1810 around 80 per cent of English people lived in the country. A hundred years later that figure had reversed, with 80 per cent living in towns. It was a mass migration to the smoke and filth – a swift economic shift, forced upon many whose rural livelihoods were no longer viable. Try doing a sword dance when you're up to your ears in factory grease. Try bringing in the May when you're up a scaffold, building a bridge.

The Industrial Revolution, its dirt and its swarming masses of soot-clad oiks, created among the lettered a heady nostalgia for the pastoral life. Ah, to be in the country, they sighed, where simple folk go about their quaint ancient ways, possibly leaning against a haywain while fording a brook. How exotic and beautiful such a life must be, they twittered, and what a tonic for our urban ennui. Let us wear tweeds immediately and write about daffodils, they cried. The latter approach had worked for William Wordsworth earlier in the century, although history does not record his position vis-à-vis the tweed. It had worked for Samuel Taylor Coleridge too, for Alfred Tennyson and for William Morris. Now the artistic greats of the industrial age were jumping on the bandwagon. Let us write about the animals and the elements, cried City banker Kenneth Grahame, let us muse upon the wind and the willows. Thomas Hardy agreed. Kipling too. We are all urban people, they said, and we want to do something that brings us back in contact with the land . . . As writers what can we do? Well we can write these books. They were influential. Where have all the maypoles gone? people were asking. Whatever happened to merrie olde England? There was a definite and deliberate attempt to revive country traditions, a nostalgic process historians refer to as Merrie England. 'Get your effigies out,' the intellectuals cried. 'Cover up the tits and cocks, mind,' they added. 'We're not barbarians.'

The Victorians 'sanitized the traditions they revived,' Sonia was telling me, a judgemental tone in her voice, as though there were any difference between Victorian revivals and those of the twenty-first century. The ten-foot effigy of the naked woman, her giant breasts and vulva proudly fashioned from the fruit of the land, is entirely a figment of the collective imagination of a group of urban actors. There is nothing wrong in this. It's fun, it's showy and exciting, but it is only the reflection of a different set of values. It's the same nostalgia, in different clothes. We live in emancipated times. Modesty is out, breasts are in.

Actually, the breasts were off. They went hurtling through the air as the actors climbed up the effigy, ripping off the vegetables and tossing them into the audience, in the manner of pantomime dames. I caught a wrinkled pepper, though I dared not imagine what part of her anatomy it had once been. It was fun, but I couldn't help thinking: *so what?* The food being strewn had been bought from shops. The action was symbolic, the effigy more so, but what did it symbolize? What were we supposed to take away from this? Were we to go home and plant bagel trees? The leaflet I had bought told me to use a composter, but I'm an urban person – I don't have a garden and the compost heap in my local park has been closed down due to new restrictions on composting imposed by the government.

Before the industrial advances of the nineteenth century, the autumn cereal harvest was the most important part of the working year. Early writers describe the last sheaf of corn, crowned with flowers, being paraded in a cart, accompanied in some records by a piper. Other harvest-end customs noted by our ancestors include the naming of the last sheaf and the competitive launching of scythes at it, with celebrations when the tuft finally fell. Such descriptions have added fuel to the idea of a corn spirit, but there is no evidence of such a cult anywhere in Europe. Modern scholars now pooh-pooh the idea, as the evidence all points towards practical roots for the customs.

A wench appeared at my side, laden with soul cakes. They were free, she smiled, if I sang her a song. This was a nice, proactive reversal of the souling custom and it appealed to me. Hundreds of years ago, children begged for cakes on All Souls' Day, singing a song in return for the reward. 'One for Peter, one for Paul, three for Him who saved us all.' Nothing very pagan about that one. Some say the souling custom was the 'origin' of Hallowe'en trick or treating. That origin theory again: the idea that, whatever trick or treat might look like now, it was really, originally, souling. Either way, the soulers had to knock on doors and offer their song in hopes of a treat. Now, in the age of marketing, this wench was actively soliciting my custom lest I give my song to a competitive rival. Thank you for choosing Wench Soul Cakes. I sang her 'Living Doll'. She gave me the cakes. She seemed happy with the transaction.

I looked at the effigy. Stripped of her vegetable produce she was just a bit of burlap on a stick. I had been taught from an early age about the evils of graven images. The Christian Church is against them, but a man needs to eat. Could a few pumpkins and a loaf be so very wrong? Historians have unearthed English records of harvest-end customs as far back as the Middle Ages, but no further. We can only speculate on pagan practices. The Romans worshipped a corn goddess, Ceres, but there is no evidence that she was honoured in England.

I left October Plenty, humming 'Monck's March' to myself. But, thanks to my old teacher Gibbons and his ceaseless hymn practice, the tune will for ever be 'George Fox', the Christian sentiments of the latter mingling uneasily with the folksy connotations of the former. Like the actors in October Plenty, Sydney Carter had adapted a tradition for his own ends, in this case to propagate Christianity. Back in the early twentieth century, a similar thing was going on.

While many music hall performers composed cod folk songs around this time, Cecil Sharp, Ralph Vaughan Williams and others changed the words of many of the 'authentic' songs they collected. Where they believed the sentiments would offend public morals, they toned them down. Where the vernacular was too base, they added literary pomp and selective tweeness. They harmonized the melodies with all the starch and stiffness of their collars and performed them in the upright salons of the moment.

They were also extremely selective in what they noted down in the field. They ignored the working-class music halls of the cities and anything derived from them. Urban song couldn't possibly have any meaning, they thought. Instead, they collected songs from the country, taking flight into the hinterland in search of the dying embers of oral tradition. What they failed to see, though, was that in some cases the halls had beaten the collectors to it. A song such as 'Dorothy Drew', the one about the Manchester calico printer's clerk, may have been 'collected' from some toothless hag in a cereal barn, but it was created by Harry Clifton, a London music hall act in 'ow's-yer-father greasepaint. It was a comedy spoof.

A mock folk song: a canny supplier reacting to consumer demand. Clifton also penned a song called 'Paddle Your Own Canoe', an expression unique to him, which has nonetheless been absorbed into our linguistic tradition as a phrase to describe self-reliance. He also wrote the 'authentic' folk song 'On Board the Kangaroo' and the bawdy jig 'Lannigan's Ball'. How many more, I wonder, share a similar root? Clifton, it is reported, often bought in songs from jobbing writers, adding his byline when he performed them. Could it be too far-fetched to imagine that my own great-grandfather, the Manchester calico printer's clerk turned music hall act, may even have supplied him with 'Dorothy Drew'?

Sharp, Vaughan Williams and their contemporaries did sterling work collecting music. But the urgency they imagined was in part an illusion. It's true that without their efforts, many songs might have been forgotten. But 'folk music' itself was never dying. It was only changing. The oral tradition was being replaced by audio recordings. Folk music is not something that used to happen and then stopped. It happens now. Only these days, the songs don't go 'I was hot-shot eager to rifle her charms, a guinea, says I, for a roll in your arms.'

When I surfaced from the Tube I saw fireworks exploding in the sky. They popped and crackled, lighting up the dark windows with reflections. The bonfire season would soon be upon us. But that would be next week. As I turned into my street, a hooded figure slipped out from a doorway, a mobile phone pressed to his ear.

'Yo, boss, trick or treat. Give me five pound.'

I gave him my last soul cake and heard it drop to the floor as I walked away.

When I got home there was a message from Doc. I should get myself to Trafalgar Square. Something was up with the morris.

13 | The Battle of Trafalgar

Trafalgar Square was full of morris. It used to be pigeons but there's been a concerted effort of late. The council and the mayor are against the pigeons. No one wants them, except one person – and the man with the wagon selling pigeon feed has been given his marching orders. Enough's enough. Pigeons are out, morris is in.

It was a curious sight. Doc had said there was to be a protest against the Licensing Bill and I had rushed out. I had imagined the streets full of bladders, the byways bulging with she-males. Baldrics standing side by side in glorious union against the oppressors. Placards in the air, bells about the ankles, loping horses menacing the police cordons. I had imagined battalion upon battalion of melodeons, pipes, tabors and sticks. What a racket. What a force. There are enough morris dancers in England to make a serious and colourful protest. At last their day had come. I couldn't wait.

When I arrived, however, and put my hat on against the drizzle, the sight was all too familiar. The gaggle of dancers lolloping about in the puddles hardly filled the square. There was no focal

point, no banner, no sense of continuity. No sense of community or union. What should I have expected? The words morris and organization are mutually exclusive. Half of them were in the pub over the road and those who were going through the motions in the square weren't really talking. Each team kept to itself. There was no cross-side chat. No inter-bladder bonding. I didn't see anyone I knew and this worried me, as I'd seen enough morris sides over the last few months to keep me in flower-bedecked acquaintances for months. I could only assume that the vast majority of sides had not turned out. I was disappointed.

Suddenly, though, something happened. A man in a suit, tie and worsted overcoat appeared to be organizing the rabble. Gradually the dancers assembled on the steps in front of the National Gallery, filling them with colour. The man held aloft a piece of paper and read from it. The wind was too strong to make out what he was saying. There were cheers and the crowd dispersed. Blink and you'd miss it. I grabbed the chap in the worsted.

'Hello,' he said. 'I'm Lord Reevesdale. I got the exemption.'

'That's nice. Exemption from what?'

'Licensing Act. Morris are exempt. They can morris wherever they like.'

Act? It seemed the bill had gone through, although Lord Reevesdale and the English Folk Dance and Song Society had succeeded in freeing the morris from its rigours. I wondered about the small print.

'They have to be in full morris regalia and doing a dance,' he said.

Ah. And what about music and singing?

'Yes, all that's fine if it's associated with the morris.'

'And if not?'

'No. Couldn't get it. Tried. Government wouldn't have it.'

So the morris was safe. But folk sessions in pubs were still in peril. English traditional music was effectively banned.

'It's a shame,' I said.

'Bloody shame. Nice to meet you.'

Lord Reevesdale went to shake some other hands. I heard him repeating: 'I'm Lord Reevesdale. I got the exemption.' He posed with a horse, and a journalist pushed me out of the way to get the shot. It would make a nice colour piece or a hundred words for the 'and finally' column somewhere.

14 | Doc

In contrast to Trafalgar Square, Doc Rowe's small flat in Clerkenwell is full to bursting. Every inch of available space that isn't taken up with video players, TV screens, cameras and tape recorders is stacked high with their output: bank upon bank of audio and video cassettes, books, files, folders and dossiers reach from floor to ceiling. It reminds me of Ron Shuttleworth's room in Coventry: the result of a lifetime's collecting. Doc is fiddling with his computer. The screen shows hundreds of digital video clips. He clicks on one and a street dance comes to life.

'I've still got my first tape recorder somewhere,' he says, vaguely gesturing toward the mounds. It's probably in there somewhere, under a groaning sack of papers, in a box, under a bag of wires or a collection of camcorders waiting to be fixed, hidden behind a book or a dozen pamphlets clinging together under an elastic band. His first recorder was too cheap. It didn't bear reliable witness. 'Since then I've always understood the importance of having the latest equipment.' He's not a rich man. People give it to him, or lend it. Whenever he needs to update, somehow it happens.

Doc has been collecting since the early sixties. But this isn't the collection. The collection is currently at Burton Street School in Hillsborough, Sheffield, where benefactors to the Doc Rowe Collection Support Group ensure the rent on the room is paid. One day, supporters hope an institution will see the collection for what it is and volunteer to house it. So this is just the material he hasn't yet found time to view, edit and file. There's enough in this flat to last him until the end of his days, and yet still he goes, year after year, collecting more. Through Doc's collection you can watch a tradition evolve and change, in living colour. His work can tell the story of an entire community, its trials, its feuds, the little things that bind it together or push it apart.

This is what he does. That's it. He's not interested in money, although sometimes people give it to him. He's a well-known face all over the country, but he's not a member of any morris team, any folk club, ring or federation. He can be seen at any number of events, if you look hard enough, blending into the background, never taking part, never becoming part of the story, just quietly filming, shifting from place to place.

'I've always been a nomad,' he says, chuckling faintly at the romantic expression. 'People sometimes invite me to join things but I can't get involved with groups. I only let them down.'

Doc grew up in Torquay in Devon. But he never acquired the accent. His father was local but away at war. His first received voice was that of his mother, who had come from London. He became fascinated with local dialect and caught the travel bug, hitching from place to place, meeting people. He loved the accents and the variations in custom. 'At the same time the educational establishment and the BBC were telling you that you had to speak a certain way. But I was always attuned to the vernacular and how comfortable it all was for everyone. In some ways these things, these customs or whatever you want to call them, have always been in opposition to the establishment.'

He's not on a mission. He doesn't have any grand theory about why he does what he does. But once he met a man who had an idea. 'You're just looking for your roots,' he said. But Doc isn't so sure. He's driven not so much by a need to know what's underneath as by a tireless fascination with what's on top. A qualified teacher, Doc – or D. R. Rowe – has taken many jobs to fund his work, from manual labour to university teaching. He used to sing around the folk club circuit, and even performed magic tricks, but this is where he feels most comfortable. Watching and documenting the living tradition, endlessly renewing, evolving and changing. He says that he's getting older, that his health is not so robust, that sometimes he's too tired to go to an event. I get the sense that this saddens him more than anything else, that if he could he'd carry on filming until he dropped, having spent his life looking in from the outside.

We go for a drink and swap stories for an hour or so. It's the last day of October. The pubs and shops have Hallowe'en displays. Some will tell you Hallowe'en was really – *originally* – Samhain, a Celtic pagan festival. As though Hallowe'en is a flimsy fake of the real thing, or a corrupted relic of something better. But the thing for Doc is that, whatever the truth of that, today it is simply Hallowe'en. 'The kids'll be out trick or treating later,' Doc says, fumbling in his bag. 'Damn, I should have brought my camera.'

15 | Go, Move, Shift

Thomas Hardy, in a stirring passage in *The Return of the Native*, describes November bonfires as being 'rather the lineal descendants from jumbled Druidical rites and Saxon ceremonies than the invention of popular feeling about Gunpowder Plot'. This isn't true, of course. There would have been no winter bonfires in England had the hapless Catholic conspirator Guido 'Guy' Fawkes not been found under the Houses of Parliament, up to his ruff in gunpowder on November 5th 1605. But to Hardy, caught in the grip of Merrie England romanticism, the urge to light up and burn the Pope seemed as instinctive and primal a reaction to the drawing in of the nights as the absent-minded pulling on of a tank top or the purchase of a flame-effect gas heater. 'Black chaos comes,' Hardy wrote, 'and the fettered gods of the earth say, Let there be light.'

Well, yes, and let there also be Co-Op beef broth and fleecy mittens. Let there be a new series of *A Touch of Frost* and a bowl of warm Ready Brek for supper. Like all these November essentials, the onset of winter really isn't the onset of winter without something to warm the cockles and buoy the spirits. In this case it was the ritual torching of pariahs and I was intending to get my dose at Lewes, the effigy-burning capital of England.

To be frank, I wasn't that interested in papal immolation. When 'the fifth' was declared a national holiday by royal statute in 1606, effigies of the pope were commonly burned in many parts of the country as a reaction against the Catholic rebels and a reaffirmation of Protestant rule. The conspirators, led by Robert Catesby, had sought to topple both King James I and his Parliament, and install a Catholic monarch. Catholics were persecuted with renewed malice in the wake of the Gunpowder Treason, as they called it then, and the venom was given legal expression in the Act of Remembrance 'in thankfulness to God for the deliverance and detestation of the papists'. But England has grown up a little since then, just a little. For most, the burning of a papal effigy is now an embarrassing anachronism, a reminder of religious intolerance, violence and misrule. Everyone has given it up for shame, or has simply sloughed it off in the general shift towards secularism, which began in the Victorian age of science. Everyone, in any case, has stopped. Everyone, that is, except the Cliffe Bonfire Society in Lewes, which remains bloody-minded to this day.

Each year the members of the society, one of five private Bonfire groups in Lewes, string up their famous 'No Popery' banner across Cliffe High Street. They mean it too. For 'the Cliffe', the fifth is about the solemn memory of five Protestant martyrs burned in Lewes by Mary Tudor in the sixteenth century. They also say it's about the resistance to the Catholic Spanish Armada and the arrival of the Protestant William of Orange to deliver us from evil. It's a sincere commemoration in any case, but I was tired of religious bickering. I was more interested in investigating Hardy's jumble of primal urges. What could the bonfires teach me about the ancient heart of my people? Would I be warmed through in Lewes? Or would I get burned? The latter wouldn't be entirely unknown.

You see, I'd been warned about Lewes. Not by folklorists but by the television news. I had switched on a few days before the fifth and accidentally chanced upon the news. It must have been a particularly slow week because the newscaster was showing a picture of someone's bonfire. Then a video link-up.

The man from the Firle Bonfire Society was on the back foot, stumbling over his words. He had agreed to be interviewed live, and it soon became clear that the journalist wasn't going to let him off the hook. Leaning forward in his seat like a pointer dog, the newscaster pushed the man to apologize and admit he had made a mistake.

England in the twenty-first century favours trial by media and Richard Gravett, a mild-mannered man from a small village near Lewes, was in the dock, charged with incitement to racial hatred. It's a serious charge and, though he looked like a rabbit caught in a set of headlights, Gravett tried to defend his committee's decision to set fire to a model of a caravan filled with depictions of gypsies.

'Wouldn't you agree that burning an image of someone is an expression of hatred?' the newsman goaded. Gravett disagreed, but couldn't articulate his reasons. He was asked to confirm that his people had been 'chanting and shouting'. Gravett would not corroborate the claim. Instead, with an audible tremor in his voice, he said: 'I think you've got to understand Sussex Bonfire.'

So that's what I was hoping to do when I walked up the hill into Lewes on 5 November. It was a crisp, clear day, but achingly cold and I didn't feel much like exploring. It's an effort to cultivate *joie de vivre* in November. October's golden leaves are beautiful, but they presage the long, barren months: bare branches set against opaque skies. In November the winter sets in, the cold comes and the earth dies. Night falls in the middle of the day. Animals bury themselves and things go still. Before the Christians came, English people called November 'blōd mōnaþ'. The old Anglo-Saxon phrase means 'blood month'. It was a time for evaluating your livestock and hunkering down. Not every animal was going to survive the winter. The weaker ones would be slaughtered, saving precious feed for those that would make it through the dark months. Like harvest, blōd mōnaþ was an important time of year and the slain animals would be eaten in a great feast, the last good meat until spring stirred.

It's natural to want a fire in November, to watch the shadows flickering against faces in the dark, to huddle close and drink hot, spicy drinks. I walked into a pub in such a frame of mind and was surprised to find it empty. I sat alone, drinking a pint of the Lewes-brewed Harveys ale, feeling that something was wrong. The need for warmth and companionship is a basic one and, if you haven't got it, November's uncompromising aspect tends to remind you. I thought of Detox Dave and his friends from the subway, a million years ago it seemed, and Cecil Sharp's gypsies. Winter is no time to be homeless or on the move. Everything in nature is telling you to keep still and put down roots.

Lewes was full of police. There's always a presence on the fifth, but no one in the town had seen the like. The barriers along the High Street had been a common sight for a long time now: a 'safety' measure the locals disdained, speaking variously of the spirit-sapping influence of the 'nanny state', or the evils of crowd control. But the sheer volume of law enforcers milling around the main drag was something new. Fluorescent jackets bobbed about. A police 'observer' with a Leica was loitering, looking people up and down and taking snaps. The shopkeepers, boarding up their windows from long habit, were sceptical.

'They say it's about health and safety,' one told me. 'But you don't have this many coppers out unless you're expecting public order offences, do you?'

'Why would that be?' I asked.

'Why do you think?' He gave me a frank look. 'Pikeys. They're expecting a backlash, aren't they.'

He meant the gypsies.

'What, because of Firle?'

The shopkeeper raised his brow in the affirmative. 'Wouldn't be surprised either. Horrible lot, that. Horrible lot.'

He meant the gypsies.

Effigies are burned every year in Sussex. Ever since 1606. Lewes and its surrounding villages set light to society's least wanted: Guy

Fawkes of course, like everywhere else, but also politicians, hum-
bugs, disgraced celebrities. Osama Bin Laden was burned once,
and Bill Clinton. TV's Ulrika Jonsson was set ablaze one year. They
also burn 'enemies of Bonfire' in effigy. Local figures who oppose
the ritual: councillors, busybodies, meddling officials. This year
was no different. Except it was.

The picturesque hamlet of Firle had problems. A group of travellers had moved onto a piece of land owned by the eighth Viscount
Gage. Not in fact, Romany people, these particular nomads had
troubled locals, it was claimed, by threatening behaviour, tres-
passing and damage to property. Some alleged theft. Residents had
complained and asked the local authority to move them on. The
council had refused to act. Although the Viscount had been to look
at them and wanted them off his land, he was afraid to engage
with the travellers.

Elsewhere in Sussex, travellers had already been the victims of
vicious attacks. Gypsies in Peacehaven had been on the receiving
end of a petrol bomb. In Crawley a lighted firework was placed
underneath a van next to a traveller's caravan, engulfing the vehi-
cle in flames. Had the alarm not been raised the blaze could have
set off nearby gas and petrol canisters.

Nothing like this happened in Firle but, come Bonfire Night,
local feeling was made public. Firle celebrates Bonfire Night before
the fifth, so residents can join in at Lewes as well. When the gypsy
effigy was revealed, a chain of events that no one in the Firle
Bonfire Society had predicted was set in motion.

The society had made a model of a caravan with the unambiguous registration plate P1KEY. In the windows were depictions of travellers and their children. Some newspapers reported chanting of 'Burn it, burn it'. Others claimed the crowds were jeering 'Burn *them*'. But, in truth, the intrepid newshounds were not actually there. They were acting on a tip-off from an angry Firle resident, one Patricia Knight, who was quoted as the witness in all the stories. Knight was a recent incomer to the village and was descended from a Romany woman. She felt both threatened and insulted by the display and complained to the local paper. From there the complaint moved to the Commission for Racial Equality. The CRE applied pressure on the police. Already under heavy fire since a television documentary had alleged widespread racism within the police force, and anxious to prove themselves, the police moved in and arrested twelve members of the Bonfire committee.

It was four o'clock and already there was a smell of smoke. I wandered down to Cliffe and went into the Dorset Arms, headquarters of the Cliffe Bonfire Society. I found it easily, it's just opposite the Jireh Chapel, the Free Presbyterian church funded by Ian Paisley. The pub was full of people dressed in navy and white stripes, like robbers. One of them was Clare Brown, secretary of the Cliffe, a young woman, sitting at the bar enjoying a drink. Not booze though.

'Anyone with a job to do stays sober,' she said, a slight reprimand in her tone. 'It's just not worth it.'

The Cliffe is the oldest bonfire society in Lewes: that is, one hundred and fifty years old. The societies were formed out of necessity. Bonfire at that time had become total anarchy, with

257   Go, Move, Shift

masked, costumed 'Bonfire Boys' terrorizing the streets with flame and firework. To understand why, we need to rewind a little.

By 1625 Bonfire Night had become an English fixture and the marriage of Charles I to Henrietta Maria simply fanned the flames. This pale, animal-loving girl was guilty in the eyes of the mob of two heinous crimes: being both Catholic *and* French at the same time. Her considerable religious retinue was costly and viewed with suspicion by the populace, which feared a Catholic infiltration. Popes and devils were regularly burned as a comment on the marriage.

Given its Protestant roots, it is perhaps not too surprising that Bonfire Night was the only religious festival to survive Cromwell's Interregnum, but its tenacity may also have been due to the fact that it was a reaffirmation of parliamentary power. By 1661 the fifth had acquired a rowdy character. Samuel Pepys records riff-raff lobbing fireworks among the people in the street, while flaming tar barrels were not unknown. Hardly surprising that the City itself was to blaze five years later.

When the Catholic James II came to the throne in 1685 the anti-papist elements were removed from the official holiday. Not that it stopped the fires, as the public holiday allowed Protestants the joy of registering their hatred of the king's religion while appearing to honour him. Around this time, displays started getting banned. James sought to suppress fires and fireworks in the second year of his reign. Faithful Anglicans kept candles in their windows, though, just in case any popery tried to sneak in while they slept. On 5 November 1688 the Protestant William III (he of Orange) landed with an army at Torbay, quashing the Catholic rule amid general rejoicing. The Bonfire prayers were swiftly rewritten in the no-popery vein and the rowdy ad hoc fires were replaced by municipal displays, amid growing civic concern about the indiscriminate lobbing of squibs and the torching of cherished property.

Towards the end of the seventeenth century, reports abound of brawling and fighting amid the flames. Windows were smashed and houses attacked by masked marauders, while the pope was often replaced with other effigies, including that of Fawkes. The atmosphere of disorder and rebellion allowed violent elements to flourish. In Lewes in 1785 the townsfolk rioted and the ringleaders were sent to a grim-sounding 'house of correction'. There were riots elsewhere too, and from this time on English Bonfire became a battle between us and them: local authorities against 'idle fellows' and 'merrymakers' (heaven forbid). In the early nineteenth century, as patronage of Bonfire events among the upper classes dwindled, the upholding of the tradition became the domain of local Bonfire Boys. These secret gangs of young men appeared in various towns around the south of England. Masked and armed, they had one aim: to keep the fires burning at all costs and to mock 'enemies of Bonfire'. It is this custom that, while it was successfully suppressed elsewhere, still burns passionately in Lewes.

In fact, so violent was the will of the Bonfire Boys that countless attempts were made by residents, magistrates and fledgling constabularies to quash the November frolics, which, of course, only added fuel to the fire. As the battles became more extreme, so the opposition to Bonfire became more determined. The suppression was absolute in many places, but the Lewes Boys recognized the need for compromise. If the custom was to continue, their riotous ways would have to change. In the middle of the nineteenth century the Bonfire societies were formed, bringing a tight and sober organization to bear against the enemies of Bonfire.

'What about the enemies of Bonfire?' I asked Clare. I was interested to know who it would be. It had been a year of war and political scandal. A year in which the cracks in the fabric of our information system were shown for what they were: the dares and follies of ambitious individuals. A year in which both truth and lies were shown to have no meaning at all. A year in which death had crept out from the shadows in one way or another. A year in which we all forgot that our futile existence was but a passing blip in the story of creation. Who would it be? Which important person?

'We couldn't think of anyone this year,' Clare said quickly, and a little too casually.

There was a silence. While the atmosphere was still heavy, I said, 'Firle's been in the news a bit, eh?' Clare raised her eyebrows and gave me a frank look.

'Well, they've said it all for us,' she said at length, pursing her lips and looking away. 'We don't need to say a word.' Someone at the bar chuckled assent. I finished my pint and left.

I passed hamburger stands and fair rides on my way up again. In the centre of town, by the war memorial, spectators had begun to congregate as costumed characters busied themselves. The Grim Reaper slipped into the Crown Inn and got himself a pint. A Roman centurion appeared from one of the narrow twitterns and crossed the road in a hurry. Another figure crouched in a pith helmet, adjusting his shoelace. A Greek goddess, Zulu warriors, Confederate soldiers. They were busy, important people with jobs to do. They walked with purpose, their faces set. There was no time for joking. I asked a Greek god what Bonfire meant to him. His response was curt.

'If you lived in Lewes, you'd understand.'

'Were you born here?' I asked.

'No, I'm from Brighton.'

'Oh.'

It was the same in the tourist office. There was a queue of tourists wanting tickets for the Cliffe display. They were met with a sharp and unhelpful response from the woman behind the desk, who nonetheless revealed in her expression a quiet delight in being unable to oblige. The Cliffe was a ticket-only display. But you couldn't buy tickets on the day, only in advance, and then only from selected pubs and shops in Cliffe. Basically, it wasn't for strangers.

When you looked through the programmes, you got the same message: 'For many people Lewes Bonfire is an annual event that provides a free spectacle to thousands of spectators who flock to the town . . .' began the Cliffe programme. 'I'm sure many strangers to the town will not realize . . . In the Cliffe we are not a carnival, nor are we here to provide an evening of family entertainment. We are the Cliffe, and we are Lewes Bonfire at its best.'

The Waterloo had similar sentiments. 'Waterloo Bonfire Society's answer to the jibe that we are just a carnival society is a firm "No." . . . The Waterloo Bonfire Society celebrate the discovery of the Gunpowder Plot on 5 November 1605. This Society is not, has never been, and will never be a carnival society.'

So, whatever was about to happen, one thing was for sure: no one was supposed to be having any fun. I grabbed a bite to eat. The young waitress was friendly so I asked her about the societies. She said: 'I was born in London, so I'm not allowed to be in them really.' Outside on a street corner I found a young man from the Commercial Square Society who was willing to chat. I asked him how he had become involved with Bonfire.

'If you're a Lewes boy, you're in it, basically,' he said. 'It's tradition, isn't it?' He had been in the Borough Society. 'But it's fashion. Mates got me into Commercial Square.' He turned around to look at the Crown Inn. The building was decked with a banner wishing good luck to the Waterloo Society. People were spilling out onto the street in their striped shirts.

'Look at that lot. Waterloo. In their rugby shirts. They'll take any old crap in there.'

I wondered if he meant members.

'Yeah, the membership. They take all the crap we won't touch.'

Time was getting on and I had been invited to a party. My hosts owned a bookshop in Lewes and had lived in the town for two decades. The party was on the other side of the road. The police were barring my passage in most directions and the crowds were pressing against the barriers. The smell of cordite in the air was getting stronger and I had forgotten my press card. If I didn't cross the road now, I never would.

I made a break for it and the crowd seeped in to fill the space I had left. A man with a trolley full of flashing lights was trawling the kerb, offering his wares: 'Need any lights, ladies and gents? Two pound your lights, now.' The door opened and Alan ushered me in. Upstairs there was a table laden with good food and wine, and two large bay windows that opened onto a balcony.

'Yes we get a pretty good view from up here,' Alan said, chomping celery. 'Do go out onto the balcony. I stood on it this morning, it's quite safe.' I teetered on the brink, a glass of wine in my hand. Below me the crowds were six deep, pavements blocked, bodies pressed against the glass shopfronts.

'If the fifth falls on a weekend it's even worse,' said Jenny, Alan's wife. 'There's double the numbers then. You can't move at all. It can actually be very frightening.' No wonder people board their shops up. I met Alan's friends – middle-aged professionals from Lewes and its surrounding villages. Affluent, middle-class incomers, entrepreneurs and seekers of idyll. Friendly, well-spoken people. I joined one man on the balcony in a cigar, while he tutted at the police below in their yellow jackets.

'Just look at it,' he said. 'Twenty years I've been coming and I've never seen that many police. It's overkill, isn't it?' He flicked the butt of his cigar down towards the helmet of a fluorescing constable.

'Hm,' I agreed, pulling my head back quickly from the parapet.

It didn't seem quite right to me, but then I had never seen the Bonfire parade. I had no idea from what I might need protection.

Then the fires came. We all crowded onto the little balcony as the dour column advanced, torches held aloft. First the Borough Society, in the guise of Zulu warriors, followed by hordes of striped lackeys, who carried barrels and picked up torches from the ground, disposing of them safely. 'You can't just join and be a Zulu straight away,' Jenny was telling me. 'There's a hierarchy.' Wasn't there always? 'You've got to work your passage.' I asked her how. 'Oh, it's a year-round job,' Jenny said. 'Fund-raising, making torches. You've got to give your all and offer your skills.' She wanted me to understand.

It sounded like a pain in the neck to me. I could imagine giving my some, or perhaps my quite a lot, if they were nice people. But my all? Forget it. I have other things I want to do. There seemed something stifling about that. Perhaps if I had lived in Lewes I would have understood. Or perhaps, like Alan and Jenny's son, who now arrived late from London, if I had lived in Lewes I would have moved away as soon as possible.

The brass band, far from giving off a carnival atmosphere, was playing 'Land of Hope and Glory' as it advanced on the war memorial. Before it reached the monument, it segued neatly into a jolly little medley of 'Pack Up Your Troubles' and Chopin's 'Funeral March'. The Borough Society wheeled a giant tableau of Bush and Blair with the slogan, 'Where Are the Hidden Arms?' The band reached the memorial and gave a quick 'Last Post' followed by two minutes of silence.

Or near-silence. The crowds, pushing for a glimpse, didn't all share the same level of solemnity.

'Time was,' said the chap with the cigars, a note of censure in his voice, 'when that silence would have *meant* something to people.' I looked at the monument with its First World War paraphernalia, poppies and slogans. The comment made me angry.

'Well, the whole thing becomes a bit meaningless, doesn't it,' I snapped, 'when soldiers are in Iraq right now? It's not as if we're learning anything here.'

I felt a bit stupid after that, so I drank wine and watched the lady samba band cavorting below. Carnival? Not carnival? Could it possibly matter? More of them came, their flaming torches singed our chins as they moved below us. The fire seemed to go straight inside the body and warm it. The sparks flew and shone against the black of the windows, the smoke filled the air, inflaming our nostrils.

'It's all very pagan, isn't it?' said one woman. I looked down. I saw a Cliffe woman dressed as a Celtic warrior princess in a horned helmet, blazing stake in one hand, mobile phone in the other.

'Sort of, yes,' I said. 'I mean – I know what you mean.'

Hardy's description of November bonfires had possibly influenced a folklorist called Henry Jewitt who, in 1903, published his unsubstantiated theory that bonfires on the fifth were 'really' – that is to say, 'originally' – pagan Hallowe'en or Samhain fires. It followed, in his assumption, that the effigies burned were 'memories' of human sacrifice. It's not true, not remotely. Samhain fires were lit in Wales, Scotland and the Isle of Man, but not in England

and certainly not in Sussex. It's pure fantasy, but it's compelling fantasy. We want it to be true. The fire speaks to us in winter. Of course it does. It speaks of primal urges: warmth, light, the elemental things. Through these things comes to us an idea of how our story, our prehistory, ought to have been. Human sacrifice? To a god of warmth and light? The sun? Could it possibly be as Edward Woodward and Christopher Lee would have us believe in *The Wicker Man*? Well, one thing is certain: we won't find the truth at Lewes Bonfire.

The chap with the cigars was telling me how one of his staff had objected to the Cliffe bringing round their 'No Popery' pamphlets to his shop. 'She's a Catholic, you see. Didn't find it funny. I don't mind at all though. You've got to accept that's the way people are. Same with the pikeys.'

'The what?'

'The pikeys – I mean, they've got to understand, these politically correct lot, that this is what's been going on here for aeons. You're not going to stop it. See, that's why you've got all these police here. They're expecting something to happen. The pikeys have already threatened to have their revenge.'

'Is there a large travelling community here?' I asked, using the neutral words allowed by the Commission for Racial Equality.

'Oh yes. Well, there's two lots. There's the Romany lot, but they don't give any trouble. Then there's this lot of bloody tinkers. Evil. They're just evil. They left an awful mess.'

Perhaps. The reports are so varied. No one seems that interested in getting to the truth of it. Did children really defecate on the step

of the gamekeeper after killing two hundred pheasants? Did the travellers really steal, defraud and vandalize? If they did, it might support the Firle Society's claim that the effigy had nothing to do with race but was a simple protest against antisocial behaviour, that the fact of the travellers' origins was irrelevant. We are not going to know: when the police came to arrest members of the Firle Bonfire Society on suspicion of incitement to racial hatred, they didn't check the travellers' caravans to see if the locals' allegations were founded or not. To judge from the reports, there has been little reason on either side. So we won't know how harshly this group has been judged. As long as one set of people wants to live in their own way, there will always be another that seeks to repress it, that refuses to understand, help or even tolerate.

Twelve were eventually arrested at Firle. If they are convicted, they face a maximum of seven years in prison. The implication of all this is that the nomadic people of England, whether they are born into the Romany culture or a travelling family, or even if they adopt the nomadic way as a lifestyle choice, are allowed a separate racial identity and formal protection for their way of life. Those who are born into the Sussex Bonfire culture are denied such recognition and are held in contempt for living as they do. It's almost a kind of creeping, subtle racism all of its own. 'Those gyppos don't know any other way, do they? But you lot, with your houses and jobs, money in the bank – you *proper* English – you should know better.' That's how it seems to me. I can't make any sense of that and I think of Ewan MacColl's 'Moving On Song':

> Born on a common near a building site
> Where the ground was rutted by the trailer's wheels
> The local people said to me
> You lower the price of property
> You better get born in some place else
> Move along, get along
> Move along, get along
> Go, move, shift.

Crackers explode in the street. People shriek and cheer. Sparks fly, smoke billows and fireworks light up the street. The heat is fantastic. The atmosphere awe-inspiring. And yet – I feel curiously underwhelmed by the proceedings. I don't know if it's the gypsy undercurrent. Locals are saying Patricia Knight has already been ostracized for her stand. Perhaps it's the pomp. The worthiness. I don't fully understand how or why Bonfire Night became a war elegy. It's an odd brew, a strange mix. The fires, the feelings, the stiff upper lips. A curiously English brew all the same.

Then there's the Cliffe. The stink of religious intolerance taints for me an impressive parade. The Cliffe claim they are not intolerant, but it's hard to misread the slogan 'No Popery' unless they have simply misspelled their dislike of fragrant dried flowers and herbs. Still, they look fantastic, in horns and furs, coming out of the flames like Viking marauders. It's a reversal of the usual trend, where Protestants suppressed the ritual and display of customs that flourished under Catholic rule. The boot here is on the other foot. But the costumes have no significance. They're just fancy dress. And the spiritual dichotomy, this Catholic and Protestant thing. It gets ever so old. In fact, that's our oldest unbroken English tradition: blind hatred in the name of light and love. The whole thing, frankly, could *do* with a bit of paganism.

But the warmth of the firelight helps me to forget the uneasy undertows. I can understand how Hardy must have felt stirred up watching this. How he must have let his imagination run wild. Because the truth is too depressing. It must really, originally, have been something much, much better and much more in tune with the earth.

In fact, I was soon to get my dose of the elemental. I was to come closer to the earth than I had thought possible. But first, the Christmas season was almost upon us, and I was in need of a humour injection.

16 | Big Head and Little Wit

It was December and I had been invited to a folk music party in Weston-super-Mare, the fading resort on the lower Severn estuary known by Somerset locals as Weston-super-Mud. There are two immediate reasons why a fun-loving person might decline this sort of invitation, but there were more reasons why I was keen to go. First, it was an opportunity to try out my new-found folk repertoire in the West Country, home of the Wurzels, the novelty group who brought us the hit single 'I Am a Cider Drinker', performed on a banjo to the tune of 'Una Paloma Blanca'. Second, I had heard that a pantomime production of *Jack and the Beanstalk* was currently running at Weston's Playhouse Theatre.

Popular variety entertainers in the autumn of their stage lives, such as the Krankies, now make a decent living in enclaves such as Weston-super-Mare. They play to crowds of largely immobile, bingo-happy old-timers and hyperactive children in the first throes of trauma. I hadn't seen a pantomime since I had been in the latter category and wanted to experience it again before I fell, muttering, into the former.

Nowadays, panto is the closest thing we have to the music

halls. It was also the closest thing I had to the world of my great-grandfather, Percy Delevine. Since unearthing his past I had found myself increasingly drawn to the music hall and to Victoriana, as though I might learn something about myself there. I had riffled through old playbills on market stalls looking for clues, I had scanned page upon page of old variety and performing arts magazines. I had found pictures in books, a photograph of Percy at a royal command performance. Percy with the magician David Devant, Percy with Leoni Clarke's Boxing Kangaroo, Percy on board an ocean liner bound for the New World. Gradually, a sketchy outline of his story had emerged. Cecil Sharp, who had also once sought his fortune in the antipodes, had shunned the halls when collecting folk songs. The urban working classes couldn't possibly teach us anything about ourselves, he had thought. I had been finding otherwise.

There was another reason for coming to Weston. I had long found it hard to return to the West Country. Although I did so regularly to visit my family, such trips often carried a bittersweet taste. For me, the landscape I had enjoyed as a child had become stained with memory. I had not found my place there and if the act of leaving had given me confidence in my own identity, it had also formalized my dislocation. So far, my travels in England had taken me to parts of myself I hadn't known before. But the more you uncover, the more you want to look. There was still a piece of the jigsaw to find.

So I set off for for the coast, where the late December air, I hoped, would be sticky with candyfloss, the sky would be luminous with neon, and the maudlin songs of yesteryear would be piped from discreet loudspeakers along the front and the pier. I packed my melodeon and my bike onto the train and settled in. I had forgotten to bring a book and I found myself thinking about Christopher Rich.

Rich was, by all accounts, an arse. According to one acquaintance, the man was an 'old snarling lawyer, a waspish, ignorant pettifogger, who disregards the rights of all'. Others were less charitable and he was variously described as a thief and a villain. In fact, his only friend seems to have been his accountant, Zachary Baggs.

In 1690, a year after William of Orange had landed in the south and seized the throne, Rich saw an opportunity to exploit the weak leadership at the Theatre Royal, Drury Lane. The theatre had lost its way and Rich bought the royal patent for £80. Drury Lane was one of only two houses with a licence to stage commercial theatre productions and so represented for Rich a lucrative opportunity and a chance to gain a position of power. Having taken possession of the patent, Rich insinuated himself into the office of manager in the time-honoured way: by bullying and manipulation. Once there, he cut wages, deducted money for spurious reasons and hired only cheap, inexperienced actors who he then charged for instruction. Anyone who stood in his way, complained, criticized or looked at him funny was threatened with legal action.

One of his more odious inventions was the notion of payment by 'profit-share'. Would-be actors in need of a break were hired for no salary on a promise of shared benefits when the books balanced. But Rich and Baggs would always claim that each production had made a loss, denying the players the right to see the books and offering to sue them if they had a problem. Consequently, Drury Lane under Rich was a hotbed of discontent, with actors permanently on the verge of rebellion.

And rebel they finally did. The Lord Chancellor agreed to 'silence' Rich for withholding profits, but the fiend refused to come out of the theatre. So the army was sent in to drag him from the building. Muttering and licking his wounds, Rich retreated to a demolished theatre site at Lincoln's Inn Fields, with his patent, vowing to rebuild that house and profit anew. He had invested a considerable sum and many years in restoring the theatre when, in 1714, shortly before he laid the last brick, the old bastard dropped down dead, leaving the theatre and the precious royal patent to his son John. John Rich finished the theatre and opened it the same year, just as the German George I came to the throne. Under John Rich the pantomime was to take shape.

When my train finally terminated at Weston, a man's voice came over the tannoy and suggested I make sure I had all my personal belongings with me when I left. I had been thinking of leaving my squeezebox on the train, but I thought his idea was better. Clutching my things and shivering against the cold, I made for the pub. The only other customer was an elderly man in a flat cap who regarded me with mild amusement, but the bar was cosy and unpretentious. It was a good place to get outside of a pint of Smiles and ruminate on John Rich.

John was an eccentric figure with a penchant for cats. He had also inherited his father's unpopularity. He hadn't been to school and, as a result, spoke in a rough mix of malapropisms and coarse dialect, which didn't exactly win him the respect of his high-minded actors. He compounded this by pretending never to know anyone's name. In fact, John Rich had a profound dislike for thespians and their caprices and contrived to bring them down a peg or two at every turn. He interrupted one upcoming actress during an audition to talk about his cats.

'That little fellow, my pratty Nykin-poop there, is nat less than fifteen year,' he told her.

He gained a reputation as an uncouth philistine. As a result, Lincoln's Inn Fields had trouble attracting the best players and was not doing too well. Its peformances were shabby and so were the actors. Locked in a downward spiral, young Rich cast about for a money-spinner. He hit on Harlequin.

This masked mime character had come from the Italian *commedia dell'arte* tradition of the sixteenth century, along with Columbine, Pantalone, Pulcinella – who eventually got his own show as Punch – Scaramouch and Pierrotto, the clown. The *commedia* had its own roots in a tradition of ancient Greek miming dancers, the *pantomimi*. The Greek words *panto* and *mimos*, meant 'all in mimic'. By the end of the seventeenth century, however, Arlecchino had more or less disappeared in Italy and was being kept alive by the French. French troubadours then brought him to England.

The English didn't really get it at first. It wasn't until the early part of the eighteenth century that Harlequin caught on. Raucous, unrestrained and noisy, the English harlequinades were riotous and often violent spectacles of knockabout comedy. They could certainly pull in the crowds, but were pooh-poohed as vulgar by the established dramatists. John Weaver, dancing master at Drury Lane, was well aware of the pantomime's classical roots and was unimpressed with the current incarnation.

To counter it, Weaver staged a performance that he hoped would revive pantomime as a classical art form. Drury Lane advertised in 1717 'a New Dramatick Entertainment of Dancing, after the Manner of the ancient Pantomimes, call'd The Loves of Mars and Venus'. But Weaver couldn't compete at the box office with Rich's harlequinades and his next composition tellingly included a comedy crocodile.

There followed a period of bitter rivalry between Rich at Lincoln's Inn Fields and the cultured chaps at Drury Lane. When one house had a success, the other copied it, adding in some random element to move it on. As the crowds flocked, each theatre seemed to be competing on quantity, with more and more 'Grotesque Characters', strongmen, acrobats and special effects being added to the bill in a bid for novelty.

Pantomime became all the rage, and not just with the working classes but with the monarch, the aristocracy and men of fashion. Rich's theatre, ever one step ahead of the 'London hactors' at Drury Lane, was established as the main pantomime house, and the man himself rose in stature.

In 1732 a house at 10 Downing Street was presented by George II to Robert Walpole, the first prime minister. But this event is of minor consequence to us, coming as it does in the same year that Rich, flush from his pantomime successes, opened the lavish Theatre Royal in Covent Garden. This was to prove more of a pull for thespian talent. One actress who came was a Dublin-born beauty called Peg Woffington. She caused a sensation in her breeches. Rich himself well recalled the meeting: 'It was a fortunate thing for my wife that I was not of a susceptible temperament.'

She was hired. Her legs became the first female pair to appear in tight trousers as the principal boy in a pantomime: a startling tradition, which, horribly, lives on.

Rich was now a man of considerable influence and standing, though his eccentricities showed no sign of abating. London's wits and men of conversation flocked to his side in his private chamber at Covent Garden. A culture of great conviviality developed in this oak-panelled room, and in 1735 Rich was moved to form the Sublime Society of Beefsteak, a gentleman's club with the motto 'beef and liberty'. It was dedicated to 'the fostering of good fellowship by the eating of beef-steak' and had its own song which celebrated 'the jolly old steakers of England'. The club, which at various points counted among its members William Hogarth, David Garrick, Samuel Johnson and the Prince Regent, enjoyed a long life. The odd Jacobite rebellion, war against France or adoption of the Gregorian calendar came and went, but the steakers munched on at Covent Garden for a good century after the death in 1761 of their founder. An English gentleman knew his priorities.

Then, in 1794, a London-born comedian called Joseph Grimaldi entered the scene, changing the face of panto for good. Grimaldi's acrobatics, song and comedy, brought the clown character to centre stage and relegated Harlequin to the sidelines. He elaborated on the clown's make-up and costume, adding his own quirks. His were the big shoes, the ridiculous face paint, the false bald head and Mohican. His was slapstick and, thanks to Grimaldi, who was not averse to stuffing his pockets with bunnies and geese, or floating above the stage on a wire to get a laugh, by the end of the nineteenth century pantomime had become very silly indeed.

Fortified by my pint and my ruminations, I left the pub and made for the seafront. Dusk was just creeping in when I reached the promenade and, in the distance, I could make out the Bristol Channel. A smear of brown, half-river, half-ocean, somewhere in the mud flats beyond the Grand Pier. The island of Steepholm crouched in the middle of it like a rabbit in a puddle, beyond it the squat disc of Flatholm and beyond that, Wales. I smelled the air, hoping for the tang of salt. There was a cloying smell of dough and fat coming from the doughnut shop at the entrance to the pier, and a reek of onions. All English seaside resorts are different, but all have one crucial thing in common. Sea. Frankly, this puts Weston on the margins. I wondered why people had ever come here.

When the fad for health-giving holidays by the sea began, Weston found itself a little out of the zeitgeist, until it came up with a novel solution. 'Come and get your mud,' the canny locals cried. 'Good for the skin and all that ails you.' And people came.

There were a few families still on the beach, well wrapped up as their children fiddled with the dirty sand, mud and donkey droppings. A pair of teenage boys were showing off to a girl among the grimy pier legs, slinging black silt at each other. The loudspeakers on the boardwalk were playing a tune from the twenties.

> Weston fair Weston, beautiful Weston
> Queen of the rolling sea
> Sunshine and pleasure, laugh at your leisure
> Restful to you and me.

The whole place was filled with an elegiac gloom, helped by the growing dusk. The dreary music, the murky beach, the drab fascias of hotels along the front. It started to spit with rain and a wind got up. I looked through the windows at the warm glow of empty lounges, last decorated in the seventies. Dour-faced barmen standing motionless, staring at the net curtains. The closer I got to the end of the pier, the louder came the electronic din echoing from its amusement arcade. A vast room filled with one-armed bandits, change machines and expressionless, shaven-headed men with earrings, having the kind of solitary, money-losing fun someone else had designed for them. I tried to imagine what a Christmas pantomime would be like here.

Of course, the first pantomimes weren't a Christmas speciality at all. They were the everyday bread and butter of competing theatres. Nor were they aimed, as they are now, at children – a fact demonstrated by the Grimaldi performance of *Harlequin and the Forty Virgins*, during which, it was reported, a dumb man regained the power of speech. Nor did they begin by telling folktales. Medieval romance and classical stories were the original fare. It wasn't until the turn of the nineteenth century that folk stories entered, when Grimaldi had one of his greatest successes with a production of *Mother Goose*. It ran and ran. On the back of this, other fairy tales such as *Jack and the Beanstalk* joined the fray, where they competed for prominence with stories and characters now obscure, such as Mother Bunch and Number Nip. *Beauty and the Beast; or, Harlequin and Old Mother Bunch*, played in 1869. A year later Handel composed the 'Mother Bunch Polka'. Sadly, it was Barry Handel the Englishman and not the celebrated composer.

During the nineteenth century, pantomime borrowed heavily from the comical song and dance routines of the music halls, which were rising in popularity. Singing stars of the day were added to the panto bills in a bid to draw ever-bigger crowds, bringing well-known songs with them. Rival performances of 'burlesques' in the unlicensed theatres gave pantomime two more crucial ingredients: topical satire and audience participation. Grimaldi was a master of the latter, singing bawdy songs with saucy words – such as 'gin' – left blank for the delighted audience to fill in. Amid this, poor old Harlequin was gradually phased out.

The Victorian era also saw the breeches gain in popularity. The curious streak of prudishness that has become synomymous with Victorian England forbade the showing of body parts. But didn't a nice pair of female legs look good in boys' trousers? This period also saw the entrance of the dame, a man in heavy, showy drag. It is interesting that this time, in which a decent fellow covered up a table leg for fear of corrupting the flesh, also gave rise to the notion that modern folklore was a relic of pagan fertility cults. The actual ancient Greek pagans were too busy with pantomime among the pillars to get involved in drums, fire and frenzied dances. Could it be that the Victorian embarrassment about sex and Frazer's barbaric heathens were somehow linked? Was it, in fact, man's fear that the beast within him was only ever one midnight dance away that drove the scholars to their ludicrous theories? Pantomime, during this period, became less bawdy and more family-oriented. The pieces were coming together.

I left the front and headed inland. Before long I found myself at the wrought iron gates of Grove Park. A sign said 'Public Convenience'. It had come at a convenient moment. But despite my need, nothing could have prepared me for the Grove Park public lavatory. The first thing I saw were the flowers. All around me, on every horizontal surface, were little vases, filled with gaudy, plastic flowers. No sooner had I spotted these than my eyes came to rest on a selection of posters of military aircraft, Blu-Tacked to the spotless walls. And that was not all. The planets of the solar system, a periodic table of the elements, articles from local papers, photographs, drawings, key rings, assorted kitsch: all were displayed, tied, hung and festooned from every available space. A cheerful, hazy light shone through the crystal-clear skylight windows and played coquettishly upon the flowers. A clean, citrus fragrance hung in the air.

I was dazzled. What a lovely place to linger and build an Airfix kit or start some knitting. Perhaps have some friends over.

A handwritten notice said all of this was the work of Pat and Iris, and invited the visitor to leave a tip. Another notice said the toilet had won awards. As I left Grove Park, with its sweeping grassy banks and dignified bandstand, and made for the Playhouse Theatre, I tried to imagine the award ceremony for Best Public Toilet and wondered why no TV network had had the vision to cover it.

According to the billboard outside the Playhouse, the big pull for *Jack and the Beanstalk* was 'International Film Star Antonio Fargas (Huggy Bear in *Starsky and Hutch*)'. He was to play a character called Fleshcreep, evil henchman of the evil giant.

The benign King George, I read on, was to be played by Paul Moriarty '(George Palmer from *EastEnders*)', and Katy Reeves '(Celeste from TV's *Down to Earth*)' was to appear as Katy Cucumber. On the poster she gripped a cucumber suggestively. Lower billings were given to 'TV's *Pot of Gold* comedian Paul Burling' as Simple Simon, to 'BBC Radio Devon's own Douglas Mounce' as Dame Durden, and to Daisy the Cow. The leading lady and gent did not even get a picture, but something else was amiss here: 'Direct from *Grease*,' Christopher Thatcher was to play Jack. What was this? A man playing the lead boy? Pantomime, I breathed to myself, is not what it used to be.

It never was, of course. The *Tatler* in 1831 complained: 'It is agreed on all hands that Pantomimes are not what they were.' But the form had been in a state of evolutionary flux from the outset. Given that panto – much like John Rich himself – had never had any artistic pretensions, its job had always been to please the masses. It had to move with the times or suffer the consequences. A production like that costs a lot of money. Sometimes, to draw the crowds, you have to make concessions. It was then that I noticed a logo in the top right corner of the poster. This production had been sponsored by Tesco.

Inside I was greeted by Brian Wiggins, who was front-of-house manager for the evening, working with his wife, Janet. Janet told me that their daughter, Sian, was stage-managing the production.

'It's her first proper job in theatre,' Janet said. 'She's on proper Equity rates.'

Another happy difference from the days of Rich. I took my seat as the lights dimmed and the house band struck up a rock version of 'Somewhere Over the Rainbow'.

Katy Cucumber was first on from stage right and introduced herself as the 'vegetable fairy'. Interesting. Next, Fargas appeared stage left as Fleshcreep.

'I will play my part with maximum street cred, to fill you all with dread,' he rasped. I could feel the dread mounting even as he spoke the lines, but he was taking no chances. Without pausing for breath, he launched into a performance of 'Don't Stop Moving to the Funky Funky Beat'. He was accompanied in this by the 'Pantomime Dancers: Children from the Tina Counsell School of Dance'. The girl on the end was spinning round the wrong way.

The King appeared.

'What would you say to a small port?' someone asked him.

'Hello Southampton,' he boomed.

If there was laughter it was drowned out by the sound of the drummer playing the international symbol for a punchline. Wait, there's more.

'I'm so poor my daughter was made in Taiwan!' Drums.

Kings are always broke in panto. That's the rule. Was it too much to hope that this could be an erudite reference to the Fisher King of medieval romance, the sick king ruling over his waste land? Could Jack be the Grail Knight, sent to restore health and prosperity? Could there be a link between the death and rebirth motifs of the mummers' plays and the panto? Could I be watching something that linked back directly to pre-Christian vegetation rites? Were we, the audience, participating in some kind of crop-related ceremony? Could pantomime, whatever it looks like now, could it really – *originally* – have been the mummers' play?

Well, clearly not, the history is all there. My imagination, like that of Jessie Weston who first made similar allegations, was running wild. True enough, the medieval romances formed the basis for all modern storytelling, but I was starting to see connections everywhere.

The dame came, a barrel-shaped vision, mincing in precariously with a large supermarket shopping trolley. Traditionally this has always been a wicker market basket, but times change. On the front end, surrounded by festive tinsel, was a large sign which read 'Shop at Tesco'. The dame manoeuvred the trolley so that the sign squarely faced the audience and addressed us.

'Hello, boys and girls. I've been doing some shopping, boys and girls. Yes, I've been to Tesco.' She then took various food products out of the trolley and threw them into the stalls. Traditionally this should really be a chicken and a necklace of carrots (allowing her to crack the joke 'this is eighteen carrot'), but a box of stock cubes from a three-for-two multi-buy offer will do.

The prosaic and the parochial, though, are both in keeping with pantomime's heritage. In 1843 the act forbidding the staging of commercial theatre without a royal patent was repealed. Drury Lane and Covent Garden no longer enjoyed exclusivity and pantomime theatres sprung up in all the London suburbs. These did well and by the beginning of the twentieth century, pantomime had spread to the provinces, finally reaching the coast and the burgeoning holiday trade where it mingled its juices with the variety numbers. It seems fair to assume that it was due to the increased competition that by 1919 only the Lyceum Theatre in London's West End was staging regular shows. Christmas specials had been a fixture for some time, but by the end of the nineteenth century, they appear to have become the rule.

During the twentieth century, pantomime became both slicker and tamer. Fewer and fewer characters were run through with red-hot pokers by Harlequin. And as the now standard repertoire of *Aladdin*, *Mother Goose*, *Dick Whittington*, *Cinderella*, *Puss in Boots* and others established the familiar stock roles of Buttons, Widow Twankey, Wishy-Washy, King Rat and the rest, the multicoloured buffoon was dropped altogether.

In the first half of the last century, pantomime was very much the province of variety perfomers and comics rather than actors. This really was the heyday of the form we know today. In the latter half of the 1900s, as variety entertainment dwindled in popularity, panto became seasonal work for TV presenters, Australian soap actors and the odd declining 'International Film Star'.

The Weston production was carried by Simple Simon – the clown, the Grimaldi figure. He kept up a constant battery of celebrity impressions and held the audience, even when heckled with 'You made my sister cry!' He assumed a craven expression.

'Under New Labour we will have a fantastic New Year,' he cried in a masterpiece of mimicry.

'Oh no we won't,' came the delighted response.

During the 'It's behind you' sequence – where each member of the beanstalk-climbing party was abducted in turn by a gorilla – Simple Simon kept up a pleasingly asinine version of 'Yellow Submarine' with the house band. A small boy in the audience was tearing out his hair. 'No, no, no,' he cried in despair as the clown foolishly missed yet another kidnapping through marching on the spot in his dungarees to the psychedelic sounds of yesteryear.

Finally the story was over and it was time for children to be summoned to the stage. Four tots were helped up to sing a verse each of 'Old MacDonald'.

'What's your name?' asked Simple Simon.

'Four,' replied a very small girl.

'It's OK, you can talk to me,' Simon said. 'I'm not a video.' All the kids got goody bags. 'You all know they come from Tesco, don't you,' Simon said.

'Yeerrrsst,' the audience chimed, and the pantomime was at an end.

Catholics and Protestants. Christians and pagans. Hinduism,

Islam, Judaism and Jedi. The range of beliefs in modern-day England is rich and diverse. In the past such plurality was divisive and dangerous. But shopping now unites us all in worship. Suddenly, at his curtain call, International Film Star Antonio Fargas made a very special speech. 'I wanna thank you all for carrying on your tradition,' he said. The crowd applauded. Praise be to Tesco. Give us this day our daily bread.

I got up to leave. I had decided not to look for mummers this Christmas, although this was the traditional time. The more I looked at the folk scene, the more I realized I was constantly watching revivals created by enthusiasts. The folk way was a lifestyle choice. It was one I enjoyed, one in which I felt at ease, but did it tell me much about my own roots? Folk song, dance and drama evolve. They're handed down from generation to generation, shaped and reshaped by natural selection. According to the tastes of the people. There was a reason why mummers' plays fell out of popular fashion while panto lives on. And the music hall was in my blood: my own roots were closer to pantomime than mummery. As I reached the foyer and picked up a programme of forthcoming events, I felt a presence at my side.

'That man Starsky Hutch telly,' said a large woman with drool at the side of her mouth.

'Yes,' I said.

She gripped my arm.

'It's the same,' she cried. 'The same.' Her eyes had gone very wide.

As I burst out past Brian and Janet Wiggins into the brisk

December night, the woman was still calling after me. 'The same
. . . The same . . .'

There was frost on the ground as I made my way to the party and
my bicycle wheels crunched over little frozen puddles. It was a
clear, dark night. The stars were out and one shone brighter than
the rest as I reached my destination, a humble terraced house near
the seafront. Before the rise of Christianity, December was still for
some a time to celebrate a special birthday – that of the sun. It was
the winter solstice, when the nights began to grow shorter. The
sun was returning: a time for new beginnings. Pagans, in at least
some parts of the world, it seems, celebrated the event with lights.
The practice appealed to the Roman emperor Aurelius, who made
sun-worship an official cult. As such it spread across the empire,
only losing favour in 323 CE, when the incumbent emperor
Constantine converted to Christianity. There's little evidence to
suggest a definite sun cult in the British Isles. More widespread
was the decorative use of greenery in midwinter, the decking of
halls with boughs of holly.

Inside the house, Bob was having trouble with Holly, his dog.
Well, strictly speaking, it wasn't his problem. The thing was, she
was perfectly well trained, but if you put food down on the floor
she assumed she was being fed. So, if the woman who was now
suggesting through pursed lips that it was ill-mannered of 'someone' to have brought a dog along to a party where food was being
served was frankly stupid enough to put her food on the floor, she
deserved all she got.

I liked Bob. He used to live round here, ran a pub in Somerset up on the Mendip Hills. He had the lilting voice to go with it and said 'zider' for 'cider'. Now he lived up in the Forest of Dean with his wife, Tess. But they came back for these folk sessions at Dave's.

Dave played banjo in a folk band in Weston. Every year he had these parties. People came and the music struck up in an informal way, people taking turns when it suited them. The time I'd put in with the Greensleeves Morris had paid off and the melodeon and I were now friends. I took part. The music belonged to me too. Dave had made pizza. Good pizza. Holly the dog had loved it.

In between jigs, reels and songs I got talking to Tess. I told her about my search for English roots. I told her how one thing had led me to another, how dressing as a horse and wearing bells had seen me denounced as a heathen, how the green man had chuckled at this in the pub in Adderbury and how I now needed to find a connection to the land. Could I really make a link between folklore and pagan fertility rites, or was it all just the mitherings of a group of self-hating Victorians traumatized by their own sexuality? Was there an answer? People are scared of getting close to what they need. That's what I'd heard Mike Gilpin say, back in Swaffham. The phrase kept reverberating. Tess said she might be able to help. She said I should visit her up in the Forest. I said I would.

Suddenly a song struck up.

'Let's have a wassail,' someone said.

Wassail. Wasael? The word Ron Shuttleworth had used.

Hearing it, I knew where I had to go next.

17 | Every Twig, Apples Big

Passing through Bridgwater has never been the same for me since the disappearance of British Cellophane. I don't know if the factory management had a row with Quality Street or what happened, but it seems that suddenly the bottom fell out of the market for see-through coloured plastic wrappers and that was it. Never more would the picturesque, if lost, Somerset town of Bridgwater smell like a pit full of dead things.

Somehow I find the loss of the smell just as sad as its presence. In its heyday the odour was an all-pervading *bête noire*, a guilty deed that hung heavy in the atmosphere staining all hope, a curse that almost certainly influenced the creation of at least one bypass. And now, it's just another fading memory of the glory days, like the peeling stucco on Weston seafront. It's as though all those nostrils bridled for nothing, all those lungs objected in vain. If decades of olfactory punishment and forbearance can't at least result in worldwide recognition for shiny plastic, what is it all for? I ask you. I must have made the same trip hundreds of times when I lived in these parts. Fleeing the city. Its alienating hum. Now I'm here again, on a different sort of journey, and I wonder if I have much further to go. I stop the bike and drink in the air. It's sweet, and the wind shakes the rushes. Time to move on.

The chain ticks and the wind squeaks. Cecil Sharp chased his gypsies around here, desperate to give a photograph to a travelling woman, to give something back. It's cold today, though the sun is out and the sky is clear. I round a corner and smell the sea. The Bristol Channel lurks at the foot of a hill, a grey warning. At Kilve I veer off onto the sea path, past the tail end of the hunt, the men in their red finery, the hounds still sniffing hopefully among the boulders. This stretch of Somerset coastline is brutal. The land falls away into the water with a sense of ill grace and temper, giant boulders and sheets of flat rock the only real beach. I reach the little port of Watchet at about three, ready for some food, and try my luck in a pub. But they won't serve until six. The one customer at the bar is staring at me and for once I don't feel like talking, so I move out to the back and watch a family walk along the harbour wall, hair blowing in the wind. I count about seven different signs around the water's edge warning of the imminent end of the land. 'Caution: Sea's Edge'. 'Warning: Do Not Climb On Rocks'. I think just one would suffice: 'The End of the World Is Nigh'. But my favourite is on the slipway, itself an architectural device named for its function. The sign says 'Danger: Slippery Surface'. With all these potential hazards and nothing to protect us for all those centuries, I wonder how we ever evolved far enough to invent the signpost.

Next door, in Skipper's restaurant, I hunker down with a copy of *Vogue* magazine from the summer of 2002 opposite a gas heater, two of its three bars glowing pink and orange. Beyond me, at a table covered with baskets of ceramic tiles, a portable television and a giant, cured pig's trotter, sits an old woman with a book in her hand and a dog at her feet. The golden retriever is called Max and he looks up with a lopsided grin, tongue lolling. The warmth causes the moist air to condense on the windows in a thick fog. The only other diners sit beyond a partition of shelving and spider plants, a young couple talking in polite, distant tones, kindling a relationship or fanning its embers to the slightly gloomy sound of the Chopin nocturne coming from the kitchen. For £5.95 I could have cod and chips. For £6.95 I could order one of the garish, over-saturated photographic prints of the local coastline that are Blu-Tacked to the walls. I like Skipper's restaurant. It feels like someone's home. A man appears. I order lasagne and coffee, and when it comes, still bubbling from the grill, it warms me enough to give me courage.

Out on the beach, I walk over the loose rubble and flat rocks onto a plateau of coarse sand. My feet sink and water fills the cavities. I walk a while towards Minehead Point, way off in the distance, and watch the sun go down over the headland, throwing up streaks of mauve and orange. Somewhere between here and there, tonight, in a dark orchard, we're going to bless the sleeping apple trees that they might bear fruit another year.

Well, I tell a lie, we're going to wassail them.

Wassailing. It's about time I got to it and now, 'old twelfth eve', is just the time to do it. It's 17 January and a short ride inland takes me to the tiny village of Carhampton – pronounced 'Cramped 'un' – and more specifically to the Butcher's Arms pub. I've come here because Carhampton claims to have the oldest unbroken was-sailing tradition in England. The word wassail comes from the Anglo-Saxon words *waes* and *hael*, meaning good health. Wassail is a word to cheer as you pass a bowl of drink among friends, a toast. Hael – like Hele, the Giant at Cerne Abbas. It's the oldest of words. It's 'hale', it's 'health'. We're going to drink the orchard's good health. And doesn't this surely imply a connection? From ancient to modern? A direct link? I feel as if things are accelerating and coagulating. As though I'm approaching a breakthrough. Can't we believe that the wassailing of trees is, because of its name, genuinely descended from a pagan ritual? Aren't we getting some-where finally?

Historians seem to agree that the word does indeed precede Christianity, although the earliest records of the activity come much later. The wassailing of fruit trees is first recorded at St Albans in 1486 and then at Fordwich in Kent in 1585. Historians note that the custom at this time was already being performed as a service by freelance wassailers, for money, drink or food. It crops up again in the writings of Robert Herrick. He describes the wassailing of fruit trees in Devon to procure a good harvest. John Aubrey completes this early picture, noting the placing of toast on the roots of trees in the West Country. By the eighteenth century, writers were recording the words of wassailing songs performed at the ceremonies: hatfuls, capfuls, three bushel bag-fuls. There were multiple variants but all cropped up around the West Country – Devon and Cornwall – and the south of England. The period after Christmas was the favourite time, and following the introduction of the Gregorian calendar some local wassailing traditions found themselves eleven-day-shifted into the middle of January. 'Old' Twelfth Night, for example. Some doused the trees with beer or cider, others fired guns. Some did both and more in return for good food and drink.

On the subject of drink, in these parts cloudy, flat cider is the order of the day and as I get some in the first of the musicians strikes up. He's playing a melodeon, of course, and soon others arrive, sitting around in a circle. I've carried mine on my back, so I join in and get talking to a man next to me. He and his wife are staying here at the pub. They've come especially.

'We're trying to get out to some of the traditions,' he says. 'We've known about this for ages and finally we've come.' He joins in on the tin whistle. On his lap he has a rolled-up canvas carrier filled with whistles in every key. He's not going to be caught out. The music thumps and there's not an amplifier in sight. In a few months all this will be illegal. I hear Dorset reels, cider-drinking songs, morris dances: English music. I recognize some of the tunes now and busk those I don't. When the session lulls I venture a few sets of dances and the others join in. It's seamless. No one would guess that a year before I wouldn't have known where to find such folk tunes, hadn't so much as touched a melodeon or felt the shadow of a morris dance stir within me. Now I feel they are as much mine as anyone else's and love them all the more for that. It's vigorous, buoyant music with a sound all of its own. And like everything else I've seen this year, you could just as easily go to the other pub, the quiet one in the other part of the village, and be none the wiser. It's a subculture, a fantastic, living, evolving subculture, which belongs to the English and to which the English, whether they recognize it or not, belong.

I begin to glow with a warm sense of belonging myself. Though the English tunes provide a focal point for this feeling, my joyous experience of community has more to do with letting go. Music has been a part of me since I was a child, but the mechanics of sharing that music have never been easy for me. I have always been driven by a fundamental urge to exhibit what I have created, to watch it inspire people to laugh, sing or dance. But the act of mounting a stage to perform creates an odd division between the performer and the audience. It is as though by climbing up above your peers you simultaneously seek and consent to this division and to the unbearable scrutiny that must follow. The complex politics of approval-seeking claim that experience and applause is the tool with which you measure your worth to the wider community. Such a division makes no real sense to me, which I suspect is why I have never felt at ease on stage. I become paralysed by the sense of being watched too closely and, despite the mask of a costume or a stage persona, I fail to open up and let the music out freely. Instead, I become trapped inside myself, a prisoner still of my own inhibition. But here, in the round among these folk musicians, no one is watching me especially. They play along, some dance or tap their feet. But I'm just a bloke in a pub, no different from them. The effect this has on me is at once overwhelming and deeply reassuring. It's an honest connection, a direct bond between equals, and it is interesting that this is happening to me here in the West Country. It's the place in which, earlier in my life, I failed to make the necessary connections, failed to become 'no different' from my neighbours: a place in which I was always effectively on stage.

At eight, a man with a shotgun appears and marches through the bar. People get up and follow him and, for want of a better plan, so do I. Outside we go, round the back and into the orchard. In truth, 'orchard' is a bit strong a term for the apple tree that squats sheepishly in the garden, but, someone is telling me, it did use to *really* be an actual orchard. In the old days. You know, *originally*. Frankly, I don't care, because the landlord has just given me a cup of home-made warm cider, mulled with ginger, and I cup the spicy drink in my hands, enjoying the heat from the bonfire as it singes my whiskers. Sparks are flying off the blaze of old pallets towards the top of the field where the men with guns stand poised.

> Hat fulls, cap fulls, three bushel bag fulls,
> And a little 'eap under the stairs . . .

When the song is finished there is a volley of shots and the singing begins again. The guns are fired after every song, to ward off maggots, worms, agues and spirits, so the locals are saying.

'We're going to douse the roots with cider now,' says the old boy who led the singing. 'We didn't want to waste any, though, so we've drunk it first.' The crowd chuckles at the gag. The men soak slices of toast in cider and pin them to the tree. Then, more singing. Strong, tuneful singing, in four-part harmony. It's impressive. To think it has been handed down from father to son.

'Well, of course,' a lady is saying to a friend behind me, 'it's an old pagan ritual *really*.' I turn to listen. 'Like all of these customs, it *was* a fertility rite originally.' There's Frazer again. How he persists. But could he be right this time, if you live in the country and you bless a tree in the hope that it will bear fruit? And since pagan really only means 'peasant' are you not performing a pagan fertility rite?

But the really important thing is not its antiquity, but simply that it is done. A tradition performed by people from the village, passed down from one generation to another. Isn't it? I sit down again inside. The chap next to me wants to try my melodeon so I lend it him.

'Carhampton man?' I ask, casually.

'Taunton,' he says. 'Shh, don't say it too loud. You?'

'Bristol,' I say, a little surprised to hear the word come from my mouth.

'Oh, that's even worse. My condolences.'

'Yes. The others here, though,' I gesture towards the musicians. 'They're local, right?'

'Well, that lot at the bar might be . . .' I turn around. The pub is crammed now. Packed. A solid mass of heaving people. The musicians, though, are bunched together, hemmed into a corner, playing in the round. They make a loud noise and the drinkers are singing along. Pints are spilled, chaos reigns. '. . . but this lot here are from the Minehead Hobby Horse.'

The Minehead Hobby Horse?

The folk revival.

By the early part of the nineteenth century the custom of wassailing had begun to disappear from England. It had had its day. It vanished from most of the country and, eventually, from the west. Gone. Historians note attempts at revivals in Devon in the 1920s, but none stuck. Only here in Somerset has the revival taken root. The Carhampton 'rite' has now become a fixture, as has a similar event hosted by the Taunton brewery, the people who make the unremarkable Blackthorn cider for mass consumption. One historian writes somewhat concisely of the Carhampton wassailing that 'the folk singing afterwards is well performed and the friendliness of the atmosphere notable'. He also notes usefully that the rhyme – hat fulls, cap fulls – is the standard version that was printed in 1813 and widely disseminated. The custom of wassailing in Carhampton is not an unbroken tradition but a definite revival. Revival yes, tradition nonetheless.

They're a great crowd and they know how to play. Despite my enthusiasm, I can't help but feel a bit let down intellectually by the fact that I'm still dealing to some extent with the folk revival mafia, the legacy of Ewan MacColl, Martin Carthy, Fairport Convention and the rest. But this disappointment is a little shallow. In the search for authenticity, then, only an unbroken tradition will do. But the truth is that a growing number of modern people are recognizing that the ancient custom makes sense to them today. New wassails are beginning all the time in people's back gardens or public places.

People travel here from the surrounding towns and villages to keep up this tradition, lest it fade. In the old days wassailers were itinerant too. I can't work out whether it matters or not. I can't work out if it means anything to be 'authentic'. Does a tradition have to be unbroken to mean something? Can't an act or an event connect you with the land somehow, with truth, with nature, even if we make it up right now? The significance of rites like wassailing has passed out of our daily lives because, despite the best efforts of CAMRA, cider like Blackthorn comes in cans from Tesco. Customs like this don't survive on their own because now we can buy own-brand 'Value Cider' in four-packs and bleep it onto our loyalty card, earning valuable points to be redeemed against future food and lifestyle purchases. Cash in our credit for a Dido CD, some batteries or a 'Finest'-range Tiramisu. We're not peasants any more, any of us. We do different things.

'See that man there?' the man with my squeezebox points to a diminutive fellow playing a tin whistle in the corner, as though butter wouldn't melt.

'I see him – '

'Inland Revenue adviser to the Cabinet.' He raises his eyebrows at me, as if to say, 'Not a lot of people know that . . .'

I like the wassail. It makes sense to me. It makes sense to bless the land, to take care of it. It makes sense to build a rapport with the land. But it doesn't go deep enough for me. It doesn't answer enough questions. I've been picking at this question of pagan rites for so long, this question of fertility and life regenerating, without ever coming close to the source. Isn't it time I just bit the bullet and asked the pagans? Clearly. But to do that I have to do something they don't much care for around here.

I have to go – as they say round these parts – 'over the bridge'.

18 | Catkins

Two minutes after the Severn Bridge touches down on the marshy estuarine flats of Gwent you whizz past a comely sign with a red dragon welcoming you to Wales. 'Croeso y Cymru'. It's a nice feeling: England on one side of Britain's longest river, Wales and all its glory on the other. There's a sense of having crossed a divide, of having left something behind and gained something new. Then, two minutes down the hill out of Chepstow, you pass another sign, welcoming you to England. It's an anomaly: cross the tiny River Wye and the Offa's Dyke path that forms the border and you find yourself in a strange no-man's land, the isolated Gloucestershire backwater that is the Forest of Dean. Cut off from its grown-up siblings of Cheltenham and Gloucester by the vast flood, the forest, along with its few rude settlements, is closer to Wales and its ways than much of England. It's an appropriate place to meet England's druids.

The weather has not been on my side. February arrived with a freezing vengeance. As I passed through Weston again on my way up the coast, high winds nearly had me in the sea. I take everything back. Weston-super-Mare at winter high tide with a gale behind is not to be mocked. The waves were over the houses at Anchor Head, the water slate-grey and deadly, the sky dark with menace. One false footing, a slip of the pedal, and you'd become part of the sea, returned to earth in an instant, one again with the elements. It's a sobering thought. Now, as I cross the Severn, listing badly in the jostling air currents, struggling for breath, it begins to spit with rain again. I'm hot and wet and cold, all at once, and the silhouettes of barren trees jut out of the soil as I make my way up the Lydney road. Ravens perch high in a tree, watching, croaking. They echo across the dead fields. I'm sick of it. It's been miserable for weeks and it seems like winter is never going to end.

But it is precisely this need that is driving me into the forest. There are people here who I think can help me. We're meeting under the ground, below the earth. A year ago I would not have done this, I wouldn't have known it could even be done, but one connection has led to another. This is the thing. If you start asking, really seeking, people start telling. Doors open. And everything so far seems to have been gently but firmly nudging me towards this.

The rain eases up as I reach Milkwall and the little grey house that is my first stop. Holly the dog barks and Tess comes out to meet me, grinning. On the porch there is a slate that reads 'Merry Meet, Merry Part and Merry Meet Again'. Odd language. It's warm inside and there's coffee. Bob bounds down with maps and books; there's so much of the forest he wants to show me, but we'll only have time to see a bit today. Holly is excited so I rub her ears manically to calm her down. Tess's friend Siggy appears with a guitar. Tess gets out her fiddle and it's clear they're not going to let me go anywhere without swapping some tunes. So I take out my melodeon and start to play the 'Shepherd's Hey' to warm us up. A few months ago I didn't even know the tune, but it seems to belong to me now. It trips out of the squeezebox as if it were the most natural thing on earth.

'Ooh,' sighs Siggy. 'That one always makes me think of summer and morris men.' Me too. I look into the damp garden to examine the weather. There's a pentagram on the fence, the five-pointed star that marks out the magician, made from twigs, with foliage around it. There's also a foliate head, or green man, peeping out from the border hedge, and a small altar on the patio. I want to ask about them but we're busy with the music. The two women are teaching me a Wiltshire six-hand reel and a rollicking version of 'Constant Billy'. It's good to sit and play these tunes. They come quickly to my fingers now. I suppose I've heard them so many times on my travels that, by osmosis, they are already in me. My own repertoire is not so wide, so I teach Tess and Siggy two jigs I wrote myself. The first I call 'London Fields', named after a dismal park in Hackney. The second I call 'The Dog Rose', after a well-known weed. They like the jigs and record them on a rickety old cassette player. They plan to learn them. I don't tell them I wrote the tunes. I like the idea of releasing them into the wild, into the oral tradition. If I'm lucky someone will pick them up from Tess's fiddle and play them somewhere else. That's how it works. It's a form of natural selection. The best tunes persist. And persist. I wonder how far mine will get.

We're having fun and we could go on, but Bob and Holly are getting restless for the wood so we pull on our hats and take off. Bob leads me over the road, down a rough path bordered with bramble and sleeping bracken. The ground is wet as we walk over leaves, twigs and patches of grass. Bob points to a few dark bricks, peeping out of the undergrowth.

'This used to be the Milkwall station,' he says. 'That's where the platform was, see there?' There's only the faintest hint but you can just make out where the building had been. 'This was the track.'

'What, here?' There's only a grassy path with a fast-running, foot-wide brook.

'Yup.' Bob's happy. He's grinning and talks nineteen to the dozen. He's been happy since he moved up here. He used to work for the electricity. But they kept cutting and cutting. In the end he was doing everyone's job. In the end he had had enough and quit. He came up here for some peace. Sometimes he spends all day out here, up and out at nine with Holly, back in the evening. The forest is such that you can take off in any direction, walk for miles and always come home by another route. 'Look, they've pulled out some of the old sleepers there and used them as part of a fence.' It's true. You can see how the forest is creeping over the old stones, reclaiming itself, clawing back the land from us.

'When you've had buildings go, the first things to grow back are the bracken and the brambles,' Bob says, full of glee. 'Then you get the silver birch.' We come to a clearing and Bob points to a collection of old, broken stone walls across the other side of a ditch. The forest is all over it, the rust colour of the bracken and the mauve fuzz of the birch meld together with hanging catkins, while ivy has claimed the stones.

Birds flit in and out of the branches. Long ago, during the Industrial Revolution, this site used to be Darkhill Ironworks. It was where Robert Mushet, the pioneering metallurgist, discovered how to make steel from iron ore. The age of steel, and all it made possible, began here under the briars, another level down in the earth, in another age. There were iron ore mines all over this area, the cavities are still there, deep below the forest floor. Railways took stone and ore from one place to another. It had been an industrial hot spot. A busy place of progress, technology and competition. Mushet, afraid rivals might steal his secret, hid the slag from his mines under great piles of rocks. Now trees grow out of the cracks, and bracken covers them, but if you push the leaves aside you can see the dark, bubbly waste, hidden under the forest. Sometimes you see a lump of floating rock in a stream. The sudden sight of one takes me back in memory to a Cub Scout camp in nearby Parkend, a school trip to Biblins on the Wye, family days out at Symonds Yat: happy summer days along the valley which seem a very long time ago.

We stumble over tramlines, partially submerged in the soil. There were tracks all over the area once. Now the Strategic Rail Authority is reducing 'services' to Lydney. The forest is more cut off than ever. On the way back we stumble across an old boiler, covered in rivets. It's broken, in fragments, with only an edge here and there poking out of the foliage. The bracken has claimed the rest, made a nest, a soft mound you can walk on. A floor. Soon the birches will grow, their roots gradually meshing and trapping the metal underground. Bob points to a dark hole in the underbrush. When I look closer I can see it's the very top of a stone archway. The forest has risen up, cutting it off. I peep in and see water filling up the cavity. It used to be the entrance to a mine. The floor I'm standing on is spongy. Just leaves and twigs, layer upon layer.

We make it back to the house in time for lunch. Tess and Bob take care to find local food from organic farmers, they say. It feels like the right thing to do. They've built a massive Tesco at Lydney, but Tess and Bob have revolted. It's good food and Bob takes out a couple of bottles of Gold Miner, a stunning beer brewed in the forest. I'm ready to fall asleep, but there's no time for that. It's time for something else.

It's time for me to wear snowdrops and catkins, join a group of witches, and call in the spring from an underground cavern.

No rest for the wicked.

Tess and Siggy lead me over the wood. I'm wearing the flowers in my bobble hat. I realize that part of me feels mildly silly. But it's the bobble hat part. The catkins part of me feels perfectly at ease. I'm in the forest. I'm wearing the forest. I've accessorized the forest. What could be more natural? We're walking across the bracken, along paths only Tess can see. Everything is moist. There's something in the air, like a feeling. I confess to Tess that I don't really know what to expect.

'Nor do I really,' she explains. 'We've never come to a big group event before, we usually just do things on our own.' Today's ceremony is largely the work of someone called Veronica, I learn.

She's the new head of the Gloucester branch of the Pagan Federation. 'They used to do it all in Cheltenham. It's so good that they've come over to us for this. You don't feel so cut off.' Committees, committees. It's the human condition. The ancient druids were hierarchical. Hierarchies are in nature, in the variations of species, the orders of animals. You can't escape it.

I'm thrashing stray brambles out of my path as Tess is telling me about Oimelc. Pronounced 'Immulk'. 'It's a Celtic celebration. It's about the first stirrings of spring,' she says. 'About the turn. We're not at spring yet, but things are turning. The first flower to push through is the snowdrop.' The French call it *perce-neige*, the snow piercer. 'The invite said it was robes optional,' says Tess. So we are hedging our bets – literally – by wearing plant life. 'They *did* say it's going to take an hour and a half,' Tess says, a little warily. 'I can't think for the life of me what they can do that's going to take an hour and a half.'

Nor I.

Finally we reach Clearwell Caves. Not really caves but old mines. They are mostly out of service, but Ray, who owns them, has kept them as they were. You can see him striding purposefully about the clay floors, head-torch beaming from his hard hat. It's a tourist attraction, Forest of Dean style. That's to say, low key. They charge you £4 to get in and leave you to it.

There are a few people milling about outside, wearing pentangles, clearly our people. One young woman, slow of voice, is telling Tess what she knows about the day's event. 'Well, I think we're all going to get in a circle and, you know, if the spirit takes you . . .' A bit like a Quaker meeting, then. Only robes optional. And with catkins. I can't wait.

But wait I must. It's half an hour before the ceremony is due to begin and various key people have yet to appear. There's still no sign of the 'minstrel', who appears to have got snarled up in traffic. Bob arrives and we stride off down the wet paths, underground. He's telling me that they still pull out the odd bit of stone. 'It's mostly for new houses, if they want to use local stone,' he says.

We come to a halt in a small hollow. People are greeting each other, taking off coats, putting on robes. Some robes are white, like ecclesiastical surplices. Others are clearly props from *The Lord of the Rings*. A hooded girl carrying a tea light close to her face walks past me. A small, energetic man with a handlebar moustache, bald head and an impressive robe and staff is buzzing about. 'Nearly ready,' he's saying. There's something round the corner. Something we're not supposed to see yet. We're supposed to wait here, but I can't help myself. I sneak round the bend.

I see a wide, circular cavern, lit by hundreds of candles, each stuck to the rock face with its own wax. The little lights give the impression of tiny hollows in the stone. In the centre of the circle is a small altar. I'm transfixed. I don't know how long I stand there, but little by little people join me. Soon there's a crowd. A tall man with long grey hair appears in a cloak. He's holding a staff. He is clearly Gandalf taking a break from his film commitments. A broad woman with frizzy grey hair approaches him. She's wearing a white robe with a green design on the front. She also wears a kind of beatific smile, like Mother Earth. She's Veronica, archdruid of the Cotswold Druidic Order and head of the Gloucester branch of the Pagan Federation. A committee leader.

'Keeper of the portal,' she addresses the man. She asks him to let us 'in'.

'By what right?' he asks.

'By the right of our ancestors,' she replies. He lowers his staff.

'Enter.'

Strictly speaking we could have gone in anyway, having paid our £4, but I gather such freelancing would not have been entirely holy. So one by one we file in after Veronica, describing a circle clockwise on the cavern floor. Four robed figures have taken position at each quarter of the circle. There must be about thirty of us.

Us, yes. We're in this together.

We stand in the circle, in the candlelight.

And wait.

19 | Robes Optional

I'm not sure what we're waiting for. But I'm anxious to get on with it. Not least because, now that my eyes have become accustomed to the gloaming, I have spied a raffia tray full of flapjack on the floor near the altar and I'm certain that one piece has my name on it. But Veronica says we can't begin until there is peace in all four quarters of the earth. I get the feeling we'll be here a long time.

'Peace in the east,' she calls.

'There is peace in the east,' comes the confident response from a young man in a white robe. Hasn't he read the papers? In the desert formerly known as the Holy Land the squabbling territorial battles that form the basis of the entire Old Testament rage on. It was supposed to be about gods then, but it's really an argument without end: who owns the land? It's an understatement to say there is unrest in the East. But it's not just a battle of religions any more. Western capitalism has taken on Eastern spirituality. The quest for that holiest of grails, oil – the salt of the earth – has met with resistance from religious tradition. And East is meeting West with all the fury and terror the holy scriptures can offer. We're all drawn in. We're all affected. There's a quickening, a coagulation.

A globalization. It's not enough to rule your country any more, leaders want to rule the world. And it's no longer the bravest who prevails. It's the richest. The oiliest. Since religious terrorists from the East dared to smite America we have watched the grisly crusades of a damaged leader who, wounded, lashes out. A sick king, sitting amid his ruins, fishing. For what, we do not know. Enlightenment, like peace, is still a long, long way off.

But I realize Veronica's gesture is symbolic. Forget the turmoil our leaders have created for us – we are to be at peace within ourselves.

Frankly, that could take a little longer.

In a flash, I understand the pull of religion. Any religion. Any system that exchanges ritual and prayers for inner peace is clearly working in our favour. Those who work against it are clearly as afraid as those who use it to justify their terror. In truth, it's less like a flash and more like a thatched roof giving way to the elements.

Earth, water, fire and air. Return, return, return, return.
Earth, water, fire and air. Return, return, return, return.
Earth, water, fire and air. Return, return, return, return.

Back in the grotto, Geoff and Dave, the two high priests of the Coven of the Sacred Wellhead, are leading a chant. 'Earth, water, fire and air . . .' We all join in. All except one man with a haversack who, having paid his £4 to potter around the caves, has clearly seen more than he cares to.

'What *is* this?' he spits, leaving the circle and making for the dark, narrow tunnel that leads back up to daylight. I don't blame him. We're a hundred feet below the surface of the earth in a damp hollow flickering with candles. Many are wearing robes and those of us who are not have attached plants to ourselves. Some are hooded and at least one is dressed as Gandalf, his long mane glinting in the candlelight. There are occult symbols, a crystal ball, an altar and an awful lot of flapjack. Put it all together and your imagination can do the rest.

And what fuels such imagination?

In order to succeed and survive, as indeed it did, Christianity had to make a damned fine job of scaring us against magic, or at least against such magic as was carried on outside the Church. In truth, medieval Christianity employed a raft of magical symbols and rites. Holy water, consecrated candles, the blessing of medallions and icons. These were all believed to ward off evil. Even Sir Gawain painted a pentangle on his shield before setting off on his quest to tackle the Green Knight. To him the five points of the star represented the five wounds of Jesus. The point was that if magic took place within the Church then it was safe and good – a burning bush here, a parting of the Red Sea there. But if it took place outside the Church, then logically it had to be evil, as the Church had registered good as its exclusive trademark. In the case of Christianity, evil took only one form: Satan, who had been created by God and allowed to exist as a tempter. Evil in the world was the work and domain of this devil, and it followed that those who practised magic in defiance of the Church had to be in the service of Satan. Hence the persecution and execution of 'witches'.

A few hundred years ago I would have been burned or drowned or hanged, or all three, for partaking of the oat-based snack in the company of magicians – no question. The last execution for witchcraft was as recent as 1712, the year the piston engine was invented.

And I dare say the gentleman who is now heading swiftly for the exit, his rucksack bobbing on his back as the candlelight casts long shadows on the rock face, is thinking along similar lines to the medieval Christians. He probably thinks he's stumbled upon a bunch of satanists. But he needn't be quite so alarmed. Modern paganism and the worship of Satan have no connection. Satan is a creation of the Christian faith and paganism rejects the Christian faith. There may be some willing to assert that flapjack is the devil's oatmeal, but this group is not among them.

Modern paganism is really a group of relatively new religions, based on ancient religions, which worship female gods. Pagans believe the natural world is divine in itself. In other words, God in heaven didn't create nature in seven days or less; rather, the goddess is nature. Mother Earth. They are pacifists and they all identify with the pre-Christian religions of Europe. By definition, a pagan can't be a satanist.

So, as I stand hand in hand with witches, I feel no apprehension. I'm helped in this, though, by a general shift in attitude towards the witch, begun in the nineteenth century. The liberals and socialists of the period that produced the search for Merrie England, the early folklore collectors and Frazer's The Golden Bough, also helpfully redefined witches for later use. They believed the old hags persecuted in medieval times were actually practising a life-affirming pre-Christian religion which had survived unbroken. The intellectuals reshaped 'witches', turning them into role models who resisted the power of the squirearchy and the Christian Church. From this it is easy to see why, for example, the anti-capitalist movement of today is so keen to identify May Day with an ancient pagan celebration. To those who looked to paganism as something organic and vital, linking them with the timeless goodness of the land, something ancient, rooted and sound – and to those who saw in folklore customs the remnants of a fertility cult that bound humanity to its ancestors and its environment – the witch was a friend.

The oldest and best known of the modern crop of pagan faiths is Wicca. Wicca is a magical religion. It worships a goddess of the earth and the night sky and a male god with antlers. The figure of the witch is central to Wicca, as it believes 'witches' were in fact the priestesses and priests of the religion.

But what is Wicca? The word is an old English term for wizard, and the religion was brought to market by a retired customs officer called Gerald Gardner, who claimed to have stumbled across it in Hampshire. He maintained that he had found a surviving strain of benign medieval witchcraft. From about 1950, Gardner became the publicist for a fertility religion based on this 'find', which came to be called Wicca and for which he composed spells and rituals. The rites of Wicca are linked with the seasonal cycles and the phases of the moon. Magic – or *magick* as Wiccans prefer to render it – is seen as a force for good. Despite Gardner's claims of an ancient find, there is no evidence to suggest that Wicca pre-dates him. That is to say, it's always possible that he invented it.

In fact, there's no evidence for any unbroken pagan religions in Britain, but, in contrast, there is a lot of evidence that paganism has been revived. The roots of the revival show themselves around 1800, in the Romantic period, blossoming into a continuous tradition by the middle of the twentieth century. But how are such religions 'revived'? The truth is that historians know almost nothing about the pre-Christian religions of the British Isles. Modern pagans have had to make it up.

Druidry is another invented pagan religion which focuses on the figure of the ancient soothsayer of north-west Europe. Not knowing much about the real druids, those who now identify with them have had to recast them to some extent. Since that reinvention, the druid has been viewed as a pacifist and a seer, both mystic and earth-centred. A wise person and a leader in both religion and magic. Or *magick*. I know all this because on my way here I visited Ronald Hutton, a historian and the world authority on modern British paganism.

'We don't know anything about the beliefs and rites of the ancient druids,' Professor Hutton told me, his long mane of hair glinting in the afternoon sun, 'because the druids left no writings – *deliberately*.'

Deliberately?

How could he possibly know that? . . .

•

I don't know about magic. Paul Daniels rather put me off it. But however you feel about the idea of witchcraft, whether you are open to it or not, calling the spring is nothing sinister. It's something I have been doing anyway, in my own way, ever since winter set in. Winter's long. We all call out for spring, whether we do it out loud or not.

But here in the earth, Geoff and Dave, Cheltenham's only all-gay witchy couple, are taking it to extremes. They are swaying from side to side, swinging their arms high in a kind of fervent disco dance, their shadows dancing on the walls as we chant. They're calling for the end of winter, the end of the barren, dead land and a return to sense and reason, to warmth, life and understanding.

I can't quite bring myself to join in with the disco swaying, indeed few can. But I have no problem joining Geoff and Dave in their call. It makes perfect sense. I feel safer here, inside the ground, inside nature with these beneficent loons than I do outside, in civilization, under the protective wing of my insane political leaders.

Veronica, the second woman I've met today with unusually slow diction, explains that Oimelc is a celebration to mark the turning of the seasons. She says the symbol of Oimelc is the snow-drop. It makes sense, they're just peeping through. But who says so? History only records the name of the festival, in an Irish story, and the meaning of that is the subject of debate. Historians tell us we can assume the festival pre-dated Christianity. But after that we're on our own. There are no clues as to the rites that were

practised at that time. We don't know whether it was really – you know, *originally* – meant to mark the beginning of spring.

Next, the 'talking stick' is passed around the circle. Each person takes the staff and is expected to address the circle with whatever they wish to share. Some wish the group a 'happy Oimelc'. Some trot out inspirational words. Tess and Siggy sing a duet, a Welsh song about miners. Tess has always wanted to sing it underground and this is the perfect moment. One man contemplates the stick for an age, then mumbles something incomprehensible, to which he is answered 'Blessed be' by a multitude of voices.

A man in an Australian bush hat vents an Eastern 'purification mantra', for which he is granted a 'Blessed be'. The woman I met outside the cave chooses to lope about the centre of the circle shaking a rattle while moaning ecstatically, to wake up the spirits. There are a few indulgent titters, but that's fine. 'Blessed be,' they say.

Next there's an extended role play event where three women – a maid, Mother Earth and a crone (Veronica plays Mother Earth) – pretend to be goddesses and various people speak lines to them. Veronica stumbles over hers.

It looks like a school play. It's good to dress up. It shows a level of commitment to the faith and lends the occasion a touch of glamour. Personally, I love it. But I'm more the dressing-up-as-a-horse sort.

We take Communion. They don't call it that, obviously, that's for Christians, but we all sip mead from a shared cup and take something to eat. It's the same gesture. We're sharing and giving thanks. Only here, we are thanking the land for the land. In Mongolia they fling vodka onto the snow before getting drunk, as their offering to God. Here we sprinkle a little mead and flapjack onto the damp clay. Veronica says we are giving a bit of the land back to the land, but she hasn't thought it through. The flapjack's only going to go mouldy. Before you can say 'so mote it be' there'll be a fine crop of toadstools. Oh, perhaps she has thought it through.

Then, finally, at long last: the flapjack is unleashed.

They're giving out the free food.

One by one. It's taking ages. A hooded girl intones, her voice filling the cave. The dutiful little boy in the white robe who is giving out the bounty says 'Blessed be' to each participant in turn. Except me. I'm disappointed; the flapjack needs more syrup in my opinion. I'm not an expert, but I know what I like. Afterwards we chant 'The Druid's Prayer'. It's a bit like the Lord's Prayer, except that no one knows it by heart, so we read it from the typed slips Veronica has distributed. Oh, and then someone's daughter is offered up.

I choke on my snack as the little scrap is led across the circle, but it turns out she's only being offered as Veronica's 'handmaiden'. She'll be trained in the ways of nature and – always handy if she ever wants to become a fat millionaire – astrology. The kids are happy enough. It's no more bonkers than going to church and at least they get to take part. Even so, the rituals, the stylized language and the home-made aesthetic make me feel a little as though I've stumbled on a Buffy-literate version of the Bible Club. I've been to both now and there are some similarities. But there is a fundamental difference that I want to mark.

No one here is trying to recruit anyone else. Quite the reverse. These believers would rather people sought their own answers and followed their own paths.

And no one here is trying to say their beliefs should replace yours. In religion, that's refreshing. We join hands and cry 'Ho!' To wake up the spring.

•

Back at Tess and Bob's house the instruments are out again. We've gained Liz, another friend, who's just taking off her velour robe, encrusted with clay from the mine, and tucking into the homemade bread and pizza Bob is proudly setting down. Not on the floor, though, as Holly is getting aroused by the smell. In between numbers the women talk a little about their attitudes to paganism. In the late 1990s, Ronald Hutton conducted a survey and counted nearly one hundred and twenty thousand individual pagans in the United Kingdom. The government census counted only about forty thousand. This might show an unwillingness to own up to one's 'path', but the pagans I have met today are only too happy to talk about their beliefs. Liz likes prayers. Praying means something to her. It helps with something. She feels closer to the earth than to other gods. So she prays to the earth. Siggy isn't bothered about the prayers. She just wants to feel closer to nature and to accept that she is part of it.

Outside there's a chill breeze. I don't feel the spring has answered our call yet. But I'm open-minded. The trip here has certainly brought me closer to the land. It's hard to get past the fact that Wicca and druidry have no solid, unbroken connection with my ancient roots, but even so it's done me good to see this fertility rite come to life under the earth. It's another part of the puzzle that fits into place. I know the fertility rites I've seen today are not ancient. They are as much influenced by modern folklore as the early folklorists were influenced by imagined paganism. But, fact or fiction, by trying to connect with the earth, by trying to make sense of their shared past, and by feeling uplifted, cradled and protected by what they find, these people are doing something instinctive. And it's this impulse – whether it blossoms into dressing as a horse or dressing as Gandalf – that is timeless. When I began my own journey I felt I had too many questions, as though the answers were too fluid.

Now I feel as though things are solidifying.

Drones

And so I sit with my hurdy-gurdy, looking out of the window at the drizzle. The mimosa tree next door is in bloom and the wind shakes the yellow flowers. They dance. A pair of jays has appeared in the tree these last few days. They flutter in and out, flashing the blue streaks of their wings as they settle on a branch and disappear into the foliage. It's rare to see a jay in the city, and a pair, nesting – it must be a sign of something. And so I sit, looking out of the window, watching the drizzle, with my hurdy-gurdy.

Moronically turning the handle.

Listening to the drone.

Waiting for the magic spring.

My journey is coming to an end. There's only one more place I can go now, the ultimate place, the first and last of places, where things will come into focus, align themselves. Where the light will dawn, I'm sure.

Time to push on, closer to the source.

322   *The Magic Spring*

20 | Avalon

Glastonbury is a town colonized exclusively by people who came to the Pilton festival in 1970 and missed the bus back to Bath. Take a walk down the main drag and you'll see what I mean. The garish shopfronts are painted by hand in psychedelic colours, broadcasting names like 'Goddesses and Green Men'. Rakish figures in ponchos and dreadlocks lurch across the road and disappear into doorways. Men in headscarves, combat trousers and giant boots stand motionless at intersections, eyes glazed, the ethnic print on their shapeless South American tunics dull with ground-in dirt. Many appear to be wearing bed linen. I was there once, fifteen years ago. Outsiders find ways to fit the description. Now I'm here again, looking through new eyes. All the windows have feathers and wind chimes hanging in them and you can't find a piece of meat for love or money. Mung beans, hummus and tofu seep from the rainbow-coloured eaves of every organic crêperie, every vegan café. In every fireplace a corn dolly, in every dream home, a chickpea. Spiritual healing flows from every fountain, every 'pagan well'. Every holistic treatment from reiki to 'purple healing plates' is accounted for. Tired, depleted, at the end of your tether?

Why not try a spiritual massage? Bored of your clothes? Why not answer this ad:

> Excellent quality and barely worn
> PAGAN/FAERY/WITCHY CLOTHES
> AT BARGAIN PRICES
> Also rare pixie/elf-type shoes

'My fear is my teacher, breathe, breathe, breathe.' Glastonbury is a cornucopia of meaningful delights, crystals and answers; landmarks for the spiritually enlightened, for every seeker, every traveller, every puckish wisp of rebellious spirit. Yes it is. Tradespeople have seen to it. Sour-faced women in kaftans sit behind counters peddling mass-produced models of Pan for £70. Get a clay mould of a green man, hurriedly painted with too large a brush. How about a massive hare, staring at the moon? Or a moonstone, a rune stone, a riddle or a prayer? Spell books for teenagers, spell books for cats. Joss sticks and oils. Candles, candles. A wicker man, ready to burn, no assembly required. Every accessory for every soul from the Buffy enthusiast to the full-blown priestess. It's all here at a price. Look at it glow. One shop offers 'Books, Dragons'. A big arrow directs pilgrims towards the till.

It's been a clear day. Crisp, not too cold. The sun has been out, and now as it starts to descend it shines on the windows of Avalon Dry Cleaning and Avalon Ladies' Fashions, on the dull, red-brick houses of Avalon Estate, the bolted door of the Avalon Hall community centre, on Avalon Electrics and Avalon Radio Cabs. There's a glow. You would think it was spring time, but it's only a blip. The trees are still barren, the ground is still dead. Spring is still far away, but Glastonbury allows you to hope. The atmosphere is unique to this place. You'll never see a sunset like it. In the night, when you look up, you'll never see the heavens open before you as frankly, as if the sky wants to give you the peace you're looking for. And as you travel over the flat land, over the narrow runnels, across the flood plains, over the scrub and brush, there's really only one place to aim for, only one place to stand.

I've been meaning to come back here ever since I found a site on the Internet. I had been trying to make contact with pagan

325   *Avalon*

believers but wasn't having much success. Then I stumbled upon the Sisters of Avalon. They seemed to be everything I was looking for. I really thought they would have some information for me. The sisterhood fetishized Glastonbury Tor. The Tor is the striking dome of land that juts out of the Somerset Levels, right here in the middle, the only hill for miles around.

Long, long ago, so the legend goes, when the knights of Camelot – Lancelot, Gawain and the gang – sat at the Round Table, when campaigns were planned (such as how to get this grail or that) and issues of the day were debated (e.g. 'Who would you rather trust, a Green Knight, say, or God?'), their king, Arthur, came to the Isle of Avalon and died there. Avalon is where Joseph of Arimathea brought the Holy Grail, and Glastonbury has laid enterprising claim to the Avalon title ever since the twelfth century, when the monks of the abbey found a way to rekindle the pilgrimage trade and their own ecclesiastical power after a fire had razed their building to the ground. They came across the buried skeleton of a man and a blonde woman on their land, concluded the couple were Arthur and his queen, and let it be known. The pilgrims have been coming ever since.

In Arthur's day the levels would have been flooded marshes. Saturated bog beneath the water. The Tor and its surrounding hillocks would indeed have been a genuine island, rising out of the shiny water like Excalibur. A fortress, a refuge, a destination and an answer.

That was the idea, anyway. The Sisterhood of Avalon worshipped Celtic Welsh goddesses only. That was because in the days of

Avalon – you know, *originally* – the Celtic goddesses would have been the dominant deities. That's what the sisterhood said. Avalon. Sweet Avalon. The end of all grail quests, of all romantic missions. One day, the website said, the Sisters hoped actually to go there, to make their pilgrimage to Avalon, their own holy grail, lost in the heart of England land. Until that time, there were always the reasonably priced fantasy novels by Marion Zimmer Bradley, which were available at Wal-Mart and upon which their Californian religion was not even remotely based, as you would know if you had read their frequently asked questions. I wrote to the Sisters. I said that I had grown up near Avalon, that I knew it had powers, that I would swap my knowledge for theirs. They never wrote back.

People are scared of getting close to what they need.

That's what I'd heard, anyway.

I can't remember the last time I walked up the Tor. I must have done it many times at different stages of my early life, but each memory seems to be lost somehow. I can never remember the way. Every step should take me closer, and yet the Tor, its lone, turreted tower sticking up darkly into the sky, never seems to come towards me. I keep walking, over fields, over stiles. My shoes cake up with mud. The light's failing now and the receding sun burns amber behind a row of trees. The ash keys in silhouette make peacock feathers of the branches. It hasn't rained today and yet the earth is still moist. It never really dries up much here, and it's constantly churned by the heavy boot prints of seekers making their way to the Tor.

328   *The Magic Spring*

Like me. Hoping for an epiphany. There's a beautiful silence here and a stillness, and that helps.

At last the mound appears before me. It's a steep climb and the dusk is creeping in fast, casting an aura of pale mauve and yellow all along the horizon. The deep sense of spirituality is heightened by St Michael's Tower, perched at the zenith, pointing up to the heavens, to the cosmos. It looms above me as I climb. It seems to be emitting a low drone, a constant hum, somewhere deep, somewhere earthy. It hits my resonant frequency. It seems crazy, but I'm sure it's real. I think about what Mike Gilpin said to me in Swaffham, about drones.

'People are scared of getting close to what they need.'

That's what he said, anyway.

But what do I need?

I grew up around here. I walked these fields as a child. Now, on this hill today, I am at a hiatus in my life. Before the future can begin, I need to fuse finally and truthfully with my past. The winter has been long. Before the spring can send up shoots, I need to accept my roots for what they are. I'm not really from London – that was just where I was born. I'm a product of this place. For better or worse, this land, these hills are what shaped me. The West Country never let me forget I was a gatecrasher and I left to look for somewhere that felt more like home. But home isn't really a place. Home is a state of peace. Before I can settle somewhere, anywhere, I need to let this landscape back into my life.

The humming gets louder as I climb. I wonder for a moment if I haven't gone mad, whether the noise is really in my head. But no.

It's definitely coming from the tower. I reach the top of the Tor and hesitate. I look around. You can see across three counties. There's the market town of Street, home of Clarks Shoes and the discount store where children are bought unfashionable cheap footwear they will want to burn and bury. There is Taunton, home of Babycham, the pear-based beverage you bought your first girlfriend, knowing no better. There's Crook Peak, high on the Mendip Hills, where dads in anoraks stand flying radio-controlled aircraft, and shifty outsiders like me hunt for magic mushrooms among the moist earth, looking for an escape. Over the ridge, the old slavers' port of Bristol crouches in a natural depression, a constant cloud above it.

The stranger is taboo in every culture, from Frazer's 'primitives' to our brave new world of detention centres for asylum seekers. It's a tradition that transcends all political boundaries, all folklores and all religions, a tradition that unites humanity as one. Fear, the universal sickness. We've been at loggerheads, the West Country and me. When connections fail, sometimes we stop trying. But the wilderness is big, there's room enough for every bough and berry. My time among the pagans has given me confidence in my place in nature. Now, like Bob's bracken and birches, I reclaim my land.

Avalon, the first and last place in all England. From here on the Tor I can see it all. From here I could go anywhere. But first, I make for the arched door, for the drone. I can see daylight through the other side and the setting sun explodes upon the old stones in a mash of browns and orange. One step, two.

And then I see him.

A single hippy with a didgeridoo.

He sits cross-legged on the cold flagstones, his eyes closed, his head nodding to a rhythm only he can hear. At peace with himself. Some of that halcyon feeling now works its way into me.

Ley lines, crop circles, runes and rings. Wicker, Wicca, feathers and stones. It's miserable in winter. Miserable and cold. Is it any wonder we reach out for something? Fires, pyres, ritual and romance. Witchcraft, woodcraft, folk song and dance. Anything to light up the dead earth, to galvanize a little life and give respite from the waste land. A return to light and colour. A return to feeling.

Roots are funny things. The more you hack away at them, the deeper they seem to go. What you thought was dead and gone stirs in the wet soil and shoots out where you least expect it. Life renewing. I think about the people I've discovered over the last year: Dick, Doc, Ron and the mummers, Ant and Simon, Trigger and Trotter, Steve and the morris, the mollies and rappers, the gurners, wassailers, the green man and preacher, the pagans, the witches and me.

LIMERIC
COUNTY L

Further Reading

Alford, Violet. *Peeps at English Folk Dances*. London, 1923.

——. *Introduction to English Folklore*. London, 1952.

——. *Sword Dance and Drama*. London, 1962.

——. *The Hobby Horse and Other Animal Masks*. London, 1978.

Aspin, Chris. *The Woollen Industry*. Princes Risborough, 2000.

Baring-Gould, Sabine. *Songs of the West*. London, 1905.

Brown, Bryan J. H. *Weston-super-Mare and the Origins of Coastal Leisure in the Bristol Area*. Weston-super-Mare, 1978.

Bryant, Arthur. *Samuel Pepys: The Years of Peril*. London, 1935.

Bull, Angela. *The Machine Breakers*. London, 1980.

Burke, John. *An Illustrated History of England*. London, 1974.

Burns, Francis. *Heigh for Cotswold: Robert Dover's Olimpick Games*. Chipping Campden, 2000.

Burrow, J. A. *Medieval Writers and Their Work*. Oxford, 1982.

Cawte, E. C. *In Comes I: An Introductory Leaflet to the Mummers Play*. London, 1972.

——. *Ritual Animal Disguise*. Cambridge, 1978.

Chandler, Keith. 'Chipping Campden morris dancers: An Outline History'. <www.rootsweb.com/~engcots/MorrisMen>.

Cibber, Colley. *An Apology for the Life of Mr. Cibber*. London, 1740.

Dallas, Karl, and Fantoni, Barry. *Swinging London*. London, 1967.

Dickens, Charles (Boz). *Memoirs of Joseph Grimaldi*. London, 1838.

Dunbar, Janet. *Peg Woffington and Her World*. London, 1968.

Edwards, Gillian. *Hogmanay and Tiffany*. London, 1970.

Ensor, R. C. K. *England 1870–1914*. Oxford, 1936.

Etherington, Jim. *Lewes Bonfire Night*. Seaford, 1993.

Fees, Craig (ed.). *Memories of an Old Campdonian, by F. W. Coldicott*. Chipping Campden, 1994.

——. *A Child in Arcadia: The Chipping Campden Boyhood of H. T. Osborn, 1902–1907*. Chipping Campden, 1997.

Fox Strangways, A. H., with Karpeles, Maud. *Cecil Sharp*. London, 1933.

Fraser, Antonia. *The Gunpowder Plot*. London, 1996.

Frazer, James George. *The Golden Bough*. London, 1922.

Frow, Gerald. *Oh Yes It Is: A History of Pantomime*. London, 1985.

Gayne, G. R. *Wassail! In Mazers of Mead*. London, 1948.

Goldenberg, Christine. 'The Composition of Jack and the Beanstalk'. *Marvels & Tales: Journal of Fairy Tale Studies*, 15, no. 1, 2001.

Harding, Patrick. *Christmas Unwrapped*. London, 2002.

Hutton, Ronald. *The Pagan Religions of the Ancient British Isles*. Oxford, 1991.

——. *The Rise and Fall of Merry England*. Oxford, 1993.

——. *Stations of the Sun: A History of the Ritual Year in Britain*. Oxford, 1996.

——. *Triumph of the Moon: A History of Modern Pagan Witchcraft*. Oxford, 1999

——. *Witches, Druids and King Arthur*. London, 2003.

Jenkins, Elizabeth. *Jane Austen: A Biography*. London, 1938.

Karpeles, Maud. *Dances of England & Wales*. London, 1950.

——. *Cecil Sharp: His Life and Work*. London, 1967.

——. *An Introduction to English Folk Song*. London, 1973.

Kenny, Colum. *Fearing Sellafield*. Dublin, 2003.

Koenigsberger, H. G., and Mosse, George L. *Europe in the Sixteenth Century*. London, 1968.

Lang, Andrew. *Myth, Ritual and Religion*. London, 1913.

Latham, Robert, and Matthews, William (eds.). *The Diary of Samuel Pepys*. London, 1985.

Lloyd, A. L. *Folk Song in England*. London, 1967.

——, and Vaughan Williams, Ralph. *The Penguin Book of English Folk Songs*. Harmondsworth, 1959.

Millar, Ronald. *The Green Man*. Seaford, 1997.

Newman, Paul. *Lost Gods of Albion*. London, 1987.

Opie, Iona and Peter. *The Classic Fairy Tales*. Oxford, 1974.

Opie, Iona, and Tatem, Moira. *A Dictionary of Superstitions*. Oxford, 1989.

Ordish, Thomas Fairman. *Early London Theatres in the Fields*. London, 1894.

Page, Nick. *Lord Minimus: The Extraordinary Life of Britain's Smallest Man*. London, 2001.

Paxman, Jeremy. *The English: A Portrait of a People*. London, 1998.

Peel, Frank. *The Risings of the Luddites*. Heckmondwike, 1880.

Salberg, Derek. *Once Upon a Pantomime*. Luton, 1981.

Scruton, Roger. *England: An Elegy*. London, 2000.

Sharp, Cecil J. *Folk-Dancing in Schools*. London, 1912.

——. *English Folk-Song: Some Conclusions*. 2nd edn. London, 1936.

Shuttleworth, Ron. *Introducing the Folk Plays of England*. Coventry, 1984.

Simpson, Jacqueline, and Roud, Steve. *The Oxford Dictionary of English Folklore*. Oxford, 2000.

Taylor, Timothy. *The Prehistory of Sex*. London, 1996.

Thomis, Malcom I. (ed.). *Luddism in Nottinghamshire*. London, 1972.

Thompson, Graham (ed.). *Border Ballads*. London, 1888.

Toulson, Shirley. *The Winter Solstice*. London, 1981.

Trevellyan, G. M. *A Shorter History of England*. New York, 1942.

——. *English Social History*. London, 1944.

Tylor, Edward. *Primitive Culture*. London, 1871.

Walker, Ernest. *A History of Music in England*. Oxford, 1907.

Weaver, John. *A History of Mimes and Pantomimes*. London, 1756.

Weston, Jessie L. *From Ritual to Romance*. Princeton, 1920.

Woffington, Margaret. *Memoir of the Celebrated Mrs Woffington*. London, 1768.

Zipes, Jack. *When Dreams Came True: Classical Fairy Tales and Their Tradition*. New York and London, 1999.

Zipes, Jack (ed.). *The Oxford Companion to Fairy Tales*. Oxford, 2000.

The *Tatler* essay, 'The Gentleman: The Pretty Fellow', is reprinted in Abrams, M. H. (gen. ed.). *The Norton Anthology of English Literature*, 5th edn. New York, 1986.

Acknowledgements

I would like to offer my sincere thanks to Susannah Godman, my dear friend and agent at Lutyens and Rubinstein, for customer care beyond the call of duty and for her judgement and vision. I owe an enormous debt of gratitude to Clara Farmer at Atlantic Books, both for commissioning *The Magic Spring* and for editing it with the sensitivity, humour, affection and probing intelligence that made the writing of this book a richly rewarding experience. Thank you to Toby Mundy, Daniel Scott and everyone at Atlantic for publishing the book with creativity, flair and enthusiasm far beyond my best hopes. Not for the first time, I am indebted to Alan Jessop and his team at Compass. May the force be with you.

I am grateful to Louis Barfe, Alex George and Aoife Mannix, who read my first draft and encouraged me. Thank you to Doc Rowe and David Atkinson, who also read my manuscript and who gave me much help in understanding English folklore. Thank you to Ronald Hutton for taking time to answer my questions, and to Steve Henwood both for unwittingly setting this book in motion many, many years ago and for helping me nail it down at various pubs in Soho. Thank you to Brian Wilshere for all his early input, and to Valerie Thatcher, John Lane, Elodie Picquet and Josie Fletcher who encouraged me to write. Other sustenance, musical, physical and spiritual, is down to Chris Allen, Josie Cadoret, Robert and Chris Chisman, Conrad and Elizabeth Collinge, Isabelle Endreo, Eric 'Ian' the Stag, Bob Flag, Alex George, Mike Gilpin, the Greensleeves Morris, Dan Hernandez and Jacqui, Geoff Hiscott, the staff at Hobgoblin, London, Bob and Tess Hunt, Jane and Nick and Arlo Joyce, Mark Lawson and his Hoodeners, Chris Leslie, Andrew and Eliana Lewis, Brian and Angela Lewis, Georgia Lewis, the staff at the Music Room, Oxford, Alice Philipson, Simon, Ant, Rosie, Molly and Flora Pipe, Steve Rowley, John Russell, Peggy Seeger, Harry and Mary Shackleton, Alan, Jenny and David Shelley, Ron Shuttleworth and the Coventry Mummers, Andy and Felicity Sutton, Ana Carolina and Milena Teixeira-Santi, Heather Tyrell, the Wessex Morris, Raj Yagnik, and Roy Young. Thank you for your help/encouragement/hospitality/generosity/creativity/music/ friendship/food/belief/transport/companionship/money.

But the most important contributor by far is Rosa, whose love, support, calm, company, enthusiasm, encouragement, note taking, train booking, map reading, cycle repairing, song singing, horse making and spirit of adventure made this journey possible from the outset. Despite her invisibility, she is in every scene of *The Magic Spring*, modestly out of shot. Thank you so much.